AF646535

Medical Anthropology

About the Author

Gaya Pandey (b. 1954) was Professor in the Department of Anthropology, Ranchi University, Ranchi (Jharkhand). After passing M.Sc. in Anthropology from Ranchi University in 1979 with first division, he joined at A.N. Sinha Institute of Social Studies, Patna as Doctoral Research Fellow, University Grants Commission, Government of India for his Doctoral Research Programme. He was awarded Ph.D. degree by Ranchi University in 1984 and got honour to join UGC Centre of Advance Study, Department of Anthropology, Ranchi University, Ranchi in February 1985. Ever since he served in the department as a teacher and as a researcher till his retirement in February 2019. During his 39 years of service as Researcher and Teacher, he has contributed two and half dozen articles in Journals of national and international repute and in edited books. He has to his credit publication of 24 books in Hindi and English medium on different branches of anthropology which have been included as course books in different universities in India where anthropology is taught. Some of his books are *Manav Shastriya AnusandhanVidut Ewan Taknik, Jatil Samaj ka Manavshastra, Bhartiya Manavshastra, Manavshastriya Sidhanta: Shastriya Ewam Adhunik, Bhartiya Jana Jatiya Sanskriti, Developmental Anthropology, Bio-cultural Evolution, Jaivik-Sanskritik Udvikas, Bhartiya Pragaitihasik Manavshastra, Sampreshanatnak Manav Shastra, Chikitsatanak Manavshastra, Neo Anthropological Theory, Social-cultural Anthropology, Indian Prehistoric Archaeological Anthropology, Communicational Anthropology and Anthropological Research Methodology: Theory and Pratice.*

Medical Anthropology
A Text Book

Gaya Pandey

CONCEPT PUBLISHING COMPANY PVT. LTD.
NEW DELHI-110059

© Author

All rights reserved. No part of this work may be reproduced, stored, adapted, or transmitted in any form or by any means, electronic, mechanical, photocopying, micro-filming recording or otherwise, or translated in any language, without the prior written permission of the copyright owner and the publisher. The book is sold subject to the condition that it shall not, by way of trade or otherwise, be lent, resold, hired out, or otherwise circulated without the prior publisher's written consent in any form of binding or cover other than that in which it is published.

The views and opinions expressed in this book are author's own and the facts reported by him have been verified to the extent possible, and the publishers are not in anyway liable for the same.

ISBN-13: 978-93-88937-86-3 (HB)
ISBN-13: 978-93-88937-87-0 (PB)

First Published 2021

Published and Printed by

Concept Publishing Company Pvt. Ltd.
Since 1974
A/15-16, Commercial Block, Mohan Garden,
New Delhi-110059 (INDIA)
T : 91 11 25351460, 91 11 25351794
E : publishing@conceptpub.com; *W* : www.conceptpub.com

Cataloging in Publication Data--Courtesy: D.K. Agencies (P) Ltd. <docinfo@dkagencies.com>

Pandey, Gaya, 1954- author.
Medical anthropology : a text book / Gaya Pandey.
pages cm
Includes bibliographical references and index.
ISBN 9789388937863 (HB)
ISBN 9789388937870 (PB)

1. Medical anthropology—India. I. Title.

LCC GN296.5.I4P36 2021 | DDC 306.4610954 23

DEDICATED TO

With all sincere regards, I dedicate my this book to my mother Late Ansuia Devi who made departure for her heavenly abode on 22.1.2018 on the day of Basant-Panchami. But *Sanskars* she inculcated in me and her blessings will always be a guiding force for me in future.

Preface

Medical Anthropology is a sub-branch of Social Cultural Anthropology in which health, disease and treatment related behaviours of people are studied. It deals with pan-historical and cross-cultural medical knowledge of the communities. This book deals with medical cultures of health, disease and treatment practised in India. This subject is taught in Under-Graduate and Postgraduate Departments of Anthropology in different universities of India. Although there are some books in English and Hindi in which some aspects of Medical Anthropology have been discussed, but they do not cover the entire syllabus taught under the subject Medical Anthropology. Therefore, attempts have been made to cover the entire syllabus of this subject under one cover. The purpose of the book is purely to benefit the students and scholars interested in the study of Medical Anthropology. The simple language and systematic presentation of subject matter will definitely benefit the readers.

The book has been written with the support and good wishes of a number of persons of different levels. Hence, it is my pious duty to extend my thanks to them individually and collectively.

First of all I extend my sincere gratitude to all those scholars and experts whose contributions on the subject have benefited me much in completion of the book.

I acknowledge my thanks to all teachers of the Department of Anthropology, Ranchi University, Ranchi (Jharkhand) whose suggestions provided theoretical and methodological lead in accomplishing the task of writing this book. I am thankful to all UGC JRFs and SRFs, Rajiv Gandhi JRFs and SRFs, Maulana Azad JRFs and SRFs and other research scholars of the department who encouraged me much in completion of this book in English.

I extend thanks to my family members—wife Smt. Indu Devi, Daughters—Sudha, Suman, Sarita and Anu, son Shekhar and Grandsons—Kushagra and Harshit without whose cooperation, it was impossible for me to do the work of book writing.

I am thankful to Sri Ashok Kumar Mittal and his Publishing Team, Concept Publishing Company Pvt. Ltd., New Delhi for getting the hand written manuscript printed with meticulous care.

Department of Anthropology
Ranchi University, Ranchi

Gaya Pandey

Contents

1
Medical Anthropology

Introduction

Now-a-days, Medical Anthropology is an established sub-branch of Social Cultural Anthropology. It is a sub-branch of Social Cultural Anthropology because it deals with pan-historical and cross-cultural study of disease, illness and treatment.

Mankind has been acquainted with diseases and their treatments since time immemorial. With the passage of time a number of beliefs, practices, behaviours, knowledge and habits got attached to diseases and methods of their treatment.

Today we are living in space age and we have varieties of knowledge related to diseases and their methods of treatment available on line. We have been able to understand causes of diseases and their treatments. Now-a-days we have multiple medical systems by which we can cure our diseases and lead a healthy life. But for Stone Age people, who were struggling hard to maintain their existence, it was quite natural that he looked towards natural objects, magic and religion for illness and their cure. As he experienced different seasons, life cycle, bodily accidents, natural events like flood, starvation, epidemic, earthquakes, storm, fire, untimely death, his knowledge about health, illness and cure went on increasing. As the time passed, the plural systems of medicine, concept of folk medicine, medicine man, midwifery, Jharkphuk, witch doctor, Puja-path and food control became integral part of cultural system of mankind living in different parts of the globe as communities.

We can say that man is such a being who laid the foundation of health, disease and cure. In remote struggleful days, he had to pass through troubles in order to save life. Gradually the concept of health got attached to wealth. The healthy persons were recognized as wealthy persons. The wealthy persons were those who were successful in struggle of survival. In every society this proverb is often quoted that 'health is a wealth'. Healthy person can go anywhere, work anywhere and maintain his existence. But unhealthy person is deprived of movement, work and wealth. He becomes burden on his family. He spends all earning on his family and finally leaves this world. Along with him, his other family members also become poor. Thus, it is quite natural that mankind had attempted to know the causes of illness and ways of their cure so that ill persons could become cured and contribute in the society. Some causes of illness and ways of curing were unscientific, some were semi-scientific, while few were scientific. These unscientific, semi-scientific and scientific behaviours gave rise to the concept of health, disease and treatment and began to be practiced as traditions. They are found existing even today.

In every folk, tribal and peasant communities, there are health healers who attempt to cure patient by their unscientific, semi-scientific and scientific traditions. In every family of the community, aged women are regarded as family doctor who possess knowledge of different kinds of diseases, folk medicine and food control. Every individual experiences health, disease, treatment, folk medicine and food control in different periods of his daily life. In our country India, it is rightly said that every Indians are philosopher and doctor by birth. Whenever an individual suffers from disease, he/she receives varieties of suggestions from relatives, friends and other community members.

In the beginning the concept of health, disease and cure of mankind was based on traditional knowledge. In every community there were medicine man, midwife, bone fracture expert, vein expert, massage expert. They had traditional medicinal knowledge of local flora, fauna and natural object. They used to prepare folk medicine on the basis of flora, fauna and natural things. They used to cure patient by providing folk medicine. Many of them were also *Jharphuk* experts and witch doctors. Besides folk medicine, they used to cure patients by *Jharphuk* and *Puja-path* which brought psychological satisfaction to the patient. They possessed knowledge of *Jari-butti* and used to preserve them. They did not disclose names and places of *Jari-butti* because they feared that they would be made extinct. They used to handover the knowledge of *Jari-butti* and treatment to their eldest son or eldest daughter if there were no son or eldest nephew in case of childless.

In traditional system, the treatment of diseases was not only continued to the use of Jari-butti (herbs) but also removal of evil spirits causing diseases through *Jharphuk* and *Puja-path.* Even today in traditional society, attempts are made to cure patients by folk medicine, *Jharphuk, Puja-path* and food control.

As the time passed on mankind gave rise to revolution and entered in the stage of civilization. The rise of civilization paved the path of system in every sphere of life. Urban civilization developed on the bank of rivers in the form of well-planned towns, trade, market, rulers, army, priest, physicians and a number of classes based on expertise. The rise of civilization established system for identifying and curing diseases. In early civilization, traditional medical systems and medicines were developed. When we entered the modern era, modern medical systems came into being. Modern medicines were also invented.

All medical systems and medicines have their unique characteristics. But their objectives are common. They all attempt to diagnose and cure diseases for wellbeing of humans. That is why they all have maintained their existence.

Today the concepts of individual health, folk health, community health, public health, rural health, urban health, child health, women health, youth health, reproductive health and others are prevalent. For various concepts of health, disease and treatment multi-speciality and super-speciality hospitals and medical colleges have been established. There are plurality of medical systems. Each type of medical system has its own concept of health, disease and medicine. But they are working for maintaining health of people by curing various kinds of diseases ailments.

The concept of health is not related only to diseaseless body of an individual. Rather the concept of health has social, mental and spiritual dimensions. An individual is healthy when he/she is physically, mentally, socially and spiritually fit. Only physically, socially, mentally and spiritually fit persons are able to contribute in development of society and nation.

Today each nation has the concept of health demography which attempts to explore sex ratio, fertility, morality, malnutrition, drinking water facilities and delivery of health services in rural and urban areas. It also attempts to explore some special diseases prevalent among the people such as T.B., AIDS, leprosy, cancer, malaria and others. Health demography has been helpful in formulating national health policies and various national programmes related to health and diseases.

Today, the concept of human right has been developed. To lead a healthy life is our human right. Nobody can deprive any other body from leading a healthy life. That is why our Government is attempting to maintain health of our people. A number of national and state level programmes have been launched. Health institutions have been established throughout the length and breadth of our country to deliver health services in rural and urban areas. Governmental, non-Governmental and

International agencies are involved in health related programmes to maintain the health of the people.

Implementation, monitoring and evaluation of health programmes are taken up. These steps have brought positive result. Man is such a being who identified not only disease of man but also diseases of plants and animals. He has also attempted to cure diseases of plants and domestic animals. He has given the concept of ethnobiology which is again divided into ethnobotany and ethnozoology.

From the above account, it is quite clear that the subject matter of medical anthropology is very wide. It covers the concepts of health, disease treatment and medicines of different communities cross-culturally. It also covers health demography, health statistics, health institutions, health development programmes launched by the Government and health delivery system in rural and urban areas. Ethnobiology practiced by the people also comes under it for the purpose of study.

The present book, 'Medical Anthropology' has been written taking examples from our country India. In fact, it attempts to explore medical systems of India.

Subject Matter

The subject matter covered under this book is as follows:

- Concept nature and characteristics of health
- Medical systems of India
- Health in Texts and traditions
- Magical beliefs: Disease and treatment
- Scientific facts: Disease and treatment
- Folk classification of diseases and folk treatment
- Impediments to Health
- Forest and herbs *(Jari-butti)*
- Health agents
- Health statistics
- Health promotion programmes
- Folk Biology: Folk Botany and Folk Zoology

Beginning of Researches in Medical Anthropology

Medical anthropology emerged as an established sub-branch of social-cultural Anthropology in 1960s, when an attempt was made to bring social-cultural anthropology and biological anthropology together. As a result of this attempt medical anthropology was established to make pan-historical and cross-cultural study of diseases and treatment. But the beginning of medical anthropological studies can be traced back to the work of E.B. Tylor, the founder of British Anthropology. Tylor in his book, '*Primitive Culture*' (1871), gave a scientific definition of culture. According to him, culture is a complex whole which includes moral, art, belief, knowledge habit, attitude and all other capabilities acquired by man as a member of society. Beliefs, knowledge, habit and attitudes were also related to health.

After E.B. Tylor, American anthropologists belonging to culture and personality school like Margaret Mead in her book, '*Coming of Age in Samoa*' (1928) and growing up in New Guinea (1930) studied socialization process and reproductive health related behaviour. She also studied the rearing and caring process of children.

The founder of functional theory and British anthropologist B.K. Malinowski in his book, '*Scientific Theory of Culture and Other Essays*' (1944) propounded the theory of need. He talked about three types of needs and cultural responses. According to him there are three levels of need—primary, secondary and tertiary. He talked basic biological needs as primary needs, instrumental or derived need as secondary need and integrative need as tertiary need. Each type of need has a cultural response. He divided primary needs into seven types in which health was also included. In order to satisfy the primary need health, there was cultural response of hygiene in every community.

The full-fledged medical anthropological studies were started in 1960s and pan-historical and cross-cultural studies of health, disease and treatment were initiated. The scholars interested in medical anthropological studies began to explore, describe and analyse women health, children health, reproductive health, adult health, adolescent health, aged health, tribal health, scheduled caste health, OBC health, minority health, food and food habit, food behaviour, growth and nutrition, plurality of medical systems, folk medicine, disease according to age and sex, health agents, health impediments, health statistics, health service delivery systems, folk treatment, classification of diseases, folk biology, ethnobotany and ethnozoology. As a result, now-a-days, the scope of medical Anthropology is very wide.

2
Concept of Health in Human Society

The form of society may be folk, rural, urban or metropolis but the concept of health is found in every society. The people of every society know it very well that healthy persons live long and contribute in the development of society. Unhealthy people have low longevity and do not contribute in the development of society. Therefore to remain healthy is essential for every individual. Members are the greatest wealth for the society and nation.

The concept of health emphasises on the need to make life long by being healthy. Unhealthy life stops the progress of individual and ultimately to the society and nation. Unhealthy life creates different kinds of hindrances.

The concept of health indicates that health is the greatest wealth. A healthy person can go anywhere to earn bread and money. He/she can find a place anywhere because healthy persons get work everywhere. But this is not true for an unhealthy or sick person. An unhealthy person does not get opportunity to work. He/she spends the accumulated wealth of his/her family. He/she does not get even loan. Thus, unhealthy persons become poor day by day.

The concept of health reveals that it is not related only to the disease-free body of an individual. Rather it is also related to social, mental and spiritual well-being of an individual. In common folk conversation, a disease-free and disease cured person is taken as healthy. Here, only physical condition of an individual is taken into account. But this is not holistic view of health of an individual. An individual is holistically healthy only when he is physically, socially, mentally and spiritually fit.

According to the concept of health, health is closely related to our habits. Healthy habits are fit and unhealthy habits make us unfit. Timely intake of food, water and rest, early to bed and early to rise, avoiding use of liquor, tobacco, cigarettes, *Ganja* (marijuna) and *bhang,* control on food are considered as healthy habits. Bad and unhealthy habits affect our health negatively.

The concept of health is also related to environment. Healthy environment affects our health positively, while unhealthy environment affects our health negatively. Our health is also related to nutrition and diets. Proper nutrition and balanced diet keep us healthy. But improper nutrition-malnutrition and overnutrition-and imbalanced diet make us ill.

The concept of health reveals that our health can be maintained by change in lifestyle, food control and medicine of various types.

The concept of health indicates that we can cure our diseases and maintain healthy life by adopting *yoga* and meditation.

According to the concept of health, jealousy, hatred, anger, and stress destroy our own health.

Satisfaction plays significant role in the health maintenance. Satisfaction provides us happiness even free of cost. The happiness ultimately affects our health positively.

The concept of health is also related to reproduction. Only those persons take part in reproduction whose reproductive health is good. The individuals with good reproductive health are able to continue their lineage and maintain population. But persons whose reproductive health is not fit do not participate in reproduction. They fail to continue their progeny and lineage.

In folk society the concept of health is also related to magical habits. According to magical belief black magicians influence health negatively, whereas white magicians influence health positively.

Not only magical beliefs but religious beliefs also influence the health positively and negatively. The blessings of deities influence health positively and curses of deities influence health negatively.

Environment also plays significant role in the concept of health. Good natural and social environment affect health positively. Bad environment affects health negatively.

The concept of health is also related to intake of pure drinking water. Pure drinking water and water resources affect our health positively. But impure and dirty water resources affect our health negatively.

The concept of health is also related to genetics. Some diseases are related to genetically and they can be treated genetically.

The concept of health is also related to sex. Some diseases spread through sexual relation such as AIDS. AIDS can be controlled by safe sexual relation.

According to the concept of health, cancer, AIDS, are non-curable diseases. But they can be controlled by medicine and change in lifestyle.

The concept of health is, now, related to human rights. To be healthy and to maintain health is our human right. No body can deny us from it. It is responsibility of our Government to keep health of every citizen. So that they can join mainstream.

DEFINITION

A number of scholars have defined health in their own ways. But here we are going to deal with definition of health provided by World Health Organisation (WHO). According to WHO, Health can be defined as physical, mental, social and spiritual wellbeing of an individual. Here, emphasis has been placed on holistic health of an individual so that an individual can contribute significantly and positively in construction of society and nation. Thus, according to WHO, health is not only a physical and biological concept, rather, it is a social, mental and spiritual concept, too.

No doubt health is a biological concept. But it is also true that health is not only a biological concept. Biological health is related to reproduction, nutrition, growth and rearing processes. Only healthy persons participate in healthy reproduction. Only healthy persons get reproductive success. It is also true that some diseases are genetically related. Such diseases can be cured and controlled by gene therapy. It is also true that proper nutrition is a must to remain healthy. Malnutrition and overnutrition affect our health negatively. Balanced and proper nutrition keep us healthy. Malnutrition and overnutrition invite a number of diseases. But in spite of all these biological facts, health is not only a biological concept. It is social, cultural, mental and spiritual concept, too.

Man is a social animal. He lives in society from birth to death. Society socializes individuals to maintain social health. Society teaches about good habit, good nutrition, good character and also about social pathology. In this way our health is a social concept, too.

In society, we live in community. Each community share common ecology and environment. Members of a community share common drinking water and other water sources. They share same type of weather, food and water. Dirty water sources, dirty house, street, drainage etc. affect our community health.

Health is also a mental concept. If we are physically and socially fit, but mentally unfit, we are not healthy. Health is closely related to mental condition of an individual. Mentally balanced individuals behave normally. But mentally imbalanced individuals behave abnormally. For example theft, dacoit, rapist, mad, abnormal etc. Thus, our mental status affects our health to a great extent.

Health is also related to our culture. Malnutrition and overnutrition take place due to our cultural practices of fasting and breaking fast. In fasting we do not take food and sometimes even water. The duration of fasting may be of 12 hours, 36 hours and 48 hours. But when the fast is over, we share more and more nutritious food several times to compensate energy loss during fasting. This affects our health negatively. Though women cook food for the family, but they share food in the last. Sometimes they do not share anything because they do not have anything left after serving food to family members. Similarly, cultural practices like child marriage, again and again pregnancy, frequent abortion affect health of women negatively. Thus, our health is related to our cultural behaviour.

Our health is also related to spirituality, i.e. purification of mind and heart. An individual is healthy, if he/she is pure by mind and heart. This purification of mind and heart can be achieved by spirituality. The spirituality purifies our mind and heart. When we join our mind and heart with superhuman power, we get an energy to control our behaviour of different kinds. Control of behaviour makes us healthy physically, mentally and socially.

From above account it is quite clear that our health is not only a physical concept, rather it is our social, cultural, mental and spiritual concept, too.

Nature and Characteristics of Health

If one goes through the concepts of health, he/she finds the following characteristics of health:

- Health is a physical/biological concept. But it is not only a physical/biological concept.
- Health is also social, cultural, mental and spiritual concept.
- The form of society may be tribal, rural, urban or cosmopolitan, but the concept of health is found in every kind of society.
- Although the concept of health is found in every society, but behaviour towards health differ from society to society.
- Diseases affect health negatively and ultimately lead towards death.
- Diseases can be controlled by treatment and one can lead a healthy life.
- Human society categorizes disease on the basis of age, sex and common category.
- In Indian society, there are multiple systems of medicine to cure and control diseases such as Yoga, Ayurveda, Unani, Siddha, Homoeopathy, Naturopathy and Allopathy.

- Members of our society are free to choose any one or more than one systems of medicine to cure diseases and lead healthy life.
- Balanced food is essential for healthy life. To eat too much and too less affects health negatively.
- Our habits also play significant role in maintenance of our health. Good habits keep us healthy and bad habits make us unhealthy.
- Sufficient in take of water is essential for healthy life. But less intake of drinking water and intake of dirty drinking water make us unhealthy.
- Pure air is essential for our healthy life. But polluted air affects our health adversely.
- Good and pure environment make us healthy. Bad and impure environment make us unhealthy.
- The health of parents also affects health of children. The children of healthy parents are healthy and of unhealthy parents are unhealthy. Thus, health is also a genetic concept. Genetic diseases are treated with gene therapy.
- Some diseases are contagious. For example cough and cold, T.B. small pox, etc.
- Some diseases are non-curable. For example cancer, AIDS, Ibola etc. But they can be controlled by medicine and change in lifestyle.
- Accordingly to belief systems, our health is affected by occult magical and religious practices. For example witchcraft, *Jharphuk,* worship.
- Natural calamities such as flood, desert, earthquakes also affect our health negatively because they bring varieties of diseases for the affected people.
- To remain healthy is our human right and no Government can deny it.
- The Government formulates and implements health promotion schemes to bring all sections in mainstream of nation. But it is not successful without public acceptance and support.
- To maintain health, there is concept of nutrition and hygiene in society. There is a need to modify them to suit the present situation.
- Leaving genetic diseases, we are responsible for our healthy or unhealthy life.

3

Indian Traditional System of Medicine

Long ago, Charles Darwin had propounded the Theory of Evolution. His theory of evolution propagated that species with useful adaptations to the environment are more likely to survive than those with less useful adaptations. This competition and urge to survive has always forced mankind to come up with newer inventions and innovate sustainable ways of life.

Today, we are living in age of modernization and also in post-modernization. No one can ignore the impact and usefulness of modernization and post modernization on our daily life. Modern and post modern innovations have made our mundane life hassle free. Faster means of communication, travelling and medicine is conquering new frontiers. The art of diagnostic techniques and treatment facilities have added altogether a different dimension to the profession of saving precious life. The other side is human interference with the nature and unhealthy lifestyle resulting in greater sufferings in terms of severe and untreatable diseases. The modern medicine system has tried to find out newer ways of treating diseases, but it has not become successful to stop or reverse the process. It is in this scenario that mankind has started looking back to the nature. Here is the role of alternative medicine and therapies. They work on principle of restoring natural balance and bringing human life back in harmony with nature.

Indian traditional medicine system has been based on this principle, i.e. focusing on holistic health, rather than treating a disease. These Indian traditional systems are as follows:

- Yoga
- Ayurveda
- Unani
- Siddha
- Homoeopathy
- Naturopathy.

Ayurveda and Yoga started their journey in India more than 5000 years ago as ancient Indian sciences. Siddha is one of the ancient systems of medicine popular in South India. Unani as a traditional system of medicine has its genesis in ancient Greece. Homoeopathy was developed in early 1800s by a German physician Samuel Hahnemann. These systems of medicines have enjoyed continuous patronage of the people over the years. Ayurveda, Yoga, Unani, Homoeopathy, Naturopathy and Siddha advocate a lifestyle which provides a healthy body, mind and over all happiness.

In recent times, all alternative systems of medicine have got global acceptance and popularity. Besides effective, cheap and no side effects, these therapies have been able to provide hope to certain chronic diseases and terminal stage patient. Modern medicine does not provide a solution or answer to such situations. Worldwide institutions have started undertaking researches to understand these systems more scientifically. Governments world over are trying to evolve policies to promote these therapies among their people so that the less privileged sections are more benefited.

In India, a full-fledged ministry was created to focuss on education and research of Ayurveda, Yoga, Naturopathy, Unani, Siddha and Homoeopathy systems. The ministry continues to lay emphasis on upgradation of AYUSH educational standards, quality control and standardization of drugs, research and awareness generation of system domestically and internationally. The United Nations has also recognized holistic benefits of Yoga for physical, mental and spiritual wellbeing and passed a resolution at its General Assembly in December 2014 to celebrate 21st June every year as International Yoga Day. 2015 marks the first year of celebration.

Now let us discuss about each traditional medical systems one by one in elaborate way.

Yoga System

Yoga is a spiritual discipline based on extremely subtle science. It focuses on bringing harmony between mind and body. It is an art and science of healthy living. The holistic approach of yoga is well established and it brings harmony in all walks of life. Thus yoga system is known for disease prevention, health promotion and management of many lifestyle-related disorders.

The term Yoga is derived from the Sanskrit root 'Yug', meaning to join, to yoke or to unite. As per yogic scriptures, the practice of yoga leads to the union of individual consciousness with that of universal consciousness. Thus, it indicates a perfect harmony between mind and body, man and nature. The aim of Yoga is self-realization to overcome all kinds of sufferings leading to the state of liberation (*Moksha)* or freedom (*Kaivalya)*. Thus, living in freedom in all walks of life, health and harmony are the main objectives of Yoga practice.

The practice of Yoga is believed to have started with very dawn of civilization. Yoga is widely considered as an immortal outcome of Indus Saraswati Valley Civilization dating back to 2700 B.C. It has proved itself as catering to both material and spiritual upliftment of humanity.

Origin and Development

The science of Yoga has its origin thousands of years ago, long before the first religion or belief system was born. According to yogic lore, Shiva is first yogi or Adiyogi. He is also regarded as first Guru or Adi Guru. According to tradition, several thousand years ago, on the banks of Lake Kanti Sarovar in the Himalyas, Adiyogi poured his profound knowledge into the legendary Saptarishis (Seven Sages). The sages carried this powerful yogic science to different parts of the world including Asia, Africa, Middle East and South America. Interestingly, modern scholars have noted and marvelled at the close parallels found between ancient cultures across the globe. However, it was in India that the yogic system found its fullest expression. Rishi Agastya, one of Saptarishis, had travelled across Indian Subcontinent, had crafted this culture around a core yogic way of life.

The evidence of seals and fossil remains of Indus-Saraswati Valley Civilization with yogic motives and figures performing yogic Sadhana suggests the presence of yoga in ancient India. The public symbols, seals of idols of mother Goddess are suggestive of Tantra yoga. Evidences of yoga are available in folk traditions, Indus-Saraswati valley civilization, Vedic and Upanishadic heritage, Buddhist and Jains traditions, Darshans, epics of *Mahabharata* and *Ramayana.* Their evidences are also found in Shaivas, Vaishnavas and Tantric traditions.

Although yoga was being practiced in the pre-Vedic period, but the great sage Maharshi Patanjali had systematized and codified the then existing practices of yoga, its meaning and its related knowledge through his *Yoga Sutra*. After Maharshi Patanjali, many sages and yoga masters contributed greatly for the preservation and development of the field through their well-documented practices and literatures. Now-a-days, everybody has conviction about yoga practices towards prevention, maintenance and promotion of health. Yoga has spread all over the world by the teachings of great personalities and yoga masters.

Different Traditional Schools of Yoga

Different philosophies, traditions, lineages and Guru-Shishya Paramparas of Yoga led to the emergence of different traditional schools of yoga. They are as follows:

- Jñāna Yoga
- Bhakti Yoga
- Karma Yoga
- Dhyana Yoga
- Patanjali Yoga
- Kundalini Yoga
- Hatha Yoga
- Mantra Yoga
- Laya Yoga
- Raj Yoga
- Jain Yoga
- Buddha Yoga.

Different social customs and rituals in India, the land of Yoga, reflect a love for ecological balance, tolerance towards other systems of thought and a compassionate outlook towards all creations. Yoga Sadhana of all hues and colour is considered panacea for meaningful life and living. Its orientation to comprehensive health both individual and social, makes it a worthy practice for people of all religions, races and nationalities.

Now-a-days, millions and millions of people have benefited themselves by the practice of Yoga from ancient time to this date.

Yogic Practices for Health and Wellness

The widely practiced Yoga Sadhanas (practices) are as follows:

- Yama
- Niyama
- Asana
- Pranayama
- Pratyahara
- Dharana
- Dhyana (Meditation).
- Samadhi (Samyama)
- Bandhas (Mudras)

- Satkarmas
- Yuktahara
- Yuktakarma
- Mantra Jaap

Yamas are restraints and *Niyamas* are observations. These are considered to be prerequisites for Yoga Sadhana (practices). Asanas is capable of bringing about stability of body and mind. It consists of adoption of various body (Psycho-physical) patterns. It provides a body position, a stable awareness of ones structural existence. For a considerable length and period of time, Asnas is widely practiced yogic practices for healthy living.

Pranayama consists of developing awareness of one's breathing followed by wilful regulation of respiration as the functional or vital basis of one's existence. It helps in developing awareness of one's mind and helps to establish control over the mind. In the initial stages, this is done by developing awareness of flow of inbreath (inhalation) and outbreath (exhaling) (*Svasa-Prasvasa)* though nostrils, mouth and other body openings, its internal and external pathways and destination. Later on, this phenomenon is modified through regulated, controlled and monitored inhalation (*Svasa)* leading to the awareness of body spaces getting filled (*Puraka),* the space/s remaining in filled state (*Kumbhaka),* and its getting emptied (*rechaka)* during regulated, controlled and monitored exhalation (*Prasvasa).*

Pratyahara indicates dissociation of one's consciousness (withdrawal) from the sense organs which help one to remain connected with the external objects.

Dharana indicates broad based field of attention (inside body and mind) which is usually understood as concentration.

Dhyana (Meditation) is contemplation (focused attention inside body and mind).

Samadhi is integration of body and mind.

Bandhas and *Mudras* are practices associated with Pranayama. They are viewed as higher Yogic practices, mainly consisting on adopting certain body patterns (Psycho-physical) along with control over respiration. This further facilitates control over mind and paves the ways for higher yogic attainment.

Satkarmas are detoxication procedures which help to remove toxin accumulated in the body and are clinical in nature.

Yuktahara (right food and other inputs) advocates appropriate food and food habits for healthy living.

Yuktakarma (Right act) leads to works suitable for the body and mind. It keeps individuals away from misdeeds and deeds not suitable to body and mind for healthy living.

Mantra jaap advocates recitation of hymns in the praise of Almighty God for healthy living.

The practice of Dhyana helps in self-realisation leading to transcendence is considered as the essence of Yoga Sadhana. A judicious combination of practice of *asana*, *pranayama* and *dhyana* daily keeps individuals healthy and disease free.

The knowledge aspects of Yoga Sadhana is being extensively researched with advantage to yoga practitioners. Psychological, Anatomico-physiological, biochemical and philosophical phenomena underlying Yoga sadhana have been commendably understood by us today. It is a matter of satisfaction for the entire humanity. Elaborate and effective means of its transmission such internet across the globe is a great stride for the propagation of yogic knowledge. The teaching methodology in yoga has also ingrained modern educational methodological rigours. There is also a world-wide growth of teaching schools of yoga across the globe. The earnest scientific and philosophico-literary research has also caught globally and is yet another encouraging sign of evolution of Yoga.

Lifestyle and Yoga

Lifestyle is the way people live and this has immense influence on status of health or disease of an individual. Since our's lifestyle generally develops early in life, it is advisable to cultivate healthy lifestyle in early childhood. Many factors determine one's lifestyle. Economic status determines the incidence of under nutrition in poor and above nutrition (obesity) in rich. Cultural values of the society dictate the dietary preferences in population. Sedentary life is a major factor for coronary artery disease, while personal habits like smoking and alcoholism determine the incidence of heart disease and cirrhosis of liver. Healthy diet, physical activity, good habits, rest and relaxation are important components of healthy lifestyle.

Yoga is the most perfect lifestyle module as it is comprehensive and holistic in nature. Yogic principles of lifestyle help strengthen and develop positive health enabling us to withstand stress better. This yogic health insurance has achieved by normalizing the perception of stress, optimizing the reaction to it and releasing the pent up stress effectively through the practice of various yogic practices. Yoga is popular now-a-days, because of its therapeutic credentials and it is being widely used as complementary medicine by practitioners of different systems of health care across the globe.

Yoga Therapy

Using yogic principles and practices for healing ailments is known as Yoga Therapy. Use of yoga practices for therapeutic purposes is a byproduct of yoga. Yogic practices are mind-centric. If one examines different references of yoga, e.g. Upanishads, Gita, Yogsutra, classical Hathayoga texts or any other yogic texts, it is clear that yoga is a discipline related to freedom of mind and its different faculties. Mind as an instrument of perception is used to transcend itself to give the perceiver clarity about its position. There is no reference of yogic tools available dealing directly with illness in yogasutra of Patanjali. But the word Vyadhi appears which is related to illness. However, direct references are available to show how Kriya, Asanas, Pranayamas and Mudras can be used to cure illness in Hatha Yoga texts such as *Hatha Yoga Pradipika*, *Gheranda Samhita*, *Yoga Yajnavalkya Samahita*, *Yoga Rahasya* etc. It is over the year yoga has developed the system for therapy purposes. They are passed on to their disciple and practiced as tradition of Yoga therapy.

THE YOGA-THERAPY: DOCTORINES AND CONCEPTS

The doctrines and concepts of Yoga Therapy are as follows:

- Doctorine of Chitta-Vrittinirodha, Kriya yogic and Astanga Yoga as found in Patanjal's Yog Sutra.
- Doctrine of Panchakosha (five sheaths/bodies) as found in Upanishads.
- Doctrine of various kinds of Shuddha found in *Patanjali Yogasutra* and *Hatha Yoga*.
- The doctrine of opening blocked channels of Vayus and Prana (Hadi Shuddhi), opening of lotuses and chakras, pranayamasm, mudras, dristis as found in Hatho-yoga and kundalini yoga.
- Workings with the mind on the lines of *Patanjali Yogasutra*, mantra yoga and hathayoga.
- Working on the lines of Karwa-Jana-Bhakti from Bhagwat Gita.

Certain aspects of Tantra yoga integrated in yoga practices.

Yoga therapy is being practiced now as an alternative health care practice in many parts of the world. The number of yoga practitioners continues to rise tremendously. Of many benefits ascribed to yoga practice, blood pressure control is among the most studies. There are several reviews regarding potential benefits of yoga for reducing blood pressure and other cardio-vascular disease risk factors, but the degree to which yoga therapy may decrease blood pressure and its modifying effects remain unclear. Yoga therapy has also been found to improve indices of risk in adults with the diabetes-2(MD), including glucose tolerance and insulin sensitivity, lipid profiles, anthropometric characteristics and blood pressure. It also leads to a reduction in oxidative damage, improve coagulation profiles and pulmonary functions. It decreases sympathetic activation in adults with diabetes and related chronic disorders. Yoga may also be useful in reducing medication requirement in patients with diabetes and could help prevent and manage cardio-vascular complications in the population. Many research papers have been published in indexed peer reviewed journals to prove the efficacy of yoga therapy in management of lifestyle related diseases. Medical researches in recent years has also uncovered many physical and psychological benefits that yoga also offers, corroborating the experience of millions of practitioners.

Mechanisms of Yoga

The following are mechanisms through which yoga works as an integrated body mind medicine:

Cleanses the accumulated toxins through various *shuddhi kriyas* and generates a sense of relaxed lightness through yogic *Sukshma vyayamas.* Free flows in all body passage prevents the many infections that may occur when pathogens stagnate therein.

Adoption of yogic lifestyle with proper nourishing diet, creates positive antitoxidants enhancement. Thus, it neutralizes free radicals while enabling a rejuvinative storehouse of nutrients packed with life energy to work on anabolic reparative and healing processes.

Yogic lifestyle steadies the entire body through different physical postures hold in steady and comfortable manner without strain. Physical balance and a sense of lease with oneself enhance mental/emotional balance and enable all physiological processes to occur in healthy manner.

It improves control over autonomic respiratory mechanisms through breathing patterns that generate energy and enhance emotional stability.

It integrates body movements with breath and create psychosomatic harmony.

It focuses the mind positively on activities being done, enhances energy flow and results in healthy circulation to different body parts and internal organs.

It creates a calm internal environment through contemplative practices and normalizes homoeostatic mechanisms. Mental balance produces physical balance and *vice versa,* too.

It relaxes the body emotion mind complex through physical and mental techniques that enhance our pain threshold and copying ability in responding to external and internal stresses. This enhances the quality of life in so many terminal cases where other therapies are not able to offer any solace.

It enhances self-confidence and internal healing capacities through the cultivation of right attitudes towards life and moral-ethical living through *yama*, *niyama,* and various other yogic psychological principles. Faith, self-confidence and inner strength are most essentials for healing, repair, rejuvenation and reinvigoration.

It works towards restoration of normalacy in all systems of human body with special emphasis on the psycho-neuro-immuno-endocrine axis. In addition to its preventive and restorative capabilities, yoga also aims at promoting positive health. This helps to tide over health challenges that occur during our life time. The concept of positive health is unique contribution of yoga to modern health care. It is because yoga plays preventive as well as promotive role in health care. It is also inexpensive and can be used with other systems of medicine in an integrated manner to benefit patients.

Yoga and Ayurveda

It is necessary to deal here the relation between Yoga and Ayurveda. Yoga and Ayurveda both are inseparable sisters. Both originated as a part of great system of Vedic knowledge. Both are based on principles of *Triguna* (*Sattva, Rajas* and *Tamas)* and *Pancha Mahabuttas* (earth, air, fire, water and space). Yoga and Ayurveda also encompass an understanding of how body works. *Dosha, Dhatu* and *Mal*—tissue waste material theory and the effect that food and medicine have on the body. *Rasa, Veerya, Vipaka* (taste)-energy-post-digestive effect concept. Yoga and Ayurveda are complementary to each other and holistic in nature. Both have a common understanding of health of body being dependant on health and balance of mind. They share virtually the same metaphysical anatomy and physiology. Which have 72000 *nadis* (Subtle channels), seven main *chakras* (energy centres), *Pancha Koshas* (five biodily sheaths) and *Kundalini Shakti* (coil powers). Ayurveda makes use of metaphysics of yoga and yoga practices to treat patient in totality. In treatment yoga advocates the regular practice of *asana, pranayama,* and meditation as well as the use of herbs, body purification procedures, food and chanting of *Mantras* for physical and mental health. Yoga and Ayurveda reveal to us the power of the body, breath, senses, mind and spirit. They cover the entire range of our lifestyle. Both recognize that keeping body and mind healthy is vital for fulfilling to aims of life—*Dharma, Aartha, Karma* and *Moksha.* Thus, Vedic medicine

(Ayurveda) and spiritual practice (Yoga) work together in bringing health and harmony to both body and mind leading to self-realization.

Yoga Teaching in Indian Universities

As per provisional report (2014-15) of All India Survey of Higher Education, there are 25 Universities and 18 colleges offering Master's degree in Yoga. The following two universities of Yoga are in UGC list:

- Lakulish Yoga University, Ahmadabad
- Swami Vivekanand Yoga Anusandhan Sansthan, Bangalore.

A committee has been constituted by the Government on Yoga education in universities. The terms of reference (ToR) for the committee included prescribing qualification of the faculty of yoga in colleges and universities and also to examine whether the existing qualification for the recruitment of faculty in colleges and universities presently approved by UGC, will need amendment.

The Committee has recommended in its report as follows:

- Appointment of Sub-committees to finalise the NET syllabus.
- Implementation of seven programmes in universities such as:
    - Certificate course in Yoga (CCY) of 6 to 12 months duration.
    - Bachelor of Science (Yoga)–B.Sc. (Yoga) of 3 to 6 years.
    - Post Graduate Diploma in Yoga Therapy (PGDYT) of 1 to 2 years.
    - Master of Science Yoga (M.Sc. Yoga) of 2 to 4 years.
    - Doctor of Philosophy (Yoga) 3 to 5 years.
    - Doctor of Philosophy (Integrated) Yoga of 4 to 6 years.

The Committee has also prescribed the qualification for faculty of Yoga. The Committee also made recommendations for promotion of yoga in universities.

International Day of Yoga

The United Nations proclaimed 21 June as the International Day of Yoga, recognizing the universal appeal of yoga. The draft resolution establishing the International Day of Yoga was proposed by India and endorsed by a record 175 member states. The proposal was first introduced by India's Prime Minister in his address during the opening of the both sessions of

General Assembly. The Prime Minister said that Yoga is an invaluable gift from our ancient tradition. Yoga embodies unity of mind and body and thought and action. It is a holistic approach valuable to our health and our wellbeing. Yoga is not just about exercise. It is a way to discover the sense of oneness with yourself, the world and the nature.

The International Yoga Day aims at raising awareness world-wide of many benefits of practicing Yoga. The International Day of Yoga on June 21, 2015 received a positive response from International Community. All 193 member countries of United Nations except Yemen participated in this International Yoga Day celebration. The Government of India celebrated International Day of Yoga on 21st June, 2015. Activities in various countries included lectures, demonstrations and mass yoga practice based on common yoga protocol, meeting with yoga clubs, community organizations, yoga concerts, Yogathons, yoga walks, films and documentary screening and photographic exhibitions. India received enthusiastic participation from people of all over the country. Two Guinness World Records were achieved. The large yoga lesson involving 35,985 participants and maximum number of Nationalities (84) participated in single yoga lesson.

The International Day of Yoga logo symbolizes the following:

Folding in both hands in the logo symbolizes yoga, the union, which reflects the union of individual consciousness with that of universal consciousness, a perfect harmony between mind and body, man and nature, a holistic approach to health and wellbeing. The brown leaves symbolize the earth element, the green leaves symbolize the nature, blue symbolizes the water, brightness symbolizes the fire element, and the sun symbolizes the source of energy and inspiration. The logo reflects harmony and peace for humanity, which is essence of yoga.

Health Benefits of Yoga in Modern Lifestyle

The modern day lifestyle has brought many challenges to health. It has become a major cause of many ailments among people across the globe.

Stress, improper dietary habits and sedentary living have led to decline in health leading to diabetes, asthma, cardiovascular diseases, metabolic disorders and cancer. Yoga can be a panacaea for all these modern day problems. Since these modern day health problems particularly the chronic NCDs are due to faulty lifestyle. Yoga is useful in combating these disorders. It emphasizes that science and spirituality are not separate entities, rather they are complementary to each other. Yoga has the potential to solve lifestyle problems and psychosomatic diseases. A series of researches and studies have been carried out across the globe to evaluate scientifically and validate the beneficial effect of yoga for prevention of diseases, management of diseases and promotion of health. Physiological, biochemical, psychological and clinical variables have been studied in controlled experiments to assess beneficial health effects of yoga. The study revealed that yoga influenced cellular and molecular aspects of health of practitioners through its effect on autonomic nervous system and endocrine system. It was observed that yogic practice brings stability of autonomic equilibrium along with strengthening of para-sympathetic system thereby minimizing wear and tear in different physiological results in relative hypo-metabolic state providing greater buffer for stress response. The study indicates improvement in physical and cognitive performance, improvement in thermoregulatory efficiency and body flexibility stress tolerance. It also strengthens our immunity preventing diseases. Yoga was also found as an adjunct to conventional medical management of hypertension, coronary artery diseases and diabetes. Yoga may be useful in reducing medication requirements in patients with diabetes, hypertension and can manage cardio-vascular complications.

Benefits of yoga can be thought at three levels:

- At the level of body, it delivers good health and wellness.
- At the level of mind, it increases focuss, relieves stress and enhances productivity.
- At the level of spirit, it elevates human value and brings peace and solace to one's life.

Physical and Physiological Health Benefits of Yoga

The yoga practice brings following physical and physiological health benefits:

- Increases flexibility.
- Increases muscle strength and tone.
- Improves respiration, energy and vitality.
- Maintains a balanced metabolism.

- Weight reduction.
- Cardio and circulatory health.
- Improves athletic performance.
- Improve immunity.
- Cardio-vascular endurance.

Psychological and Spiritual Health Benefits of Yoga

The Yoga practice brings following psychological and spiritual health benefit:

- Increases experience of relaxation.
- Provides a deeper appreciation for present moment or mindfulness.
- Allows greater control over mind and thought.
- Increases mental clarity.
- Improves concentration and focuss.
- Improves self-discipline.
- Expands imagination and creativity especially in children.
- Elevates mood and feelings of contentment.
- Increases self-awareness.
- Increases self-confidence.
- Increases optimism.
- Improves symptoms of certain neuron-psychiatric disorders including Schizophrenia and ADHD.
- Reduces symptoms of anxiety and depression.
- Encourages self-knowledge.
- Stimulates the energy centre of the body.
- Increases ability to manifest positive experience in daily life.
- Discovery or connection with one's sense of purpose or meaning in life.
- Creates a sense of being more in tune with one's inner consciousness.
- Leads to a greater sense of connectedness to others and the world.

Responsibility of Youth Population

India has a very large population of youth. It is commendable that they are taking an active interest in matters related to healthy lifestyle and development of personality. Younger generations need to adopt as part of their lifestyle for a stressfree life and to deliver better performance. Several initiatives have been taken by the Government of India for the promotion and development of yoga in recent past. The ground and successful celebrations of International Day of Yoga has increased our responsibility. The event has created huge awareness of health benefits of yoga and great demand of yoga teacher across the globe. Ministry of AYUSH has approached Quality Control of India (QCI) to certify yoga professionals. Ministry of AYUSH is planning to establish AYUSH integrated hospitals in every districts of each state. Ministry has initiated action to impart yoga training to Armed forces, paramilitary and police personnel. Yoga training programme has also been started at Griha Kalyan Kendras in New Delhi by Department of Personnel and Training. Six Central Research Institutes in Yoga and Naturopathy are coming up. WHO has also emphasized the need to involve ancient systems of medicine in the health delivery system. Here, it is to be emphasized that system of yoga has withstood the test of time and cannot be ignored simply on account of lack of evidence. Due importance needs to be given on strength and potential of yoga policy. The strategic interventions need to be done to optimize the utilization of this system. Proper administrative setup needs to be established to look after regulatory and development aspect of yoga. Only peaceful individuals can make peaceful families. Yoga is a way to create such a harmony and peace with individuals, family, society, nation and all over the world.

Assessment and Certification of Yoga Practitioners

The certification attests to the basic common understanding of practices and theories of yoga by certified yoga professionals. In a way, the certification guarantees quality of yoga professionals both in skill and knowledge. The proposed levels of certification envisage establishing a hierarchy of yoga professionals based on skills and knowledge.

There have been various speculations regarding the exact date and history of yoga. Yoga tradition is much older than the speculation. Some of the most revered scriptures in India such as *Mahabharata* and *Bhagwat Gita* have elaborated references to Yoga. Gita has identified three kinds of yoga: *Karma yoga, Bhakti yoga* and *Jñāna Yoga.* It is a ways of life which finds mention in Vedas between 1900 B.C. to 1000 B.C. The *Patanjali Yoga Sutra* has described eight-fold path of Yoga, namely *Yamas, Niyamas, Asana, Pranayama, Pratyahar, Dharana, Dhyana* and *Samadhi.*

These Yoga Sutras codify the best or Royal (*Raja)* yoga practices. These are eight limbed system—Ashtanga. The philosophical tradition of Yoga is based upon *Samkhya* Philosophy of Sage Kapila. The focus is on the mind. The second Sutra of Patanjali defines yoga as cessation of all mental modifications and stoppage of all wandering thoughts.

But in later tradition of yoga, such as *Hatha yoga* focuses a on more complex *Asanas* or body postures.

Now-a-days, yoga is also being practiced for elevating the cosmic life force or *kundalini,* through a series of physical and mental exercises. At physical level methods comprise various yoga postures or *Asanas* which keep the body fit and healthy. At mental level the techniques include breathing exercises such as *pranayama*, and meditation *dhyana*.

The popularity of yoga has attracted a large number of people globally who strive to practice yoga for achieving a better quality of life. In order to keep their faith in tact, it is necessary to impart proper knowledge base to train and guide those yoga aspirants across the world. This is possible by creating a pool of credible and competent personnel for imparting training to yoga practices. For this purpose, various initiatives were required. One initiative was to develop a system of certifying yoga professionals by assessing their competence. There was a need to develop a globally acceptable assessment system. Depending upon the knowledge, skill and maturity yoga professionals can be categorized as instructor, teacher and *Acharya.* The system of assessment should be such that an instructor could become *Acharya* through promotion scheme.

The another initiative should be issuance of a degree, diploma or a certificate of proficiency in yoga.

The third initiative should be to develop framework of institutions imparting yoga. Not all institutions are of the same standard in imparting basic knowledge and skill of yoga. The recognition of institution will fulfil the gap of identifying the committed from the compromising lot among the institutions.

The yoga school certification scheme should have provision to certify the yoga schools at different levels such as level I, level II and level III. At first level those schools are included which have capacity to impart yoga education to instructor and teacher. At the 2nd level those schools have been included which have capability to impart yoga education to at least 50 per cent yoga associations approved teaching/training programme. At the level 3rd those schools are included which have capability to design tailor made teaching programmes. They impart yoga education in *Ashram* like setting for the courses which are 200 hours duration or more.

In order to provide benefit to students passing from these certified yoga schools, the yoga professional certification school be awarded to such students by taking interview in the form of *viva voce* instead to day long theory and practical assessment.

Challenges of Assessing Competence

There are some challenges in assessing competence of yoga professional. Whether one can assess and measure the knowledge transferred from teacher to his student. The another challenge is Ceru the *Chitta* (mind) be observed itself, assessed or measured by others. Is it possible to for other person to see the *Vritti* (meditation) happening in the mind of others.

It is very hard task to certify yoga professionals. It is because yoga is identified as experimental discipline. Certifying knowledge and skill in yoga is an attempt to make yoga more and more objective. The essence of yoga is subjectively, depth and interpretation.

Some other challenges come from yoga institutions imparting education and training. In our country as well as in foreign countries there are a number of reputed yoga institutions which are engaged in promoting Yoga activities. There are also innumerable smaller institutions involved in imparting yoga activities, education and training. These courses of various institutions differ from each other time-wise and content-wise. Therefore, yoga teachers have different proficiency and expertise in skill and knowledge aspects. Practices of different institutions are also different. These differences make the discipline vibrant and all encompassing. But it also creates confusion and uncertainty in the mind of yoga learners. Whenever any phenomenon becomes popular, it involves a larger cross-section of people interpreting it in their own way. It leads to dilution when such academic and non-academic discourse completing disassociates itself from the basic premise on which it was based and nurtured over centuries. Yoga is naturally and inevitably susceptible to this danger.

Over the years, *Gurus* in India and abroad have ventured to promote their own interpretations of yoga which have readily accepted by their followers. They have provided required solace, peace and healthy practices. Sometimes such teachings were founded upon the experiences of their *Gurus* in different Ashramas or institutions.

In order to deal with these challenges, some basic principles were needed to formulate. It was laid down that certification must not destroy the essence and uniqueness of various yoga schools. It should be developed as a science, but subjectivity and experience should not be lost.

Solution of Challenges

The soaring practices and popularity of yoga over the globe got a further impetus with declaration of 21st June as International Yoga Day by United Nations. In this way, India re-established its role as world leader in Yoga. This position of India has placed a great responsibility for protecting and promoting yoga in its true and undiluted spirit.

The Ministry of AYUSH in pursuance of above identified Quality Council of India (QCI) to develop a scheme for evaluation and certification of yoga professionals. It also emphasized upon scheme of certification of yoga institutions. The QCI has expertise to develop such quality framework based on international practices.

The main focus of voluntary yoga professional certification scheme is to certify the competence of yoga professionals who work as instructors, teachers, masters, Guru Acharya and the therapeutic practitioners. The QCI scheme of certification of Yoga professionals of different levels is an attempt to encompass all diversities related to yoga professionals and institutions and to create an acceptable benchmark as regards to skills and knowledge of yoga practitioners irrespective of institutions from where they have taken formal or informal yoga training.

The certification attests to basic understanding of practices and theory of yoga by all certified yoga professionals. The certification guarantees quality of yoga professionals in skill and knowledge both. It also makes attempt to establish hierarchy of yoga professionals on the basis of skill and knowledge. The skill and knowledge are two important aspects of yoga practitioners.

The scheme for certifying yoga institutions is a step towards harmonizing the basic tenets on which any yoga training must be based. Its aim is also to establish outcome parameters for yoga teachers irrespective of institutions. In framing the syllabus for certification process, an opportunity is provided to establish and promote the spirit of yoga in its pristine purity.

The scheme has been designed to employ global standard system to ensure internationally acceptable certification. This would ensure internationally acceptable conditions. The objective of the scheme is to assist organizations and individuals to select yoga professional or yoga institution. The QCI operates the scheme on the principle of third party assessment.

QCI created a multi-stakeholder committee of experts for designing the scheme. The Committee constitutes representation of various stakeholders, namely yoga personalities, yoga schools, AYUSH Ministry of Commerce, academic institutions, consumers organization, potential certifying agencies.

There is also an advisory committee to provide over-all guidance. The scheme of certification of yoga has the following sections:

Governing Structure

It emphasizes upon the structure, components, roles and responsibilities of participating organizations.

Certification Criteria

It emphasizes the standard for certification developed by technical experts.

Certification Process

It lays emphasis upon the evaluation process—initial evolution, frequency of surveillance and requirements of evaluators.

Requirements for Certification Body

A dedicated website has been created and all informations are available on it—www.yogacertification.qci.org.in

Opportunities Incentivising the Certified Personnel

The Government of India has been supportive to QCI scheme and has been proactively promoting the scheme in various national and international platforms. The certificate issued to successful yoga professional has the Ministry of AYUSH emblem. It lends it the required credibility and status for being a matter of pride.

The Government has been considering to offer incentives to yoga professionals in many aspects such as preference in Government requirement, mandating the current professionals to get their competence validated by undertaking the QCI yoga professional certification, urging various boards like CBSE, Kendriya Vidyalaya Sangathan, to consider certification in recruitment of yoga teachers, informing Minister of Home Affairs, Ministry of External Affairs for announcing sops including ease of issuance of Visa relaxation in visa fee for encouraging yoga professionals to go for certification. The Indian Council for Cultural Relations (ICCR) has been requested to mandate that for all overseas yoga appointment.

In a measure thrust to the scheme, the Ministry of AYUSH, Government of India, has announced hundred per cent reimbursement of fee through QCI for first 2000 successful candidates pass in their first attempt.

The yoga professional scheme has been launched by QCI globally. A team of QCI visited Japan to conduct evaluation and certified 13 yoga professionals.

It is envisaged that over a period of time, universities conducting yoga courses, formal and non-formal yoga institutions/schools, health resorts, spas, yoga studies will induct only yoga professionals having certification under QCI yoga scheme.

Balancing Healthy and Stress-free Life through Yoga

People from different walks of life are now more aware about yogic practices and its role not merely in preservation and promotion of positive health, but also in the prevention and management of various diseased conditions. Scientists and other medical professionals have realized the importance of yogic lifestyle for prevention and management of stress induced and other psychosomatic disorders. The popularity of yoga has reached beyond India. Practices of yoga are performed in many parts of the globe by youth. Yoga is above region, religion, caste, creed, race and nationality. It is open for all. The United Nations has declared 21st June as International Day of Yoga.

Health is defined being a state of complete physical, mental, social and spiritual wellbeing and not merely as absence of disease or infirmity. This definition of health has been provided by WHO. Overall health is achieved through a combination of physical, mental, social and spiritual wellbeing. Here begins the role of yoga. It develops our personality in a holistic and balanced way, i.e. on physical, mental, emotional, social and spiritual planes of living at the same time. Its regular practice enhances our capacity and improves level of confidence. Yoga has the power to transform the youth in leading a more healthy balanced, stress free and meaningful life. It educates the person on does and does not five *Yamas* and five *Niyamas.* Yogic practices are easy to follow and can be integrated well in our daily routine as per the need. The industrialization and fast metropolitan lifestyle have increased health challenges before us. These health risk are pollution, stress, anxiety and so on. In dealing with these problems our lifestyle has become faster and more mechanical from early morning to late night. The dietary habits are not healthy. Preserved food, fast food, junk food, high calorie diet, smoking habit, drinking habit, drugs intake, not proper reset, lack of exercise have made us impatient which ultimately cause a number of psychosomatic diseases such as diabetes, hypertension, arthritis, backpain and others. The number of mental illnesses is increasing day by day due to these reasons. It has been found that a large number of people are suffering from depression, schizophrenia disorder related use of drugs and alcohol. Yoga as a non-invasive mode of treatment treats the body and mind effectively.

Its different practices, e.g. *Asanas, Pranayamas, Satkarmas, Surya Namaskara* and meditation help mental patients in becoming cured. Various illnesses like anxiety, fear, depression, neurosis, behavioural impairment disorder, anorexia, headache, bronchitis, asthma, diabetes, autoimmune disorders can very well be managed by the practice of yoga.

Stress and anxiety are one of the most common problems of youth. Stress may be physical or mental with external or internal causes. Major changes in life, work load at office, kin conflict, family relationship, children problem are common causes of stress. While chronic worries, pessimism, negative self-talk, unrealistic expectations, perfectionism, rigid thinking, lack of flexibility, all or nothing attitude are common internal causes of stress. These are psychosomatic disease conditions with complains like headache, insomnia, twitches, skin rashes, digestive disorder, peptic ulcers, colitis, palpitation, highblood pressure, coronary thrombosis, dysmenorrhea and others. Regular practice of *Asanas, Pranayamas* and meditation has a great role in their management. *Asnas* stabilize and relax the body and mind, open new thought process and ultimately brings changes in attitude of practitioners towards life and health. The practice of deep breathing yoga *mudra* and meditation decreases the pessimistic attitude and brings calmness, internal pleasure, and cultivates optimistic thought.

Save Healthy Lifestyle Practices

Some healthy lifestyle practices can be incorporated by youth in their lifestyle to become more healthy. These lifestyle practices make practitioners stress-free. They are food for maintenance of health and prevention of diseases. These are simple, cost effective, easy to follow, and can be integrated in the daily routine as per the need. The natural lifestyle enhances the love and affection between each other and develop a bondage of connection. It promotes calmness, tranquility and optimistic attitude to mind. Some of these practices are as follows:

Balanced Eating

The first and foremost important practice is balanced eating. Our food must be in natural form as far as possible. Our diet must consist of fresh seasonal fruits, fresh green leafy vegetables and sprouts in sufficient quantity.

These foods help in the improving our health, purifying body and rendering immune to diseases.

Fasting

Fasting is an important technique of health preservation. It is a process of giving rest to whole digestive system. During this process the vital energy which digests the food is completely used in detoxification of body. It is an excellent remedy for improving the disorders of body as well as mind. Weekly fast on fruit juices or fruits is advised to maintain good health.

Regular Exercise

Regular excercises in some form or yogic practices are essential for good health. It increases the blood circulation and makes the body flexible. It reduces the ageing process and maintains sound health. For this purpose morning walk, running, jogging, swimming, *yoga sadhana, Surya namaskara, pranayama,* gardening and other works can be selected. It depends upon our body and capacity to do exercises. Exercise activates our body, boosts energy, develop new and optimistic thought along with other physiological benefits. According to a naturologist Dr. Henry Lindbahr exercise stirs up the morbid accumulations in tissues, stimulates the arterial and venous circulation, expands the lungs to their fullest capacity, increases the intake of oxygen and promotes the elimination of waste and morbid through skin, kidney, bowels, and respiratory tract.

Rest

Apart from yogic practices proper rest is also essential for good health. Rest means quality sleep. A good sleep gives us freshness, makes us happy and light. Incomplete sleep results in stress, anxiety and deterioration of health. Hence, quality sleep should never be compromised.

Adequate Water Taking

Adequate water drinking is good for prevention of disorders and maintenance of health. Water dissolves all toxicity of body and cleanses the body internally.

Some Healthy Lifestyle Practices and Tips

Some golden tips related to lifestyle practices are as follows:

- Go to bed early at night and wake up early before sunrise.
- Take simple balanced and *sattvic* diet.
- Reduce quantity of heavy salt, sugar, oil, *ghee*, spices, heavy meals, red chilly, pickles, tea and non-vegetarian food.
- Fix the meal time.
- Take whole wheat bread, steamed vegetable and salad.
- Take breakfast of fruit, *dalia* or sprout.
- Take water half an hour after or before lunch.
- Morning and evening meditation or prayer should be practiced.
- Do internal and external cleansing of body through yogic practices or *satkarma.*

- Have faith in nature.
- Avoid habit of over-eating. Follow the principle of no appetite no food. Always avoid over-eating.
- Morning walks and maximum walk on foot.

Enriching Health and Quality of Life Through Yoga

The yogic lifestyle has a scheme of balancing internal and external lives. If life is well balanced, the capacity, expertise and success in life develop spontaneously. It is not an exaggeration to say that yogic lifestyle is the golden principle for a disease-free life. Currently yoga has become very popular and a number of organizations have started teaching yoga. But not much attention has been paid on standardising yoga and developing a scientific model of yoga therapy. Therefore, it is essential to establish the scientific nature of yoga therapy through adequate research in practical and theoretical aspects.

Our body does not consist of only visible physical form, but also possesses four unseen bodies (subtle and causal layers). Altogether each of us has five bodies or *Koshas.* They are as follows:

Annamaya Kosha

It is called as body of nourishment or physical body.

Pranamaya Kosha

It is known as energy body or bioplasmic layer.

Manomaya Kosha

It is called as mental body or Astral layer.

Vigyanamaya Kosha

It is known as intellectual body or wisdom layer.

Anandamaya Kosha

This is termed as body of Joy or Bliss layer.

Our *karmas* (Actions) and *sanskaras* (memories and experiences) are stored in these *koshas.* They form partition between individual soul and the universal self. Liberation *(Moksha)* means to release *Atma* (soul) from these *Koshas.* Without releasing ourselves with *Kosha,* we cannot become one with infinite. It is also true that the five *Koshas* are essential for our existence on earth. Without them, we cannot exist on earth. To surmount and detach from *koshas* is an extensive process of mental purification and development.

Annamaya Kosha

It is the physical body. It is influenced by our food and environment. Therefore, yoga teaching emphasizes upon positive beneficial human interactions; healthy *sattvic* diet for physical and mental development. The consumption of meat, alcohol and drugs weakens our vitality and fills us with negative vibes. A wholesome lacto-vegetarian diet provides nourishment for our body in an optimal way.

Pranamaya Kosha

It is subtle sheath of cosmic energy called *Prana* that penetrates and surrounds the physical body. It forms our 'Aura', the radiance that emanates from us. *Prana* is subtle nourishment as necessary to life as food and drink. With each breat we not only absorb oxygen but also *prana.* All foods supply us not only nourishment but also *prana.* The quality of *prana* is affected by external influences as well as our own thoughts and emotions.

Manamaya Kosha

This is mental energy sheath. It is more extensive and powerful than the *Pranamaya Kosha.* The mind and thoughts can reach anywhere without any loss of time. Therefore, it is very difficult to central thoughts. It is this uncontrolled speed of mind that creates emotional upsurges leading to speed. This is called *Adhi* which goes down to *Annamaya Kosha* for becoming *Vyadhi* (disease) through the imbalance of *Pranamaya Kosha.* Only through controlling over mind we can get control over these instances, stresses and diseases. The best method of mastering the mind is to foster good thought. Following rules of *Yama* and *Niyama* purity of mind can be obtained.

Vigyanamaya Kosha

It is the intellectual body. It can be positively or negatively oriented. This depends upon the society we live together with sensory impressions that we absorb from our environment. It is formed by experiences, socialization and education and represents sum total of all these. The intellect is not always our best adviser. It is deaf towards truth and judges egoistically in life with our desire. Of course, intellect can be a very useful tool but it also creates great hindrance. That is why we should always employ *Buddhi* (reason) and *Viveka* (correct discrimination).

Anandamaya Kosha

It is the body of bliss. It is causal layer from where the other four emerges all over *sanskaras* and *vasanas.* They are difficult to purify. This is because aspiration for fulfilment of our desires, comfort and pleasures is a powerful motivator and decisive power within us.

There are several layers of bliss encompassed by eternal unlimited supreme joy. The first one depends on certain conditions. The fulfilment of our desires and other favourable circumstances. The latter is unconditional and totally independent on external conditons. Lasting contentment and *Maha Ananda* (infinite bliss) are bestowed upon us only in union with the self. All other joys are limited and transitory. Only through *Gyana* (wisdom) we can force ourselves from *Anandamaya Kosha. Bhakti* (devotion to God) takes us close to this goal. But the final step can be mastered through the knowledge of truth. Only then we attain *Moksha* (liberation).

Yoga is recognized as forms of mind medicine that integrates physical, mental and spiritual of an individual to improve stress related illness. Evidences show that stress is one of main causes of heart disease, cancer, stroke and other chronic diseases. Hence, in yoga emphasis is given on stress management and reduction of negative emotions. Yoga is viewed as holistic stress management technique.

There s no doubt that yogic procedures are effective in treating diseases. But how does it work, what is the scientific basis on which yoga therapy works, what is the model of yoga therapy without answering these questions correctly, scientifically and logically yoga therapy would be incomplete.

The foremost truth involved in model of yoga therapy is that it considers scientific as well as total perspective on human system. The comprehensive knowledge of role of *Prana* (vitality) in functioning of human body is essential. According to the science of yoga, diseases are due to *Adhi* and the distortions in *Prana* or by deficiency in *Prana.* The science of yoga classifies diseases into two broad categories:

- Diseases caused by circumstances, and
- Diseases caused by *Prarabdha Karma* (*Adhi Vyadhi).*

In both cases the flow of *Prana* gets disturbed, but there is difference in their cure. In yoga therapy, lifestyle and perspective of life plays a crucial role in cleansing and enhancing *Prana.*

The science of yoga proves that aspects of our life are influenced by harmony of *Prana. Prana* in its different forms flows through our body. Modern science denotes *Prana* as life force, capacity to resist diseases, bio-electricity of electromagnetic energy. Actually all of these are the various forms of *Prana*. In science of yoga a comprehensive knowledge of *Prana* is required. Yoga believes that when the flow of *Prana* breaks, our gross physical body will get separated from the subtle body. In physical parlance, it is defined as death.

For a healthy and long life, conservation as well as enhancement of *Prana* is essential. The preliminary emphasis of yoga is on preservation of health. Yoga specialists believe that negligence of yogic lifestyle is the root cause of disease. If regularity is mentioned in adherence to yogic pattern of life, total freedom from the diseases is possible. Yogic technique also solve the problem of diseases caused by *karma*. Thus, yoga promises for a disease free life for everybody.

It is surprising to note that man does not use *prana* stored within him and regrets the suffering caused by the each of *prana. Prana* can be preserved by *Sanyam* (self-control) and utilize it rightly to make life blissful. But man ignores *prana* and starts leading life as an animal. The yogic lifestyle makes a balance between external and internal lives.

AYURVEDA

Origin

The origin of Ayurveda as a system of holistic health care is known to have emanated from the health and medical knowledge imbibed in Vedic literature. Dating back to about 5000 years, Ayurveda is believed to have its roots in *Atharvaveda*. It is also counted as fourth Veda and science of life. Initially transmitted in oral form from one generation to another, systematic documentation of Ayurvedic concepts, basic principles and clinical application started with two major compedia known as:

- *Charak Samhita*
- *Sushrut Samhita.*

These two *Samhitas* were written about 1000 years B.C. Other compedia of Ayurveda based by and large on *Charak Samhita* and *Sushrut Samhita* came up much later in the name of *Ashtang Sangraha* and *Ashtang Hridayam*. By the end of the first millennium B.C., Ayurveda got established with two main schools of thought. They were as follows:

- *Dhanwantri Sampradaya,* and
- *Atreya Sampradaya.*

Dhanwantri Sampradaya is known as school of physicians, whereas *Atreya Sampradaya* is known as school of surgeons. Both these great schools had their own representative collections. The collection of *Dhanwantri Sampradaya* is known as *Charak Samhita* and the collection of *Atreya Sampradaya* is known as *Sushrut Samhita*. In *Charak Samhita*, a number of chapters were written on different types of diseases and their treatment. This *samhita* provides us name of 600 medicines prepared from plants, animals and minerals.

In *Sushrut Samhita* one finds description of basic principles and concepts of surgery. This knowledge-based book provides us names of 100 tools and instruments used for surgery were practiced on vegetables and dead animals. One also finds description of 650 medicines. They were used in different types of surgery.

Tenets of Clinical Medicine

In Ayurveda tenets of clinical medicine were classified into eight specialties. They were as follows:

- *Kaya Chikitsa* (Medicine)
- *Shalya Chikitsa* (Surgery)
- *Shalakya Chikitsa* (Ophthalmology and ENT)
- *Kaumar Bhritya Chikitsa* (Paediatrics)
- *Agad Tantra Chikitsa* (Toxicology)
- *Bhoot Vidya* (Psychiatry)
- *Rasayana Chikitsa* (Gerentology)
- *Vijikarma* (Science of Virility and Health Progeny).

This health knowledge is also known as Ashtang Ayurveda. The fundamental concepts and subjects of clinical medicine are described in two triads of classical treatises called *Brihat Trayee* comprising *Charak Samhita*, *Sushrut Samhita* and *Ashtang Sangraha*, and *Laghu Trayee* consisting of *Madhava Nidan*, *Sharangadhara Samhita* and *Bhava Prakasha*. Fortunately, all the major authritative books of Ayurveda are available today. They are listed in First Schedule to Drugs and Cosmetics Act, 1940. They serve the purpose of leagal definition of Ayurveda drugs.

Different aspects of Ayurveda have evolved and documented from time to time. That is why various Ayurvedic treatises have specific objectives and subject to emphasize than the others. For example, in *Charak Samhita* there is much emphasis on philosophy of life, health and medicine and classical line of treatment for different diseases. *Sushruta Samhita* emphasizes more on surgery and surgical aspects of diseases. It also deals with systematic approach to diagnosis and surgical treatment of diseases of eye, ear, throat, nose and dentistry. *Kashyap Samhita* deals mainly with child health care. *Madhava Nidana* deals with pathological aspects and diagnosis of diseases. *Bhava Prakasha* deals with formulations based treatment of diseases and description of food items. *Sharangdhara Samhita* is replete with various aspects of pharmaceutics and dosage forms. There have been perpetual and methodical inputs to enhance the theoretical framework and applied aspects of Ayurveda with perpetual innovations, inclusions and necessary modifications from time to time. Subsequent commentaries on the original texts have clarified intricacies and complexities of the subject matters and helped to resolve the texual ambiguities and confusions. Presently, Ayurveda has reached at a stage of much clarity of its fundamental principles, concepts and application due to continuous efforts that have gone in the process of its development and evolution.

Before medieval period, Ayurveda was a recognized medical system in Indian subcontinent. The health of kings, courtiers and the people were looked after, cured and preserved by Ayurvedic medical system and lifestyle. This medical system enjoyed the patronage of kings and people. This period is recognized as golden period of Ayurvedic medical system. Majority of its principles, concepts, theories and usages were developed during this period.

The medieval period brought a rough weather towards this medical system prevalent all over ancient India. India had to face foreign invasions. Political stability in country was badly disturbed. This period witnessed new rulers who were not ready to provide patronage to Ayurvedic medical system. But this medical system maintained its existence even in adverse situation.

The Ayurvedic medical system had to suffer more during British period. This lifestyle was totally neglected. In place of Ayurvedic medical system, allopathic medical system was introduced throughout the length and breadth of country during British period. As a result Ayurvedic lifestyle suffered a great jolt. But when freedom movement started, revival of Ayurvedic system became one of the issues of freedom movement. When India became free, importance of Ayurvedic medical system was recognized. The Government of India took a number of steps to revive Ayurvedic medical system. Ayurvedic hospitals, colleges and institutes were established. CIRISM was established in 1955. Post-graduate Ayurvedic Training centre was started in 1956. Gujarat Ayurvedic University, Jamnagar, was established in 1976. Indian Medical Central Council was established in 1972. Through this Central Council, emphasis was placed on teaching and registration of Ayurvedic, Siddha and Unani medical systems. In 1971, Indian medical Homoeopathy and Yoga Central Research Council was established. Through this emphasis was placed on development of Indian medical system. Later on, this Council was divided into Ayurvedic and Siddha Central Research Council, Unani Central Research Council, Homoeopathy Central Research Council and Naturopathy and Yoga Central Research Council.

National Institute of Ayurved at Jaipur was established. Rajasthan Ayurveda University, Jaipur, was established very recently, Indian Government has announced a policy related to establishment of a Ayurvedic hospital in each district headquarters of each state. The purpose has been to provide cheap and alternative medicine to the people. Policies of Ayurveda and other Indian medical systems are available at website of AYUSH Mantralaya.

Concept of Health in Ayurveda

In our country, Ayurveda is not taken only ethnomedicine, rather it has been recognized as a holistic medical science. This medical system provides us informative, physical, mental, philosophical, moral and spiritual health of human beings. In this system attempts have been made to emphasize on living and doing works peacefully in the universe. Emphasis has been placed on correlation between nature and science. This science employs holistic and universal approach. As a result, this medical system has its special and separate existence. This medical science deals mainly with positive health and proper lifestyle. This medical system is nearly 5000 years old. Modern medical sciences have also recognized its importance. Perhaps, concepts of health which appears in world health organisation was taken from the Ayurveda.

Philosophical Background

The philosophical theory of Ayurveda is based in this fact that whatever is happening in universe is also happening in our body. This universe is made up of five physical elements—Earth, water, fire, air and ether. These elements are also present in our body in combined form. The organisation of these elements creates *Tridosha* (Three bio humors). They are *kapha, pitta* and *vata.*

Thus, according to Ayurveda, human body is like a mini universe made up of five physical elements. They are *Prithavi* (Earth), *Jala* (water), *Agni* (Fire), *Vayu* (Air) and *Akash* (Ether). Besides these five physical elements, our body consists of a most subtle element called *Chetana* or *Atma Tatva.* This is responsible for consciousness and is indicator of life. There exists similarilty and correlation between macrocosm (universe) and microcosm (human body) in terms of law of nature. The functional entities of body system derived from interaction of physical elements in definite proportions are called as *Tridosha* (Three bio humors). They are *Vata, Pitta* and *Kapha. Tridosha* when remain in the state of dynamic equilibrium, health remains maintained. But when *Tridosha* remain in the state of imbalance, health is disturbed and disease is caused. The structural entities forming the body matrix are termed as *Dhatus.* They are as follows:

- *Rasa* (Plasma)
- *Rakta* (Blood cells)
- *Mansa* (Muscular Tissue)
- *Meda* (Fatty Tissue)
- *Ashthi* (Bone tissue)
- *Majja* (Bone marrow)
- *Shukra* (Reproductive secretions).

All metabolic and biotransformation functions in the body system are in the hands of *Agni* (bio-fire) and *srotas* (channels). In the process, excretory waste called *Mala* like urine, stool, and sweat are produced. Integrated balance of *Dosha, Dhatu* and *Mala* and happiness of souls, mind and sense organs is attributed to health and the imbalance of these factors cause indisposition.

The definition of health provided in *Sushruta Samahita* is very comprehensive. It depicts the wholesome state of wellbeing and harmonious life with stable equilibrium of functional, structural and excretory entities. Health is considered as a basic prerequisite for enjoying, virtues of life. Individual, social, cultural, economic, political, religious, materialistic and spiritual gains cannot be attained without health.

Concept of Disease Causation

People can be divided into different categories on the basis of their psychosomatic structure. In order to maintain health, there is a provision to perform daily and seasonal works. If daily work and seasonal works are not performed regularly and properly, *Tridosha* develops in our body and made us ill. Imbalance in *Tridosha* is caused by improper nutrition and food, bad habit, seasonal disturbances, improper exercise, improper use of sex organs and work against the will of body and mind. Besides these factors, other factors also cause diseases. For example entrance of micro-organisms and bacteria, change in environment etc. These factors also create imbalance in *Tridosha* which ultimately leads to causation of diseases. In general situation flow of *tridosha* takes place through macro and micro channels. These channel are known as *srotas.* Body tissue gets nutrition through these channels. *Malas* (waste) come out of body through these channels. When a stoppage is created in channels due to imbalance in *Tridosha,* the body tissues do not get nutrition and *mala* do not come out of body. As a result the body gets diseased. Thus, blockage in biochannels is the mother of all diseases.

Treatment of Disease

Ayurveda provides distinct approach towards diagnosis and management of diseases. In principle, diagnosis in Ayurvedic terms is complete understanding of disease factors and process of manifestation of the disease in an individualized manner. The treatment is accordingly planned with the objective to balance *Dosha, Dhatu* and *Mala* by breaking the disease process and restoring pre-disease state of health. This involves dual diagnostic methodology of investigating the disease and individual to find out the strength of disease process as well as patient's strength. Modes and modalities are accordingly determined. Ayurvedic system studies inner physical characteristics and mental condition of the patient carefully. It takes into account the effected body tissues, *Tridosha,* place of disease, resistant capacity of patient, psychological condition, situation of digestion, and social, income and environmental conditions of patient. The common examination is known as ten-stage examination. In this ten stage examination, the Ayurvedic physician considers the following health parameters of patients. These include—

- Psychosomatic state
- Probability of disease
- Virtues of tissues
- Body structure
- Human cells
- Adaptation
- Mental health
- Digestive power

- Exercise efficiency
- Age.

Besides above ten health parameters, urine, stool, tongue, oration, skin, eyes, pulse rate and entire behaviour are taken into account in Ayurvedic treatment. In Ayurvedic medical system an attempt is made to bring balance in *Tridosha.* Emphasis is placed on regular food habit, life work, behaviour, medicine and non-medicine treatment. This is known as *Panchakarma.* Observation of precaution is also made.

Types of Treatment

In Ayurvedic medical system, one finds a number of types of treatment. For example *Shodana, Narana, Amritkaran,* food taboo, psychiatry, geriatric, digestion and assimilation. *Panchakarma* treatment is also applied. First of all, *Tridosha* are turned into liquid form and then they are forced to come out of body.

In Ayurveda, all substances are believed to have therapeutic value when used judiciously and logically. Raw materials for Ayurvedic medicines are basically sourced from the products of plants, animals and minerals. They are processed in different ways to prepare different dose forms. There is a wide range of Ayurvedic drugs categorized as herbal, herbo-minerals, and mineral-based formulations depending upon the ingredients used in them. Drugs made of mineral ingredients are grouped *Rasaudhies* which in the process of their manufacturing are subjected to certain specific process of *Shodhana, Marana* and *Amritkaran* to render them therapeutically safe and effective.

Classical Ayurvedic literature is replete with numerous single ingredient and multi-ingredients based formulations made from medicinal plants which are practiced even today. The prioritized ones are standardized and listed in National formulatory and pharmacopeia of Ayurveda. *Anupana* (drug vehicle like honey, milk, warm water, decoction) and *Bheshaja kala* (time of drug administration) are of great importance in Ayurveda treatment. The type of therapeutic procedure to be adopted for a patient is decided on the basis of state of disease and condition of patient; medicines are administered in specific dose forms with certain vehicle at specific time and interval to facilitate better absorption, drug delivery, bio-transformation, and desired therapeutic effects. Eleven types of drug consumption times are prescribed in Ayurvedic literature depending on site and nature of disease, symptomatology, status of digestion, dose time etc.

Although Ayurveda is capable of offering solutions for various diseases, but its strength areas include chronic degenerative diseases and therapeutic specialities of Panchakarma for metabolic and geriatric problems. *Kshar Sutra* for ano-rectal disorders and *prakriti* based lifestyle interventions for preventive and promotive health care.

Present State of Ayurveda

Ayurveda has always enjoyed the patronage of people and survived even in adverse time during pre-independence era. In post-independent era, Ayurveda has been officially recognized as a health care and medical knowledge system. It is amply codified and adequately organized. It has become integral part of healthcare and network of the country. Supportive policies for Ayurveda and other AYUSH systems have been evolved. The Ayurveda sector developed with specific strategies envisaged in the National Health Policy 1983, National Population Policy 2000 and Implementation Framework of National Rural Health Mission 2007. With the establishment of Ministry of AYUSH in 1995 and declaration of National Policy for Homoeopathy in 2002, focused attention has been given for inclusive growth and development of Ayurveda and implementation of programme in accordance with own genius. Favourable policies and increasing budgetary support steered the implementation of programmes during Five Years Plan in accordance with its own genius. This has influenced the Ayurveda system in improving its infrastructure, functional capabilities, services and use of contemporary technologies. Outcome of these interventions are visible in terms of enhanced institutional network, initiatives for standardization and quality control, expansion and accessibility of Ayurvedic services and awareness building about strength areas of Ayurveda. AYUSH strategies under National Rural Health Mission and Centrally sponsored schemes have helped in building up outreach, acceptability, and demand of Ayurveda at various levels of health care. Ayurvedic interventions have more and more support from Government for Research and Development activities and involvement of Ayurveda in Health care delivery system.

On the regulatory front, Ayurveda education and practice is under control of Central Council of Indian Medicines which is a statutory body constituted under the provisions of Indian Medicine Central Council Act 1970. The Council is responsible for prescription, revision and enforcement of standards of Ayurveda education, course curricula and infrastructural facilities of colleges. Today under graduate and post graduate education of Ayurveda is properly structured BAMS course of 5½ year duration including one year of internship period has been started. Three year post graduate courses in 22 specialities are conducted from recognized colleges.

Ph.D. programme and short to midterm informal courses of study are also conducted in Ayurvedic institutions. With the amendment of Indian Medicine Central Council Act 2003, no college or course of Ayurvedic study can be started in country without prior permission of the Central Government. The Central Government also has power to notify recognized Ayurvedic qualifications in consultation with Central Council of Indian Medicine. In order to meet the emerging demand for various circles, initiatives have been taken to develop and implement bridge courses of Ayurveda for training of allopathic and foreign doctors. Manufacturing and quality control of Ayurvedic Drug and Cosmetics Act 1940. Manufactures of Ayurvedic medicines have to take licence and certificate of Good manufacturing practices from the State Government. Recent regulatory amendments for ensuring quality of Ayurvedic products, include notification of guidelines for licensing different categories of drugs, revised labelling provisions for plant parts, form of ingradients, botanical names of medicinal plants used in formulations, display of use of prefix or suffix with the name of classical Ayurvedic drugs.

India has unique distinction of having a pluralistic health system consisting of allopathic system and Indian system of medicine of homoeopathy including Ayurveda. Prevailing socio-economic epidemiologic and demographic transition of country, fast changing lifestyle of people, high rate of population growth and limited resources have been responsible to make Indian health care delivery system more complex and challenging. In order to achieve health goal, management of communicable and non-communicable diseases is a must. In this scenario, Ayurveda stands out prominently to supplement delivery of preventive and promotive health services and management of chronic health problems.

Over the years, the infrastructural network of Ayurvedic functionaries has grown to 3,99,400 registered practitioners, 15,153 dispensaries, 2838 public health hospitals, 260 degree colleges with annual admission capacity of 13,152 students, 100 postgraduate centres with annual admission capacity of 2500 scholars and 7835 licensed manufacturing units.

Access to AYUSH facilities in primary health centres, District hospitals and other hospitals under mainstreaming of AYUSH strategies is National Rural Health Mission. With this strategy about 18128 health facilities in the country are reported to cater AYUSH services. In addition, Pharmacopeia Commission of Indian Medicine and Homoeopathy, Pharmacopeia Committee, National Institute, Ayurveda Research Council, Pharmacopeial Laboratory of Indian Medicine, and Rashtriya Ayurveda Vidyapeeth are playing significant role in promoting the scientific endeavors for Ayurveda.

The establishment of All India Institute of Ayurveda in New Delhi has advanced research, development and interdisciplinary education of Ayurveda. Publication of Ayurvedic formulary with 635 formulations and volumes of Ayurvedic pharmacopeia containing about 600 monographs of quality standards of single drugs and 152 monographs of multi-ingredients.

Bio-instrumentation of equipment used in administering Ayurvedic therapies is of significant interest to the entrepreneurs for which Ayurvedic institutions have collaborated with premier technology institutes. Such development in public and private sectors, research environment is growing phenomenally. The implementation of various central sectors and centrally sponsored schemes aimed at inclusive development of Ayurveda and other AYUSH systems has steered the out come in interms of quality health delivery, availability of quality drugs and professionally suited human resources, research and validation of drugs. Scientific activities on Ayurveda are also supported through schemes of other Government organizations such as Department of Science and Technology, Department of Health Research, Department of Biotechnology, Council of Scientific and Industrial Research, Indian Council of Medical Research and others. With these initiatives scientific aspects of Ayurveda are becoming more and more evident and evidence-based safety, efficacy and quality is being promoted. The intellectual property rights involved in the development of Ayurveda technologies, tools and medicinal products are protectable under the provision of Indian Patent Law.

Research and development in Ayurveda is mainly anchored under the Central Council for Research in Ayurvedic Sciences which has 30 field centres spread across the country. International activity of council includes clinical research, drug research, pharmacological research, survey and documentation of medicinal plants, standardization and validation of safety efficiency of Ayurvedic Drugs and therapies. Council has accomplished validation of 26 formulations for 17 disease conditions, documentation of 704 tribal folk claims and local health traditions validation studio, on 35 drugs for 10 diseases conditions are in progress and a target of validating another 64 drugs has been taken up. Ayurvedic Research Council and investigators in R & D institutions have reported to have been granted 17 patents and 14 patent applications are pending. Technology transfer has been done for 10 products.

Central Ayurvedic Research Council above has published about 3500 scientific papers and uploaded 23065 research articles in AYUSH research web portal. Digital Helpline for Ayurvedic Research Articles (DHARA) was launched by an NGO. It is reported to have about 54,000 articles, out of which 7336 are filtered peer reviewed on us.

National Policy on Indian Systems of Medicine and Homoeopathy was adopted in 2002. The policy emphasized the need for a meaningful phased integration of Indian system of medicine in health delivery system. It also outlined the need to secure complete integration of all plants for health development. The Ministry of AYUSH has mandated seven functional areas to steer the development of AYUSH at national and international level.

Emerging global demand and establishment of bilateral and multilateral platforms for traditional medicine and complementary and alternative medicine have provided the Ayurveda to develop initiatives of international cooperation and promotion. To achieve this objective, the Ministry of AYUSH has implemented a central sector scheme to facilitate international exchange of experts and officials, provision of scholarships to foreign for studying regular courses in Indian institution, participation of drug industry in international exhibitions, trade fairs, road shows, and registration of products for market authorization by foreign regulatory body.

With the help of this scheme, success has been achieved in establishing AYUSH Information cells in Indian Missions in Malaysia, Trinidad and Tobago, Mexico, Indonesia, Mauritius, Cuba, Russia, Hungary, and others. 115 foreign students have availed scholarships to study AYUSH courses in India from 2005-06 onwards. Ayrveda academic chairs are established in the University of West Indies, Trinidad & Tobago, and University of Debrecen, Hungary respectively. Proposals for setting up of Ayurveda chairs in Solovenia, and Indonesia are in pipeline. MoUs have also been signed with Malaysia, Trinidad and Tobago, Hungary, Bangaladesh, Nepal, Mauritius and with other countries are in pipeline for developing bilateral cooperation in the field of traditional medicine including Ayurveda. Normative engagement with WHO in the area of traditional medicine had led to two Ayurveda publications brought out by WHO itself in 2010. WHO collaborating centre designation of the Institute of Post Graduate Teaching and Research in Ayurveda, Jam Nagar since April 2013 has opened vistas to work for development and global positioning of Ayurveda.

Although Ayurveda has made inroads to many countries, perceptional differences prevails in its utility, quality and safety at global level. Ayurveda as a system of medicine is not recognized in most of the countries and its identity and practice face regulatory problems. Promoting international cooperation for addressing these concerns is the objective of Governmental efforts and to steer contribution of Ayurveda in global health care.

There is no doubt that growing popularity of Ayurveda has reached at a stage from where we can look forward to offer it for health care of people. Evidences of safety, efficacy and quality are required to the extent that productive and services meet the standards prevalent in international market. The challenge is to prove the pharmacodynamics and the bioavailability of Ayurvedic medicines and export them like pharmaceutical products. Scientific validation of therapeutic claim, development of standard treatment protocols and protection of traditional knowledge of Ayurveda from piracy and misappropriation are important aspects to pursue.

UNANI SYSTEM OF MEDICINE

Unani System of Medicine is one of the traditional systems of medicine with its genesis in Greece. Unani system of medicine is basically a synthesis of contemporary system of traditional medicine in Syria, Egypt, Iraq, Iran, China, India and other Far East countries. This system is holistic in nature and offers preventive, promotive, curative and rehabilitative health care.

Unani system started in 5th to 4th century B.C. under the patronage of Hippocrates (Borate) in Greece (Unani). This system was developed in Arab and Persian lands. It was introduced by Arabs into Indian sub-continent about a millennium ago. In India, it found its permanent home to attain the zenith of scientific development. This system has so well-assimilated with Indian civilization that it is recognized as one of the Indian systems of medicine by the Government of India. It has become integral part of our national health care delivery structure. The Government of India is providing funds and support for its multidimensional development. That is why today the country has several educational and research institutions, pharmaceutical industries and hospitals providing health care to masses at national level. In area of public health care, a large network of Unani hospitals and dispensaries is functioning across the country with the initiatives taken by State and Central Governments.

Fundamentals of Unani Medicine

The Unani system of medicine, as the name indicates, owes its origin to ancient Greece. Its fundamental frame is based on deep philosophical insights and scientific principles. The most fundamental principles are as follows.

Natural/Basic Components (Umoor-e-Tabaiyah).

This principle states that the human body is composed of seven natural and basic components. They are called as Umoor-e-Tabaiyah. They are mainly responsible for maintaining the health. These seven components are:

- *Arkam* (Element)
- *Mizaj* (Temperament)

- *Akhlaat* (Humours)
- *Aaza* (organ)
- *Arwaah* (spirit/vital forces)
- *Quwa* (Faculty/energy)
- *Afaal* (Function/Action).

It was Hippocrates who propounded the dectorine of humours. The distinguished feature of the Unani medicine is that human body consists of three types of materials—solids (*Azad),* liquid (Akhlaat, Humour) and gaseous matter (*Arwaaha,* Pneuma).

The trimatter theory postulates that the entire universe is made up of the above mentioned three matters—solid, liquid and gas. The Unani medicine system lays emphasis upon diagnosing a disease through pulse (*Nabz),* urine (*Baul)* and stool (*Bras)*. This system relies upon the theory of four elements—air, water, fire and earth and also upon theory of four humours—blood, phlegm, yellow vile and black vile. Any kind of disturbance in humoural balance in the body is responsible for disease causation. A perfect balance of humours is responsible for good health and temperament is denoted by dominant humour—Sanguine, phlegmatic, choleric and melancholic. The main aim of Unani medicine treatment is to restore the equilibrium by giving factors (drugs) of opposite temperament. There are four modes of treatment in Unani medicine system. They are as follows:

- Dieto therapy,
- Regimental therapy,
- Pharmaco therapy, and
- Surgery therapy.

The Strength of Unani Medicine System

The main strength of Unani medicine system is its holistic approach, temperament-based prescription and treatment and principles of six essential factors of life (*Aslab-e-sittach Zarooriah)* which are toning up of organs and immune system is unique feature of Unani medicine system. The Unani medicine system has shown remarkable results in curing disease such as musculoskeletal disorders, respiratory conditions, skin disorders, liver disorders, nervous system disorders and several other acute and chronic diseases.

The Regemental therapy is boon of Unani medicine system. This therapy works on the principle of modifying six essential factors of life. The regimental therapies include following:

- Dietotherapy
- Cupping *(Hijamah)*
- Leeching *(Taleeq)*
- Vein Section *(Fasd)*.

These help to eliminate morbid humours from body *(Tankiya)* and can be used alone or in combination with drug therapy.

Pain management and various skin disorder can be managed effectively with least medication by Regimental therapies. The prompt effectiveness of Regimental therapy excels it from other modes of treatment used in Unani medicine system.

Immuno modulators such as *Khameera Marwareed, Jawahar Mohra are* available which can boost up the immunity. In chronic diseases like tuberculosis, AIDS, cancer and others where a long term medication is used and required. Unani system of medicine can act as an adjuvant to minimize the side effects of main therapy, enhancing the body immunity and improving overall quality of life.

Unani system of medicine offers an effective treatment for various diseases and disorders such as GIT disorder—respiratory disorders, musculo-skeletal disorder, neurological disorders, cardiovascular disorders, metabolic disorder and sexual disorders.

Education and Practice in Unani Medicine System

The education and practice in Unani Medicine System in India is monitored and regulated by the Central Council of Indian Medicine (CCIN) established under Indian Medicine Council Act, 1970. A 5½-year under graduate course in Unani medicine leading to award of BUMS degree is governed by Indian Medicine Control Council (IMCC) Regulations, 1995. Three years post graduate courses leading to award of MD/MS degree are governed by Indian Medicine Central Council Regulations, 2007. At present there are 42 recognized colleges in India which impart education and training in Unani System of Medicine at UG level. Out of 42 colleges, 8 colleges have facility for P.G. courses. National Institute of Unani Medicine, Bangalore offers P.G. courses in Unani medicine and undertakes researches in Unani medicine. The total seats for UG and PG courses are 1861 and 135.respectively. Recently Ph.D. programme has also been introduced at National Institute of Unani Medicine (NIUM) under Rajiv Gandhi University of Health Sciences, Bangalore and Govternment Nizamia Tibbi College under Vijayawada University, Hyderabad.

Role of Unani Medicine System in Health Care

In India, there are 50,475 registered Unani practitioners providing health care services in remote rural areas across the country. There are 259 Unani hospitals with 3744 indoor bed facility. There are 1483 Unani dispensaries all over the country. The National Policy on Indian Medicine and Homoeopath 2002 ensures provision for AYUSH health care facility including Unani system of medicine in primary health care network. 11650 AYUSH doctors have been appointed on contract at primary and community health centres under National Rural Health Mission (NRHM). AYUSH practitioners including Unani medicine system are also involved in reproductive health, child health and school health programme.

Research and Development in Unani Medicine System

Research and Development in Unani System of Medicine is in the hand of Central Council of Research in Unani Medicine (CCRUM). Over the past three and half decades, the Council has emerged as a leading organization to bring out significant scientific documents for reference and use in this field. The CCRUM was established in 1979 to build up research base for Unani System of Medicine. The CCRUM has its headquarters in New Delhi with 23 centres functioning in different parts of the country.

The institution network of Council includes: 2 Central Research Institutes of Unani Medicine, one each at Hyderabad and Lucknow, 8 Regional Research Institutes of Unani Medicine at Chennai, Bhadrak, Patna, New Delhi, Mumbai, Kolkata, Aligarh and Srinagar; Literary Research Institute of Unani Medicine at New Delhi, Drug Standardization Research Institute at Ghaziabad, 2 Regional Research Centres of Unani Medicine at Allahabad and Silchar, 6 Clinical Research Units at Bhopal, Burhanpur, Meerut, Bangalore, Kurnool and Edathals, Drug Standardization Research Unit at New Delhi, Clinical Research Unit at Aligarh and Clinical Research Pilot Project at Imphal, Manipur, 2 Co-location Centres in major Allopathic Hospitals in New Delhi for providing free Unani treatment under one roof:

- Unani Medical Centre at Dr. Rammanohar Lohiya Hospital.
- Unani Speciality Centre at Deen Dayal Upadhyay Hospital.

Under clinical pharmacology activity, CCRUM has conducted pharmacological action and safety evaluation study of 130 single drugs and 120 formulations in 30 diseases.

The initiative of Department of AYUSH to set up CRISM is intended to meet increasing global concerns on the safety, efficacy and quality of Indian System of Medicine (ISM) products and promote high level research in these systems and their worldwide acceptance. The primary mission of Centre is to facilitate scientific validation and dissemination of information of ISM in particular Ayurveda, Siddha and Unani medicine through collaborative research advocacy by Department of AYUSH and National Centre for Natural Products Research (NCNPR), University of Mississipi, USA.

CCRM has developed a unit of Unani drugs for common seasonal ailments and scientifically validated the efficacies of these drugs. These are now being commercially available through National Research Development Corporation. CCRM conducted studies on healthy ageing and development of package for senior citizens. Council has also conducted multicentric trials of Unani drugs in different skin diseases.

Collaborative Research

The Council is engaged in collaborative studies with different scientific organizations and medical colleges of repute in the country including Council for Scientific and Industrial Research (CSIR), AIMS, ICMR and other prestigious institutions of the country.

The Government of India is developing cooperation with foreign countries to promote traditional Indian systems of medicine globally including Unani medicine. In this connection a landmark was made with launching an Indo-U.S. Centre for Research in Indian Systems of Medicine (CRISM) at University of Mississippi, USA, in April 2009 by the Ministry of AYUSH. This initiative of the Department of AYUSH to CRISM is intended to meet increasing global concerns on the safety, efficacy, and quality of Indian System of Medicine (ISM) products and promote high level research in these systems and their worldwide acceptance. The primary mission of the centre is to facilitate scientific validation and dissemination of information on ISM, particularly Ayurveda, Siddha and Unani through collaborative research and advocacy by the Department of AYUSH and National Centre for Natural Product Research (NCNPR), University of Mississippi, USA.

The Ministry of AYUSH has constituted a National Medicinal Plants Board (NMPB) to coordinate and support conservation, cultivation and trade of medicinal plants. Along with Indian Medicines Pharmaceuticals Limited (IMPL), Mohan (Uttarakhand), Government of India enterprises for supply of medicines to Government dispensaries and hospitals, there are good number of licensed manufacturing units for Unani drugs in private sector.

Drug Standardization and Patenting of Drugs

Standards for 298 single and 100 compound drugs under technical guidance of Unani Pharmacopeia Committee have been developed by the CCRUM. Standardization of 277 single drugs of Unani medicine in five volumes with 385 compound drugs and physio-chemical standards of Unani formation in four volumes have been published *Unani Pharmacopeia of India* in six volumes 100 monographs of compound drugs have been completed. National formulary of Unani medicine in five parts contains standards of 1228 formulations. Eight patents have been granted from the Indian Patent Office on the research conducted by CCRUM. Forty six applications are pending for grant of patent in patent office.

Based on this work, the Council has brought out two publications which are as follows:

- Physio-chemical Standards of Unani Formulations.
- Standardization of Single Drugs of Unani Medicine.

The first book carries monograph on Unani formulations. The book contains four parts dealing with 350 compounds Unani of Drug.

The second book consists of monograph on single Unani drug in five volumes. Each has standard for 50 single drugs.

The Council has also published books entitled, *Chemistry of Unani Medicinal Plants*. Since 1978, Council has undertaken series of ethnobotanical surveys in remote forest areas in different states having tribal and indigenous people. Classical Unani literatures are abound with references about the use of medicinal plants. Unmindful over-exploitation of this important resource has led to extinction of several species. Availability of genuine raw drug material is very important for the efficacy of formulations. Besides, there are also some medicinal plants/drugs whose identification is controversial. Keeping it in view, a herbal garden at CRIUM, Hyderabad has been established for plantation of about hundred Unani medicinal plants of repute for demonstration purposes and field scale cultivation of medicinal plants particularly those used in clinical trials and kit medicines.

In order to popularize medicinal plants, particularly those used in Unani medicine the CCRUM has embarked upon a vigorous programme of cultivating about 100 species in its nurseries at its centres at Aligarh,

Hyderabad, Chennai and Srinagar. Based on ethnobotanical survey in different forest zones of country, Ethnopharmacological data have been collected and compiled region-wise in seven assortments.

Traditional Knowledge Digital Library

Traditional Knowledge Digital Library (TKDL) is an important joint initiative of Ministry of AYUSH, Ministry of Health & Family Welfare, Government of India and Council of Scientific and Industrial Research (CSIR) and is being implemented by CSIR through National Institute of Science and of Science Communication and Information Resources (NISCAIR), Ministry of Science and Technology to prevent biopiracy and misappropriation of classical Unani formulations.

The main objective of globally recognized project is to prevent misappropriation of India's rich heritage of traditional medical knowledge. Details of 1,54,015 formulations of Unani medicine is available with TKDL.

Unani Drug Industry

There are 485 licensed pharmacies manufacturing Unani drugs in addition to Govterment of India enterprise—Indian Medicine Pharmaceutical Corporation Limited (IMPCL).

Manufacturing and sale of Unani drugs is regulated under Drug and Cosmetic Act, 1940 with compliance of good manufacturing practices (GM7P). Drug standardization is taken by competent institutions. For example Pharmacopeial Laboratory for Indian Medicine (PLIM), Pharmacopeia Commission of Indian Medicine (PCIM), Unani Pharmacopeia Committee (UPC) and CCRUM.

Global Scenario of Unani Medicine System

Unani Medicine System is popular in different parts of the world with different names. For example—

- In India, Bangladesh, Sri Lanka and South Africa, it is known as Unani Medicine or Unani TIBB.
- In Iran, it is called as Tibb-e-Sunati (Traditional medicine).
- In Pakistan, it is termed as Eastern Medicine.
- In China, it is known as Uyghur Medicine.
- In United Arab Emirates (UAE), it is termed as traditional complementary and alternative medicine (TCAM).
- In Kuwait, it is called as Islami medicine.

Conclusion

After going through a good deal of discussions on various aspects or Unani medical system in India, we can say that Unani medicine system is holistic in nature. It takes into account the whole personality. It does not follow reductionist approach towards disease. It is a great healing art as well as science whose theories, philosophies of nature (*Tabiat),* temperament (*mizaj)* and practice of medicine are most appropriate for the maintenance of human health.

India is a land of great ecological diversity. Its health care system reflects this diversity in its plural systems of health knowledge and practice.

In India, Unani medicine system co-exists with conventional medicine and other AYUSH systems to form a unique model of medical conflation. It is a comprehensive medical system that deals with various states of body (health and disease). It was Hippocrates the father of medicine, who in conjugation with founder of Unani medicine brought medicine out of superstition and his teachings were well adopted in modern system of medicine till the 16th century. While Arabs and Persians developed fundamental principals and core practices of Unani, but Indian scholars explained and applied them to a peerless in the land of its inception and Unani was very well comprehended in the soil of India. There was exchange of knowledge between Unani and Ayurveda. Many things of Ayurveda were assimilated in Unani by determining their temperament and actions. The continuing creativity of Indian Scholars is testified by emerging encyclopaedia of Hakeem Azan Khan and research development by Hakeem Azmal Khan. It helped Unani to become the legacy of India.

The Unani system of medicine has a long and impressive record in India. Today India is one of the leading countries in so far as the practice of Unani medicine is concerned. It has the widest network of well developed educational institutions. Comprehensive health care facilities, state of art research and quality drug manufacturing. India has reached a stage where many countries are approaching for cooperation and support for Unani system of medicine. India is a world leader in Unani System of Medicine.

THE SIDDHA SYSTEM OF MEDICINE

The Siddha System of Medicine is one of the ancient systems of medicine found in South India near Kanyakumari in Tamil Nadu. The term Siddha means achievements. Siddhars are those who have achieved perfections in the medicine. Eighteen Siddhars are said to have contributed towards the systematic development of this system and they recorded their experiences in Tamil language.

This system of medicine is closely related to Ayurvedic system, but it has maintained its separate existence. This system of medicine is also closely related to Tamil Civilization. The term Siddha has originated from Siddhi which means perfection and achievement of knowledge. The persons who were well versed and had achieved perfections were termed as Siddhars. Siddhars had obtained supreme knowledge in medicine, yoga and devotion.

A number of scholars are of opinion that, a well evolved civilization was in existence in South India before the arrival of Aryans. The spread of this civilization was on the banks of river Kaveri, Vaigai and Tamirparani. The medical system of this civilization was probably precursor of modern Siddha Medicine System. Later on, the Siddha Medicine System came in contact with other medical systems. As a result of this contact, the exchange of traits of different medical systems would have taken place. This reciprocal exchange of medical traits made Siddha medical system more rich. The medicine materials of Siddha system were metals and minerals. They were used in drug formulation. In the beginning plants and animals were used for making drugs in Ayurveda system. But later on use of metals and minerals were introduced in this system of drug formulation.

According to a tradition 18 Siddhars had contributed in the development of Siddha medicine. But their written materials are not available at all.

Philosophy of Siddha Medical System

According to Philosopy of Siddha Medicine System, there are two important elements—matters and energy—which have great influence upon the determination of form of nature of the universe. In Siddha medicine system, they are known as Shiva and Shakti. Matters cannot exist without energy. This is also true for energy because without matters energy cannot exist. Thus, matters and energy are not in isolation, rather they are complementary to each other. The universe is formed of five basic elements—*Kshitij* (ether), *Jal* (water), *Pawak* (fire), *Gagan* (sky), and *Samira* (Air). Imbalance in these elements creates *Tridosha—Cough, Pitta, Vata (Vayu).* As a result of *Tridosha,* disease causation takes place. Thus, the philosophy of Siddha Medicine System is similar to Ayurvedic Medicine System. Ayurveda and Siddha both medical systems also show similarity in diagnosis of diseases. But they also differ in some traits. In Siddha system diagnosis process is based on examination of *Ashthasthan* (eight places of body). They are pulse, ear, voice, touch, colour, tongue, stool and urine examination.

Theory and Law

So far as treatment procedure is concerned, it appears that Siddha Medicine System like Ayurveda Medicine Systems is based on the concept of Ashtang. But here emphasis is placed on three branches:

- Treatment of child diseases.
- Treatment of person.
- Treatment of ear.

Other branches like Ayurveda were not developed in Siddha. Treatment of diseases through surgery was prevalent in Ayurveda Medical System. But in Siddha Medical System one does not find mention about treatment of diseases by surgery. Notably Ayurveda and Siddha both medical systems are divided into two groups:

- Shodhanas, and
- Vamana.

Sodhana treatment was related to *Pancha Karma* treatment. One does not find any mention of *panchkarma* treatment in Siddha Medical System. Siddha Medical System was influenced only by *Vamana* treatment.

Pharmacology

The Pharmacology of Siddha medical system and Ayurvedic medical system also show similarity in concepts and merits of drug formulation. The characteristic feature of Siddha pharmacology is formulation of medicine by metals and minerals. In place of plants, majority of medicines in Siddha system were made by the use of metals and minerals.

In Siddha medical system, metal and mineral-based drugs have been divided into seven groups:

- *Uppu (Lavanam).* These medicines were soluble in water and evaporated on heating.
- *Pashnam.* These medicines were insoluble in water but evaporated on heating.
- *Uparasan.* These medicines are also like *pashanam,* but their actions are different.
- *Ratna and Uparatna.* These medicines were made by using costly gems and sub-gems.

- *Loham.* These medicines were made by use of iron. They were melted on heating.
- *Rasam.* These medicines were soft but appeared as air on heating.
- *Gandhokam.* They are insoluble in water, but when come in contact with air, they burn.

From above basic medicines, compound medicines were prepared. 35 medicines were also prepared from animals.

Besides India, Siddha medical system is also prevalent in Sri Lanka, Mauritius, Indonesia, Singapore, Malayasia and other parts of the world where Tamil speaking people reside. Tamil Doordarshan has raised its popularity in different parts of the globe.

The Siddha system of medicine emphasizes upon the patient, environment, age, sex, race, habitat, habit, diet, appetite, physical condition, physiological constitution, and mental framework of the disease for its treatment which is individualistic in nature. Diagnosis of the disease is done through examination of pulse (ratio of *Vatham, Pitham, Kapan* etc.), urine, eyes, study of voice, colour of body, tongue and status of digestion of individual patient. The system has unique treasure for conversion of metals and minerals as drug and many infectious diseases are treated with medicines containing specially processed mercury, silver, arsenic, lead and sulphur without any side effects.

The strength of the Siddha system lies in providing very effective therapy for psoriasis disorder, liver disorder, beings prostrate hypertrophy, bleeding piles, peptic ulcers and dermatological disorder of non-psoriatic nature.

Vaman (Pressure Manipulating Therapy)

It is a special kind of treatment in Siddha system of medicine. Specific points are manipulated by pressure with finger and the pain is relieved. By practicing it restricted movement becomes free and active.

The Khanam

It is an another type of treatment which includes applying oil on area of pain and swelling and massaging so that neuromuscular and musculo-skeletal pain and swelling is relieved.

The Siddha system of medicine is very popular in Tamil Nadu. Here, most of primary health and Government Hospitals are having Siddha wing for treatment of patients and their diseases. The Government of India has established Siddha wing throughout the country.

During the last six decades, there has been continuous development in Siddha medical education. This has led to the establishment of National Institute of Siddha at Chennai as apex institute having six specialities in post graduate teaching and M.D. degree. There are *Maruthuvam* (General medicine), *Sirappa Maruthuvam* (Special Medicine), *Kucanthae, Mathuruvam* (Pediatrics), *Gunapadam* (Pharmocology), *Noinadal* (Pathology), *Nanju Nool* and research in Siddha Medicine system, the Government of India has constituted a Central Council for Research in Siddha (CCRS), an autonomous body under the Ministry of AYUSH.

Education of Siddha Medicine System

Siddha like all other traditional medical systems gave way to biomedicine some 300 years back. Revival of Siddha medicine system took place and institutionalized education started in the middle of twentieth century. Diplomas were awarded in the presideney of Madras and medical registration based on hereditary training was awarded.

An integrated course along with allopathic training was in vague till 1960. Subsequently an exclusive college affiliated to Madras University was started at Palayam Kottain in Tirunelveli district of Tamil Nadu in 1964. Medical degree Bachelor of Indian Medicine (BIM-Siddha) of five and half years duration was awarded. Now, this college offers postgraduate course of three years durations in five branches. An another college at Chennai also conducts graduate and postgraduate courses leading to bachelor of Siddha medicine and surgery and also doctor of medicine Siddha. The Government of Tamil Nadu runs two colleges affiliated to Tamil Nadu Dr. MGR Medical University, Chennai. There are five private Siddha Colleges in Tamil Nadu and one in Kerala. The National Institute of Siddha imparts post graduate training. Around 300 graduates and 100 post - graduates receive degree each year.

Branches like varman, pathology, Toxicology and Pediatrics were established in post-graduation degree in Siddha medicine. The curriculum is based on the one laid down by the Central Council of Indian Medicine, New Delhi. The University of Jaffna in Sri Lanka also imparts graduate training in Siddha medicine.

Government of India strictly implements the qualifying norms for new colleges and new specialization with the objective of improving teaching standards and also broad based review of curriculum and syllabus which includes modern sciences, microbiology, medical biochemistry, Pharmacology, Toxicology and modern medicine. New diploma courses under integrated ISM Pharmacy and Nursing therapy to provide well-trained paramedics for treatment centres in pubic and private sector has been started in Tamil Nadu. Currently internees are posted to primary health centres to enable them in delivering primary care after completion and train them to work in rural environment.

Ministry of AYUSH provides financial support for conducting continuing medical education for teachers and Government physicians. College is not available. The Ministry of AYUSH is sanctioning a sum of Rs. 10 crore for establishment of the college. Taking this advantageous opportunity, the private management and State Governments may start Siddha Medical College in their area.

Research in Siddha Medicine

An apex body for research was formed exclusively for Siddha known as Central Council of Research in Siddha. This autonomous Council has one Central Research Institute for Siddha, Regional Research Institutes for Siddha and two units like Survey of Medicinal Plants unit and Clinical Research units.

Research in Siddha medicine is focused on clinical research, library research, drug development, standardization and fundamental research. Apart from Central Council of Research in Siddha, the State Department has also established centres for researches in AIDS, Cancer, Diabetes, Asthma and Infertility. Multidisciplinary researches are being carried out identifying new health benefits for known drugs and known benefits from unknown drugs. Dermatological and Neuroskeletal Muscular Disorder have been treated effectively. Clinical research shows the efficacy of various Siddha formulations in postnatal care/antinatal care, anaemia, HIV, diabetes, rheumatoid arithritis, psoriasis, cancer and polycystic ovarian disease.

Research organization is currently focusing on child survival to reduce the infant mortality, safety profile of harbour mineral drugs, drug standardization, endangered Siddha plant conservation and multiplication, literary research and survey and documentation of traditional knowledge. The research organization of India which carry research in Siddha medicine system are Central Research Institute for Siddha, three postgraduate colleges of Siddha, private universities with grant from the Department of AYUSH, Department of Biotechnology and Department of Science and Technology. NGOs working in different parts of the country, university departments on medicinal plants, phytochemistry, and pharmacology. State Public Health Department also carry out field based research activities to promote Siddha system of medicine.

Manufacture of Siddha Medicine

As many as 600 units mostly in tiny sector and small scale sector are engaged in the manufacture of Siddha medicine. Government of Tamil Nadu Pharmacies at Chennai and Thirunelveli manufacture medicine for the requirement of Government hospitals. The major Siddha industries in Tamil Nadu and Indian Medical Practitioners Cooperative Pharmacy and Store (TAMPCOL).

The above industries have increased their productions. Most of them have excess capacity for future growth. Others are in the process of improving their capacity. Most of them are manufacturers of classical formulations and increase the number of retail outlets and sales. Good manufacturing practice was implemented in 2002 and is mandatory for all AYUSH drug manufacturing units. Sophisticated instrumentation laboratories for analysis are being established by companies. There are four independent third party laboratories 100 testing quality standards with expertise in Siddha.

Formulation Testing of Siddha Medicines

GMP education is carried out continuously for quality improvement by Government body and manufactures association. Manufacture and sale of Siddha medicine is regulated by State Licensing Authority (ISM). The technical inputs for the formulation is given by competent authority of the State Directorate of Indian Medicine. The Drug and Cosmetics Act, 1940 is also applicable to Siddha medicine.

Siddha System of Medicine in Global Context

The Siddha system of medicine is also patronized extensively more particularly in Tamil speaking countries like Sri Lanka, Singapore, Malaysia, Mauritius and some parts of Indonesia. The internet, social media, electronic media particularly Tamil Television channels have created an awareness in Tamil diaspora. Siddha system could be practiced in any part of the world because it lays emphasis upon food as the basis of health. Most of the remedies for common ailments that affect human being could be managed with many spices used in kitchen and adoption of healthy food habit based on body type season and health status. It has provided simple lifestyle based practices like breathing exercise, meditation practice, appropriate postural practice for unison of body and mind. The another advantage of Siddha for its universal utility is its branch of physical manipulation of varman and thokanam which are carried out by trained and skill fully proficient practitioners manually without drugs or instruments particularly in case of trauma or postural disorders and also for pain management.

Cost Effectiveness of Siddha Medicine

The cost of Siddha drugs and treatment procedures are much less and affordable to majority of people of developing countries where universe health insurance or public health delivery is inadequate. The strength of Siddha system lies in the area of diagnosis, particularly the pulse diagnosis which is predominantly dependent on clinical acumen of practitioner and could be carried out in any location. It does not require a great clinical laboratory and costly instrument.

Most of drugs based on food ingredients, spices, and plants are proven to be safe in general. Even in case of inorganic such as coral, pearl oyster, conch shell, cowriae shell and processed calcinated copper, zinc are safe in micro particular state and doze level.

Patenting of Siddha Procedure

There are certain unique external therapy procedures like varman which is slowly gaining national attention. There is a need to validate and standardize these procedures before they are patented. Like some postures of Yoga, there is every chance that these procedures are also patented. Therefore, CCRSIS taking special interest in standardizing and patenting Siddha procedures.

Crosspathy of Siddha System

There is a felt need among Siddha physicians who run clinics in remote locations as well as major hospitals that they should be allowed to use some of the bio-medicines. Many patients go for Siddha treatment when they find no alternative. Therefore, Siddha physicians should provide pain relief and protect patient from acute distress and prevent sudden death. Now, many cardiologists recommend high risk individuals to keep certain medicine in their pockets to prevent damage in ischemic heart diseases. They are taught in human anatomy, physiology, biochemistry, microbiology, and pharmacology in their Siddha medicine course and trained in obestries. They are not seeking complete use of bio-medicine. In Tamil Nadu, Allopathy and Siddha are allocated in primary health centres. In centres where there are one Allopath and one Siddha physician, the Siddha physician has to attend patient when Allophath doctor is absent or on leave. In remote hilly regions Siddha physicians are forced to use bio-medicine. In many hospitals the Siddha physicians have to play this role during their night duty. This challenge could be overcome by bridge course for Siddha physicians.

Government Effort for Siddha System

The Central as well as State Governments both adopted a policy to promote Siddha system of medicine. They are taking every effort to mainstream this system in public health delivery. Various institutions have been established by the Government for ensuring better quality of healthcare. WHO on its part has initiated lot of efforts for strengthening various components of the system. Through central sector scheme and Centrally sponsored scheme, Public Health Initiative Scheme of Government of India, Ministry of AYUSH, Siddha projects are carried out throughout India.

In Central Government, Siddha physicians are selected through UPSC and posted in Government Health Scheme wellness centres throughout India.

Increasing Popularity of Siddha Medicine System Abroad

Siddha system of medicine is more popular in Sri Lanka where Siddha medical colleges and hospitals are available. This system is also popular in Malaysia, Singapore, Thailand, where Siddha hereditary physicians and qualified physicians are practicising it and doing noble services.

Realizing the above value of Siddha system of medicine, the noble system should be utilized further, nationally and internationally for the welfare of humanbeing.

HOMOEOPATHY MEDICINE SYSTEM

Homoeopathic Medicine System is practiced worldwide by several practitioners. Its popularity has soared recent years due to its inherent virtues as well as advancements in evidenced based researches. There is all evidence shift in the trend of public preferences for therapy selection from standard biomedicine to other systems that offer holistic and individualized treatment.

Medical science is transforming at a fast pace. The novel ideas are bringing modern science closer to the traditional one. Holistic treatment and life space investigation is becoming not only acceptable but imitable, too. It is because conventional medicine rethinks its perspective towards human health and objective behind case interrogation.

Homoeopathy is a system of health care that treats an individual gently, holistically and permanently. It has been used for over 200 years. It is known to second largest therapeutic system in use in the world. Homoeopathy originated in disregard to the crude practices of orthodox medicine back in 18th century. Dr. Hahnemann, a reputed German physician, saw leeching, bloodletting and other forms of crude practices intended to alleviate people's suffering, only adding to misery and pain. As he was an accomplished clinician himself, he discontinued this form of practice. He resorted to his skill as chemist and translator to earn his means. However, the plight of patients could not let clinician in him rest. When he was translating a chapter on therapeutic ability of cinchona bark to cure malaria of book entitled, '*Cullen's Materia*', he turned towards a new leaf in the history of medical science. Homoeopathy was eventually born as a scientific system of medicine based solely on concepts and methods derived from scientific experiments. Historically, Homoeopathy was the most lively source for later placebo controlled crossover and parallel group experiments. The first ever blind trial using placebo dates back to the 19th century Homoeopathic therapeutic trial and provings. Single blind place to controls, still used today by both contemporary and complementary and alternative medicine system, was first put to biomedical use by homoeopathy.

Principles of Homoeopathy System

The main principles of Homoeopathy system of medicine are as follows:

The first principle is 'Similia simili buscurenture'. Its meaning is that a medicine similar in action to disease acts as a stimulus to the own response of body towards a disease. It provides information the body needs to complete its healing work.

The second principle is related to body's own inherent force which means that body know what it is doing and healing response to overcome an illness is initiated from within the living organisms.

The third principle is based on application of minimum dose. It states that the stimulus of the medicine is needed in a dose just about to initiate the vitality. That's why homoeopathic medicine are given in a minimum doses. It is because they stimulate body's healing responses without producing gross side effects that are so often pit falls of other medical system.

Apart from these three principles, homoeopathy has other principles, too. These are laws of simplex which advocates about administration of simple and single medicine, law of chronic disease which describes approach to chronic case, doctrine of drug dynamisation which describes as to how medical substances are transformed to homoeopathic substance during preparation and doctrine of drug providing which is concerned with effects of homoeopathic medicine on healthy human being.

Status of Homoeopathy

Today Homoeopathic medicine system is practiced worldwide by several practitioners. Its popularity has soared in recent years due to its inherent virtues as advancement in evidenced based researches. There is an evident shift in trend of public preferences for the therapy selection from standard bio-medicine to other system that offer holistic and individualized treatment.

A recent publication reveals that both practitioners and users are rapidly growing in USA, Brazil, South Africa and in European countries like UK, France, Germany, Norway, Australia and Switzerland. Our country India tops this list with maximum practitioners (over 2.5 lakh) and a huge number of users.

Considering the huge demand for homoeopathic medicine system, our Government has extended strong infrastructure and technical support for successful institutionalization of homoeopathy in India. As a result our country India has about 187 graduate and 42 post-graduate Homoeopathic medical colleges which produce qualified homoeopathic doctor. These doctors undergo a rigorous homoeopathic medical training of 5 and ½ years before getting their degree in homoeopathy (BHMS). Higher study in homoeopathy include M.D. in homoeopathy at post-graduate level and Ph.D. at doctorate level.

Health care services in homoeopathy are provided by 215 hospitals 6812 dispensaries run by State Government and municipal bodies, 35 dispensaries of Central Government Health Scheme, 39 of Labour Ministry and 129 of the Railway Ministry. Homoeopathic treatment facility is also provided by public sector undertakings such as Thermal Power Corporation, Central Reserve Police Force, Border Security Force. Homoeopathic practitioners in India operate singly through private clinics which vary immensely in terms of available facilities, consultation cost and treatment cost. Homoeopathy treatment is also available in some allopathic hospital establishments largely through the effort of individual homoeopathic practitioner in the private sector and through collocation facility in Government sector. Further homoeopathic hospitals in India operates along with educational colleges and independently providing an array of Outdoor

Patient Department (OPD) services with radiological and pathological facilities.

Advantages of Homoeopathy

Users are attracted towards homoeopathy for its innate quality, like personalized treatment with no side effect. Medicines are gentle, easy to administer, cost effective, and affordable to the poorest of the poor. A study found out that cost per patient in homoeopathic clinic is 1/5th time less than Allopathic clinic. Being palatable, the patients of all age groups, from infants to very old can be given these medicines. Further, all Homoeopathic medicines are verified on human beings prior to their clinical application. Hence, they are clinically safe. Most single homoeopathic medicines are non-patented as their original homoeopathic use remains reserved with the old stalwarts of homoeopathy to barred their knowledge to profession without patenting the drugs.

A study reflecting the data analysis of a decade (2001-2011) of patients reporting to homoeopathic units of Government of Delhi revealed that the popularity of homoeopathy has steadly gone up with 58 per cent rise in patient inflow over a decade. The study also revealed that homoeopathy was primarily popular among the patients of chronic and subacute problem of skin, respiration, female infection, digestive disorder, and so on. Another significant finding was that children and women were common users of homoeopathic medicines. Majority of homoeopathic medicine users in the middle age of 25 to 44 years and of above average income. They were educated, too. They were capable of selecting homoeopathy as a line of treatment.

Like other medicinal systems, homoeopathy, too, has its own limitations. The scope of homoeopathy is limited in emergencies, irreversible or advanced organic changes, artificial chronic diseases resulting from abuse of medicinal system lack of vital organ in patient and unavoidable surgery.

Cross-pathy

The cross-pathy has its own positive and negative effect. If a biomedicine practitioner prescribed a homoeopathic medicine it promotes the homoeopathy system and adds to its credibility. But on the other hand, such practice takes away the chance of a trained and expert homeopath. Cross-pathy should be avoided.

Research in Homoepathy

Research is an integral part of a medical system. Researches bring newer understanding of medical sciences. With the advent of nanotechnology and cutting edge laboratory research techniques, it has become possible to prove the positive effect of homoeopathic medicines in various ways.

In recent past, homoeopathy has been researched for its viability in medical care through various means—primary one being clinical research. A review of clinical trials in homoeopathy reported from 1975-2002, found 93 studies comparing homoeopathy with placebo or other treatment. Positive effects of homoeopathy were found in 50 studies. Randomized control trial (RCT) revealed that homoeopathy was effective in various clinical conditions ranging from skin, respiratory, female to child-diseases and problems. But the data from RCTs did not reflect the true picture of the effectiveness of homoeopathic treatment. Although a widely respected format of conventional studies, RTCs do not encompass the homoeopathic features of treatment to yield result which are as encouraging as observational studies, which is more patient oriented. Homoeopathy being a holistic medicine, relies on a self regulation process where only defence mechanism of individual is stimulated to act as defence in disease.

New adaptations in RTCs are other ways of capturing homoeopathic elements of clinical outcome. Therefore, on being convinced, with initial results being encouraging. One such design is prognosis research, studying effect modifies, i.e. variables that influence outcome of treatment. As in conventional medicine prognosis research is becoming more important. This type of research becomes increasingly important in medicine since the emergence of pharmacogenomics. This principle states that medicine should not only fit the indication but also the person. Personalized medicine has always been core of homoeopathy philosophy. Prognosis research resembles diagnosis research. Several symptoms and personal characteristics increase or decrease the probability that a specific medicine will work, instead of probability of a specific diagnosis. As in most differential diagnoses about illness, the differential prognosis about successful homoeopathic medicines is based on analysis of more than one symptoms/characteristics by application of Bayes theorem and livelihood ratio.

An another category of research is basic research which investigates many intriguing questions in homoeopathy. For example, the preserve of curative powers of original substances in homoeopathic medicines in ultra diluted potencies, mechanism of actions of medicine once administered, in a biological system, human, animal or plant. Its pharmacokinetics and pharmodynamic aspects and relevance of negative control in basic researches in order to validate the finding also influence. A successful basic research is capable of setting a standard for formulating subsequent research designs at multiple levels—right from standardization of parameters of drug substance, its proving effects on individuals to clinical findings. In all basic research can set up the goals for other researches.

The peer reviewed Journal Homoeopathy published two special issues on biological models of homoeopathy in 2009 and 2010 concluded that the field of homoeopathy was exciting and dynamic. There were remarkable range of biological models of reference to homoeopathy. There were encouraging progress in terms of quality and growing number of positive findings. According to a data profile named Hombrex, India is third highest contributor of basic research work in the world with 237 publications including 30 papers in last ten years.

Committed to credible research, Central Council for Research in Homoeopathy (CCRH) an autonomous organisation under Ministry of AYUSH, Government of India was established in 1978 to undertake scientific research and development in homoeopathy. Since inception the Council is engaged in research activities. It had a strong network of 29 units spread across the country with its headquarters in New Delhi.

The main thrust research of CCRH are as follows:

- Survey, collection and cultivation of medicinal plants.
- Drug standardization.
- Drug providing.
- Clinical research.
- Extramural research.
- Documentation and Dissemination.

The researches have been published in Journals of national and international repute. The research activities of the Council are also available online of official website www.ccrhindea.org. The Council also invites proposals for collaborative research under expression of interest scheme, which can be studied at its official website. The council also publishes peer reviewed Journal. For dissemination of knowledge in this regard the Journal is accessible at www.irjh.org. An overview of research in homoeopathy in India has been compiled by Ministry of AYUSH in a dossier 'Homoeopathy: Science of Gentle Healing' available on line at www.ccrhindia.org/Dossier/index.html.

Apart from several clinical research studies, CCRH have been able to some high and basic researches in collaboration with Bose institute Kolkata on the effect of Homoeopathy medicines—Calcarea carbonicum and Thuja on cancer through gene regulation. The School of Tropical Medicine, Kolkata has explored the effect of medicine on Chorioallantoic membrane of chick infected with Japanese encephalitis and in suckling mice of premeditated mothers. The ALM Post Graduate Institute of Basic Medical Sciences, University of Madras has explored the effect of medicines on high fructose induced Type-2 diabetes. The Indian Institute of Technology, Delhi has explored a possible nano science mechanism of action of homoeopathy medicines.

But in spite of all such research advances, research in homoeopathy poses a great problem and challenges. This ranges from drug safety and efficacy studies to physio-chemical experiments with high dilution drug at preclinical level and rigorous validation of drugs in various diseases through concept of personalized medicine at clinical level. Attempts have been made to answer several questions of individual and group ventures in order to bring evidence-based scientific value of homoeopathy at par with well recognized clinical value.

There is no doubt that homoeopathy is gaining popularity worldwide and a change in its status at global level has taken place. But people are waiting for qualified homoeopathic practitioners for their day to day and chronic ailments. No matter how small the pills are homoeopathy will continue to benefit mankind and ensure restoration of health in most gentle, safe, cost effective and permanent manner.

NATUROPATHY SYSTEM OF MEDICINE

According to Naturopathy, all diseases are caused by accumulation of morbid matters (toxins) in the body due to faulty eating and living habits. Naturopathy Medical System believes that nature itself is a doctor. This medical system makes use of only natural elements to restore health of a patient by eliminating toxins.

Naturopathy medical system of building the entire being in harmony with constructive principle in nature on physical, mental, moral and spiritual plans of being. The Naturopathy system of treatment is also known by the names such as Nature Cure and Naturotherapy. In this system seven elements are used to restore health of a patient.

The treatment by seven elements are quite different from the other systems of medicines practiced at present. Those who regard naturopathy as a method of curing diseases only are mistaken. In fact nature cure is right path of living. It is an art of attaining a long healthy and blissful life.

Mahatma Gandhi, the father of nation, had repeatedly advocated the importance of nature cure in case of illness. He had realized the importance of nature cure and adviced those to follow nature cure who came to meet him. This system is so simple that when any one comes in its contact, he becomes its devotee throughout his life. In comparison to other systems of medicine, Naturopathy is very cheap. Therefore, this system of medicine can be very useful in our country for serving the people. The mass of our country can easily adopt it and remain healthy without doctors and medicine.

The main strength of Naturopathy is not only in providing preventive, but also curative and promotive services. This system has been found very effective in the treatment of various chronic diseases especially among older people above the age of 60 years.

The Naturopathy tackles the illness that cannot be healed wholly by allopathic treatment. This treatment focuses on the entire body of the patient, not just a particular part of body. A naturopath attaches significance to natural foods loaded with rich nutrition and to maintain a healthy lifestyle.

Apart from natural food sources, naturopaths offer several therapeutic modalities which have benefited millions of people across the globe.

Some important naturopathic therapies are as follows:

Hydrotherapy

This is a well known ancient therapy. In this therapy, a patient is prescribed bath at different temperatures. For example cold bath, hot bath, steam bath, immersion bath, compression, fomentation, saunas, wraps etc. They produce several types of physiological effects depending upon temperature of water, duration and area of application for different disease conditions.

Mud Therapy

Mud absorbs, dissolves and eliminates the toxins such as Eczema, Psoriasis, boils, pimples, patches, hypertension, diabetes, migraine, arthritis, constipation, gastritis, dyspepsia, anorexia, peptic and duodenal ulcers and menstrual disorders.

Massage Therapy

Massage is generally applied for tonic, stimulant, and sedative effects. This therapy is useful in improving blood circulation and relieving fatigue. It is helpful in opening the closed pores of the skin. The opening of the closed skin pores allows harmful toxins to come out of body with sweat. This therapy is very useful in all chronic conditions such as rheumatoid arthritis Osteoarthritis, inter-vertebral disc prolapse, frozen shoulder, stroke and in gastro-intestinal conditions such as constipation, dyspepsia, anorexia, CAD, metabolic disorders, hormonal disorders and neurological disorders.

Chromotherapy

Sun rays have seven colours—violet, indigo, blue, green, yellow, orange and red. These colours are employed through irradiation on body or by administering charged water and oil for treatment. The most commonly administered treatments in chromo therapy is plantain leaf sunbath, thermolium sunbath and open air sunbath. This therapy is useful for rheumatoid arthritis, osteoarthritis, Psoriasis, eczema, upper respiratory problems, anemia, paralysis, hypertension and digestive disorders.

Magneto Therapy

Magnet influences health. South and north poles of different powers and shapes are used in magneto therapy. They are applied directly on different parts of body or through charged up oil or water.

Urine Therapy

Selfurine after leaving bed or urine of cow is used to cure a number of diseases and disorders.

Air Therapy

The morning air is known as *Pran Vayu* (air of soul). Walking in morning air is helpful in number of disorders. It increases longevity also.

In addition to above modalities of treatment in naturopathy, yoga, diet, fasting, acupressure, acupuncture therapy and pyramid therapy are also very popular. These therapies are effective for treatment of nervous system imbalances such as stress, anxiety, muscle cramps, headaches, depression, pre-menstrual syndrome, infertility, obesity, pre-conception care can be treated by this therapy. It is also recommended for digestive disorders, gastrointestinal disorders, constipation, prickly bowel syndrome, immune disorders, allergies, sensitivities, weightloss, cough, cold, flu, insomnias, prostrate arthritis, high cholesterol can be cured by this therapy.

Our nation can save huge amount of money by using naturopathy. It is less expensive, better quality of care could be provided. This system of health care can be made available to masses at very cheap rate.

Health infrastructure is an important indicator to understand health delivery provisions and mechanisms in a country. Ensuring well coordinated high quality health care also establishment of a supportive health system infrastructure.

According to report of Census of India 2011, 7.4 per cent population of our country is above 60 years of age. This section is most vulnerable group requiring proper attention. The Naturopathy can play vital role for this vulnerable group. It is because it is easily accessible and affordable. 58.38 per cent population in urban areas of our country come under below poverty line. This is also a vulnerable section which requires affordable health care. Total 35.46 people are BPL.

The National Health Profile 2013 states that in the entire country there are 19,817 hospitals of which 15,398 are in rural areas and 4,419 are in urban areas. In addition, there are 1,51,684 sub-centres, 24,448 are Primary Health Centres and 5,187 are Community Health Centres in India.

Naturopathy Infrastructure

The medical care facility under AYUSH by management status, i.e. dispensaries and hospitals are 26,107.

According to information available, status of Naturopathy Hospitals/Dispensaries is as follows:

Table-1

Sl. No.	Facility	Naturopathy
1.	Hospital	107
2.	Dispensaries	97
3.	Registered Practitioners	1401
4.	Degree Colleges	17

Table-2

Sl. No.	National Council Registered	Population Served per Doctor
1.	Per doctor both Allopathic and AYUSH	1217.84
2.	Allopathic doctor	1384.43
3.	AYUSH doctor	1783.21
4.	Dental surgeon	10120.79
5.	Nurse	531.79
6.	Pharmacist	1936.94

4
Health in Text and Traditions

In our sacred texts like *Vedas, Puranas, Samhitas, Ramayana, Mahabharata*, *Sushrut Samhita*, *Bhav Prakas*, *Ashtang Sangraha*, *Astang Hridya* and *Arogya Prakash*, knowledge about health and health related traditions have been brought to our notice. Our Ayurvedic system of medicine is based on those knowledges and wisdoms. They have been and are being transmitted from generation to generation. Here we are going to describe those knowledge traditions related to health which have communicated to our folk and rural people by our Great *Rishis* and *Munis*. Now they have become not only textual traditions but also the folk and rural traditions related to our health system. The health behaviours described in sacred texts have become the health behaviour of folk and rural people. On that basis people of all houses discuss the causes of ailments and ways of their treatment in their day-to-day talk.

Our country India is a country of villages where more than 70 per cent people live in villages and practice agriculture or allied work. In our country, health related behaviours are dependent on nature. The knowledge related to those environments have been written by our *Rishis, Munis* and *Acharyas* (sages and seers) in the form of text for future generations. Our health traditions were oral in the beginning. They passed orally from generation to generation before they got written status. *Shruti* and *Smriti* were integral parts of oral traditions. Oral traditions of health is still going on among folk and rural society. But we also have our written health traditions in the form of sacred texts. In oral and written traditions, we find that our health is product of environments where we are born and brought up. Food and medicine avoidable in our environment have been beneficial for our health. In our sacred texts, it has been mentioned that means and medicine available in environment where one is born and reared are beneficial for his health.

In our *Dharmashastra* it has been written that to wear good clothes and eat good food are not sufficient for our healthy life, rather our healthy life depends upon our all those activities which we perform right from leaving bed in morning till going bed at night. From getting up in the morning to going bed at night activities must be according to nature. We can remain healthy by observing lawful bath, devotion, breakfast, mid day meal, night meal and *Brahmacharya.* Food, sleep and *Brahmacharya* (control of lust and passion) are three pillars of our health.

In our *Dharmashastra* special attention has been paid on mental health. In the materialistic age today, the mental health has become more significant. Today we are using our body like a machine. That is why a number of mental and physical diseases are occurring in our body. High blood pressure, hypertension, heart disease, peptic ulcer, loss of appetite and bronchial asthama are occurring due to mental tension and anxiety. The main cause of our ill-health is avoidance of lawful food behaviour. We can save our health definitely, if we observe lawful food behaviour. The observance of lawful food behaviour does not allow disease to occur.

According to our *Dharmashastra,* our body is main means of *Karma* and *Dharma* and our body is dependent on health. Thus, our healthy body is the main means of *Purushartha—Dharma, Artha, Kama* and *Moksha.* The healthy persons achieve Purushartha, but unhealthy persons do not achieve *purushartha.* In this way, the first aim of our life is to remain healthy. This is the most valuable wealth of our life. Our life becomes aimless without a healthy life. Our life becomes burden without health. A patient cannot do anything. He/she cannot win troubles of life. He/she cannot win enemies like (desire) and *Krodha* (anger). He cannot become victorious. Pleasure and happiness depend upon the health of an individual. Rich, poor, king-beggar, man-woman, youth-aged all need to lead healthy life. But it is possible only when we are healthy.

Good health is such a valuable thing whose value we realize when it is lost. But how can we live long, how can we achieve good health, how can we maintain good health, these are such questions whose solution is not very simple. Today, our Government is spending crores and crores of rupees on Allopathy medical system. More and more medical colleges and hospitals are being established. But it is also true that number of patients is also increasing more and more. We do not find place to put our patients on bed in hospitals. Doctors are helpless and patients are disappointed. Sugar, blood pressure, T.B., asthma and heart disease have taken an epidemic dimensions.

When we go 50-60 years back, there were no doctors in 100-100 miles. The number of patients was also less. When anybody became some ill, he/she was cured by domestic medicines and treatment. Now question arises as to why we became so diseased and we are loosing our health day by day.

This shows clearly that we have committed mistakes somewhere in our health behaviours. It seems that we have started behaving against the ways mentioned in sacred texts, told by our *Rishi-Muni* and preached by our venerable *Acharyas.* We have started treating our body like a machine and thing of consumption. We have started loving a civilization which has come in our nation from a distance of nearly 600 kms. We have given up good habits and adopted such habits which are bad. We have given up habit of rising in *Brahmamuhurta* (early morning). We have started getting up in late after sunrise. Instead of early to bed and early to rise, we have started late to bed and late to rise. We have started working for whole night and sleeping for whole day. We have given up working in contact of nature. Rather we have started working in air conditioned room. Instead of morning walks, we have started morning sleep. We have adopted tooth brush in place of brush of thin green stick *(Datun).* We have given up oil massage and exercise. We have given up milk, *ghee* and curd but we have adopted refined and Dalda. We are selling Till, Rai, Saraso in markets and purchasing refined and vegetable oils. Instead of talking water in the morning, we have started taking bed tea. We have started using tobacco, biri, cigarettes, wine, drugs etc. without any hesitation. We rush to allopathic doctors even for small health problems. We have forgotten to maintain fast and control of food. We are losing our health culture and civilization. We are also paying for it. A number of diseases are occuring in our body. That is why, today it has become essential to understand, know, think and adopt once again those health culture and civilization preached by *Rishi-Muni,* described by *Dharmashastra* and guided by *Acharya.*

In Ayurveda, it has been described that man can survive hundred years by performing work. We should follow the preachings of Lord Brahma for our hundred years of life. We should also tell the preachings of Brahma to others for hundred year. In Ayurveda, the age of a man has been determined for one hundred years. This is possible when we adopt healthy behaviours mentioned in sacred texts. It is fitness of the thing to mention here the reply of a question asked by Lord Buddha from one of his disciples to reply who was a diseaseless person. The disciple replied that a diseaseless person was one who takes proper quantity of food at proper time earned by proper means.

Now, we are going to present here those health cultural traditions which have been described in *Dharmashastra,* preached by *Rishi-Munis* and guided by *Acharyas* one by one.

Early to Rise

In our *Dharmashastra,* special emphasis has been placed on early to rise. In *Dharmashastra* the early period to rise is called *Brahmamuhurta.* One and half hour before sunrise is termed as *Brahmamuhurta.* One should get up in *Brahmamuharta* and remember all pervading and almighty God *Parmatma.* In Ayurveda, it has been written as hymns, "*Brahmamuhurta Uthisthetswasthayo Rakshartha Mayusha.*" The meaning of this *shloka* is that one who gets up early in *Brahmamuhurta,* he/she lives long. This habit increases our age, energy confidence and shining on face and body. In our *Dharmashastra,* the habit of getting up after sunrise, is treated as patient. In English language, there is a famous proverb that "early to bed and early to rise, makes a man healthy wealthy and wise". Our *Dharmashastras, Rishi-Muni,* and *Acharyas* have told us that *Pranvayu* (Life promoting air) flows in *Brahmamuhurta.* The *pranvayu* makes us immortal. One folk saying in this regard is as follows:

> *Pratah Shubh Bela Men Amrit Ki Varsha Hoti Hai*
> *Jo Jagat Hai So Pawat Hai, Jo Sowat Hai So Khowat Hai*

The meaning of above folk proverb is that immortal air (*Pran Vayu)* flows in *Brahmamuhurta.* Those who get up, obtain it and those who sleep loose it.

Seeing Good Objects

In our *Dharmashastra* curd, *ghee,* cow, baby suckling cow, mirror, *Bel Patta, Pan Patta,* yellow mustard, flowers, flower beads are taken as good objects to be seen soon after leaving the bed. Daily seeing good objects after leaving bed increases our age, energy and confidence. These are essentials for healthy living. Contrary to this, seeing of bad objects after getting up, affects our health negatively.

Water Intake

In our *Dharmashastra,* water intake in the morning is regarded as beneficial for long life and health. For this purposes water is kept in copper glass or an earthen pot at night. It is taken in the early morning soon after leaving the bed. The water kept at night in copper or earthen pot is taken in the morning before defecation. The stomach becomes clean. A number of diseases are cured such as piles, cough, gas, and eye defects.

Taking a glass of water in morning is very much beneficial for health. The water may be cold or light hot. A folk proverb related to morning intake of a glass of water is as follows:

Pratah Pani Jo Piye, Nitya Utha Hara Khay
Taja Datun Jo Kare, Ta Ghar Vaidya Najay

The meaning of this proverb is that a man can prohibit a doctor to enter his house by taking water an *Hare* (Myroblem) in the morning and using fresh *Datun* brush of green stick.

Defecation

According to our *Dharmashastra* and prevalent folk tradition, the best time for defecation is morning after leaving bed and taking a glass of water. Our stomach, heart and brain become light after defecation in morning. This habit is also helpful in controlling a number of diseases. Not defecation in morning invites a number of diseases. Taking tobacco, cigarettes, biri, tea and reading newspaper for defecation is not a good habit. Rather such behaviours affect our health negatively. Washing hands with ash, soil or soap after defecation is beneficial for health. It is also taken as a good habit.

Constipation

According to *Dharmashastra,* constipation is mother of all diseases. Constipation creates toxins in our body. Toxin creates a number of diseases in our body. In constipation our stomach is filled with air and we feel heaviness on heart and mind. We feel uneasy. We are not in a position to work. Regular constipation makes our blood and skin impure.

In order to remove constipation, our *Dharmashastra* has stressed upon following food behaviours:

- Before going to bed at night a glass of light hot milk or water should be taken.
- A glass of water kept at night in a copper or earthen container should be taken after leaving bed in the morning.
- Bread of wheat flour with chaff should be taken.
- Green and leafy vegetables should be taken.
- Pulses with husk should be taken.
- Papaya and fig should be taken.
- Light hot water should be taken an hour before or after meals.

- Fasting should be kept.
- Lemon juice in light hot water should be taken.
- *Trifla churna*-powder of *Amla, Hara* and *Bahera*—should be taken along with loaf sugar.
- *Hing* (Asafoetida) should be taken with loaf sugar and hot water.

Morning Walk

Our *Dharmashastra* places special emphasis on morning walk. In the morning *Pranvayu* (life promoting air) blows. Morning walk keeps us physically and mentally fit. It removes diabetes, blood pressure and heart diseases. We feel fresh and energetic throughout the day. One must perform half an hour morning walk regularly. Walking, running, performing exercises and yoga in morning is very much beneficial for health.

Cleaning Teeth

In our *Dharmashastra,* teeth have been described as the door of body protection. Healthy teeth keep us healthy. When our teeth are affected with disease, our body is also affected by disease. White teeth increase glaze and beauty of our face. In our *Dharmashastra,* emphasis has been placed upon washing teeth in the morning with green stick (*Datun)* after defecation. Even tea taking without washing teeth and tongue is not allowed. Our *Datun* (Green stick) should be 12 fingers long, thin and straight. The green stick is turned into brush with the help of chewing teeth. With the help of this green stick brush, all teeth are rubbed horizontally and vertically. Mustard oil and salt are also rubbed on teeth with *Datun* to make them more and more clean. After washing teeth, the *Datun* is torn in the middle into two parts and tongue is cleaned with torn thin Datun part. Now, teeth, tongue and throat are cleaned properly with water keeping in mouth. Now-a-days, tooth brush and tooth paste are used to clean teeth and tongue cleaner to clean tongue. They are made of steel, plastic and brass. They clean teeth and tongue undoubtedly, but exercise of teeth gum is not held. The teeth and gum becomes weak.

Our teeth become weak due to eating too much hot or cold food. Before and after sharing meals teeth and mouth should be washed properly. The green stick of *Nim, Ber, Babul, Jamun, Mahua, Chirchiri* and *Sakhua* should be used. The green stick of mango and guava should be used on fast and festive occasions.

Kulla (Gargling)

Cleaning mouth, teeth, tongue and throat again and again with water is called *Kulla* (gargling). In our *Dharmashastra* gargling is told as beneficial for health. It cures mouthache, teethache and pimples on faces. Gargling cures throat related disease. Gargling can be done with cold and hot water both depending on season and requirement. It is also beneficial for eye diseases.

Nail Cutting

In our *Dharmashastra* nail cleaning and cutting has been regarded as beneficial for healthy life. Dirty nails are carrier of a number of diseases. A number of germs and bacteria find their place in dirty nails. They make our food and drinking water infected and dirty. The infected and dirty food create a number of diseases in our body. We should cut and clean our nails at least once in a week. We should not chew or cut nail with teeth.

Taking Snuff

In our *Dharmashastra* taking Snuff (*Nasya)* is regarded as beneficial for the health. Taking mustard oil as snuff is beneficial for health. It keeps our voice sweet and hairs black and mouth free from foul odour. It is also, beneficial for cough and cold. We should put two drops of mustard oil in both noses with the help of a dropper. Snuff can be taken in morning, noon or evening. Taking tobacco as Snuff is harmful for the health.

Eye Health

Eye is a boon for us. If our eyes are not healthy, we have to face darkness everywhere. Therefore, special emphasis has been placed upon eye health in our *Dharmashastra.* A number of means have been described to maintain eye health. Factors responsible for creating eye diseases have also been described. For example walking in storm heat, severe cold, seeing sun, seeing glittering things, reading books in little phones, reading or writing while sleeping, reading in dim light, seeing towards dazzling light, seeing towards smoke, loss of sexual control, rubbing eyes with dirty nails and fingers, washing eyes with dirty water, rubbing eyes on something falling in eyes, washing head with hot water, cutting our hairs of nose, weeping with tearful eyes, long persistent headache and sugar disease create eye diseases. The following practices have been mentioned in *Dharmashastra* to maintain eye health:

- Walking bare footed on green grasses in the morning.
- Washing eyes with pure cold water in the morning, noon and evening.
- Using two drops of mustard oil in ears and nose.
- Seeing sun at the time of rising for sometime.
- Seeing moonlit for sometime.
- Using mustard oil, or Til oil on head.
- Using pumpkin seed oil on head during summer.
- Rubbing eyebrows gently after sharing meals.
- Using black ointment on eyebrow.

Nose Cleaning

Nose is a way through which air goes in our body. That is why special emphasis has been placed on cleaning of nose in our *Dharmashastra.* Putting two drops of mustard oil in nose during morning and evening keep our nose clean and disease free. We should never pull out the hairs of nose. They prevent germs and bacteria from entering in our body. We should not put fingers inside our nose.

Ear Cleaning

Ears are also important parts of our body. The communication reaches in our brain through eyes and our brain decodes the meaning of sound heard. The persons suffering from ear diseases do not hear the speech and communication. We should clean our ears by putting mustard oil drops in ears and cleaning ears after sometime with cotton or clean cloth. This practice increases our hearing power, and pleases our mind and heart. To keep ears disease free, special emphasis has been placed on the practice of ear boring. The behaviour of ear boring prevents the disease of hydrocele and control sexual desire. The practice of ear boring is also beneficial for lungs and breathing diseases.

Exercise

In our *Dharmashastra* special emphasis has been placed on exercise for remaining healthy. Walking, running, jogging, *yogasana, pranayama* and *Surya Namaskaras* are all known as exercise. The performance of exercise in proper ground and proper time is very much beneficial for a healthy life. Every individual should perform exercise according to his/her interest. For example walking, running, jumping, swimming, performing yoga and performing *pranayama.* The performance of exercise makes body disease free and mind pleasant. It increases our hunger and digestion. It increases our longevity. The exercise doing during winter and spring season is very beneficial. In other seasons, exercise should be done as per own efficiency. The exercise doers should take milk, *ghee* and fruits.

Describing the benefits of exercise, Ban Bhatta has written as follows:

Laghwam Karma Samarthyam Dipto Agnirmendasah
Vibhakta Dhangatratwam Vyayayandup Jayate.

The meaning of above *shloka* reveals that regular performance of exercise increases our body activities, physical and mental work ability, digestive power, loss of fats and fitness to each and every part of body. That is why exercise is essential for good health. But we should not do exercise in excess. The performance of excess exercise causes fever, T.B. and blood vomiting. *Charak Samhita* prohibits excess excercises in following shloka:

Prak Shramat Vyayam Varjiyat

The meaning is that excessive exercise is prohibited.

We should not do exercise immediately after sharing meal. Persons suffering from fever, cough, T.B. should not perform exercise.

Some laws have been formulated in our sacred texts relating to performing exercises. They are as follows:

- Exercise should be performed in open place so that body can get pure air.
- While doing exercise, we should breath through nose.
- Exercise should be done according to age and sex.
- Exercise should be done in empty stomach.
- Exercise should be done regularly and timely.
- The amount of exercise should be increased slowly.
- Exercise doers should take milk, *ghee* and fruits.
- Proper time for exercise is morning and evening.
- Taking hot milk after doing exercise is beneficial.

Body Massage

In our *Dharmashastra,* the importance of body massage for healthy life has been emphasized. As leaves and branches of a tree grow up due to pouring water in roots, in the same way our body and its different parts grow up due to massage. It increases juice, blood and flesh. Our body becomes attractive and strong. We should massage our body regularly in the morning. We should massage our body parts such as head, neck, hand, back, stomach, thigh, legs and feet. The regular massaging of entire body parts keep us physically and mentally fit and strong. It removes bodyache, too and brings good sleep. It stops crack of skin. If massaging of entire body parts is not possible, we should massage at least our head, nose, ear, forehead, navel and feet regularly everyday. Daily massaging oil in navel keeps our lips and face attractive and removes dryness. Massaging oil in head removes headache and dendrufs. It keeps our hairs dark. The massage of ears with oil increases our hearing power. It keeps ear waste out. The massage of teeth with oil makes our teeth strong. It increases the shining of teeth. The massage of feet brings good sleep. The massage of oil on joints makes joints free and removes joint pains.

The persons suffering from fever and indigestion should not do massaging of body with oil.

Ubatan (Pulse Paste)

In our *Dharmashastra* great importance is attached to *Ubatan* massage for maintaining health. *Ubatan* is a kind of paste prepared from pulses and turmeric powder. Pulse and turmeric powder are mixed and made a paste with the help of water. *Ubatan,* thus, prepared are massaged over body to look handsome, attractive and beautiful. Its use increases youthfulness. *Ubatan* is massaged over the body of bride and bridegroom to make them youthful, attractive and handsome. The massaging of *ubatan* is done as a marriage ritual. The women folk massage *Ubatan* over their body even after marriage to maintain their beauty and youthfulness. *Ubatan* purifies skin, and beautifies body. It destroys cough and obesity. It is also prepared from oat flour, turmeric powder and orange husk powder. Milk is also added in *ubatan. Ubatan* is virtuous for maintaining health.

Bathing and Health

Special emphasis has been placed on bathing in our oral and written textual traditions to remain healthy. In our traditions, it has been described that bathing increases energy, strength, beautifulness, youthfulness and longevity. It decreases body heat. It removes sweating, sleeplessness, body waste, thirst and body heat. It also controls scabies. Bile natured persons should perform bath in cold water and cough natured person should perform bath in gentle hot water. Too hot water brings harmful effect on our hairs, skin and eyes. We should do bath daily regularly. We should clean our ears, nose, hands, heads, armpits, thigh, elbow and feet properly while performing bath. Paste of milky soil should be prepared and applied overhead and other parts of body. It should be kept for some time in sun to become dry. After getting dried, bathing is performed rubbing the entire body parts one by one. Pulse flour paste is also applied over body to cleanse the body properly during bathing. Oil is also massaged before bathing. Bathing can be done in river, pond, bank of well, spring, chapakal (hand pump) and sea or lake. Bathing should not be done before or after sharing meals. In our textual traditions, emphasis has been placed on morning bath before sharing breakfast. Performing bath with milk is also beneficial for our health in certain circumstances.

Surya Namaskar

In our *Dharmashastra,* special attention has been placed on performing *Surya Namaskar* for maintaining good health. In *Surya Namaskara,* exercises are done keeping face towards rising sun. These exercises are also known as *Surya Ashnan* (Solar bath). In these exercises *Pranamas* are offered to Lord Surya in different body poses. It is a method of *Pranayam in* which an individual stands up keeping his/her face towards sun. The air of lung is allowed to come out of body and the outside air is allowed slowly to go inside the lungs. Now breathing is controlled for some time. While doing so, it is felt that the rays of sun are entering inside lungs and heart and are killing all germs present there. A *Surya Namaskar* doer also feels that the rays of sun are making his/her lungs and heart energetic and burning all germs and bacteria. Now the breathing is allowed slowly. This exercise is repeated for 10-15 minutes. *Surya Namaskar* should always be done in the morning at the time of sunrise. It should always be done in the morning at the time of sunrise. It should not be done in day time when the rays are very hot. *Surya Namaskar* makes our lungs and heart strong and increases the seeing power. In our *Dharmashastra,* Lord Surya is regarded as destructor of skin, eye, leprosy, blood, brain, bile and intestine related diseases. It destroys all types of contagious diseases. In our *Dharmashastra,* the tradition of performing Surya Namaskar and offering water to Lord Sun is prevalent since time immemorial. There are seven colours in sun rays and each colour ray is beneficial in a particular disease. For example,

- Red ray—Leprosy disease
- Violet—Blood disease
- Blue ray—Brain disease

- Green ray—Eye disease
- Sky ray—Skin disease
- Yellow ray—Bile disease
- Orange ray—Intestine disease.

Wearing Dress

In our *Dharmashastra,* emphasis has been placed on wearing dresses to look handsome, energetic, attractive, courageous, strong, and wise. In our tradition emphasis has been placed on wearing clean dresses to remain healthy and disease free. Wearing clean dress increases our name, fame, age and pleasure. It is also beneficial for skin. Dirty dresses increase infections and diseases of various kind. They create the sense of shyness, poverty and unpleasant attractiveness. Cotton dresses have been adviced. Narrow and small dresses have been prohibited.

Putting Tilak

In our sacred texts, importance of putting *Tilak* mark on forehead has been described as beneficial for good health. Putting *Tilak* of *Chandan, Rori, Haldi, Sindur,* Sunfried rice and *Bhabhut* is regarded as protector of health, wealth, age, energy, knowledge and wisdom. The putting of *Tilak* activates our all five organs. It makes them strong and positive.

Wearing Kharaun (Wooden Slipper)

In our *Dharmashastra,* wearing *Kharaun* is regarded as beneficial for health. *Kharaun* is a wooden slipper. Its use is beneficial in feet and eye diseases. It also controls hydrocele disease and increases our age. Wood is a bad conductor of electricity. The use of *Kharaun* does not allow the energy of feet to enter in the land as happens in case of barefooted.

Devotion in God

In our sacred texts, devotion in God has been attached to hour good health. According to our tradition, it is God who keeps our body healthy, energetic, strong, disease free and long. We can live long by devotion in God. Whosoever the powerful, wise, intelligent and famous individuals we know, they were great devotee of God. Those who lost the blessings of God were lost. For example Ravana, Kansha and Mahishasur. They were powerful, wise, famous and intelligent. But they were not devotees of God. So, they had to become extinct. In our *Dharma Grantha,* a number of hymns or *shlokas* are provided o please Gods and Goddesses. For example *Gayatri Mantra, Mahamrityunjay mantra, Hanumat mantra, Devi-Durga Mantra, Siddhi-Vinayak Mantra,* Goddess *Lakshmi Mantra,* Goddess *Saraswati Mantra, Surya Mantra, Shani Mantra, Rahu-Ketu Mantra, Mangal Mantra, Som Mantra, Buddha Mantra, Vrihaspati Mantra* and others. One can achieve good health and long prestigious life by performing Puj-path and offering prayer through *Mantras* or hymns. Blessing of God and Goddesses is sought in every life cycle rituals.

Blessing of Elders and Aged

In our *Dharmashastra,* emphasis has also been placed on blessing of elders and aged for healthy and long life. Elders and aged are equivalent to Gods and Goddness. Their blessing provides sound health and long pleasant life. Blessing of elders and aged are a must for good health, wealth and wisdom. The curse of aged destroys name, fame, health, wealth and wisdom. Duryodhan and Karna could not get blessings of elders, so they lost their health, wealth, wisdom and kingdom and became extinct.

Yoga and Pranayama

In our *Dharmashastra,* stress has been placed on regular performance of Yoga and *Pranayama.* Yoga and *Pranayama* are such means which keep us disease free and make us energetic, strong and intelligent. But Yoga and *Pranayama* should always be done under the guidance of a *Guru.*

Attainment of Wealth

In our *Dharmashastra,* emphasis has been placed on attainment of wealth through the ways of *Dharma* to remain healthy, wealthy and wise. It is because it is not possible to maintain family, rear family members, to lead oldhood and to maintain mental balance in absence of wealth. We cannot protect our body from disease without money. Thus, poverty is the route of all troubles. Wisdom does not find place without money. In poor condition our wisdom does not work. A poor intellectual does not find name and fame. Our all kins and friends leave us when we are poor. The poor do not have friends. Justice also does not help a poor. That is why in our textual traditions special attention has been placed on attainment of wealth. But the wealth must be attained through the ways of *Dharma* or proper means.

Intake of Food

In our *Dharmashastra,* food intake behaviour has been related to the maintenance of good health. The food intake keeps us healthy and provides us a long pleasant life. The food intake has been influencing our health since time immemorial and it will continue to influence our health in future, too. Food is the greatest boon provided to us by the Almighty God. It nourishes us and makes the energy to flow in every parts of our body. But the intake of food should be regular and under control. Without regularity and control, the food can affect our health negatively and ultimately take our life. Wisdom of a wiseman and justice of Judge become invalid without food.

The main function of food is to nourish and grow body and to compensate loss of energy in body. It also maintains heat and energy in our body. Our food must perform all these four functions. Our food should be balance and digestible. The food which gets digested easily is the best food for maintaining health. If food is costly but not digestible easily and juice creating, it is not beneficial for the health. Such foods are useless from the point of view of health.

Husk of Grain, Pulse and Vegetable

According to our sacred texts, husks of grain, pulse and bark of vegetables are beneficial for the good health. We should take husk mixed wheat and other grains flour, husk mixed pulses and rice prepared manually by *Deki* and *Okhali-Musali.* When husks and barks are taken out from grains, pulses and vegetables, a number of valuable nutrients are lost. Husks and barks of grains, vegetables and Mar (gruel) of rice are natural digestive. They contain dietary fibre and create digestive juice and help in digestion process.

Cooking Food

In our *Dharmashastra* special attention has been paid on cooking the food. There are a number of food materials which become more digestible by heating more, but there are some other food materials which become digestible on very less heating. For example pulses are cooked on more heat but they maintain their nutritious value. Ghee and spices should be mixed in the last phase of cooking to make food digestible.

Pickles, Sauce and Jam

In our sacred texts, taking pickle, sauce and jam to increase hunger has been prohibited. There is no doubt they increase our interest in food intake. But they are harmful for the health. Our natural interest in food increases when we are hungry. When we feel hungry, our interest in food increases naturally. When we feel hungry we take salt and *roti* or *mar-bhat* and salt with great interest. Artificial interest in food can be created by pickles, sauce and jam. But natural interest is created by hunger. Therefore, taking pickle, jam and sauce has been prohibited in our textual tradition. In certain cases, they have been allowed in very less amount. Lemon, ginger and curd have been allowed to increase hunger.

Harmful Food

In our *Dharmashastra,* certain foods have been declared as harmful for the health, for example uncooked, half cooked, burnt food, rotten food, left over food, fungus and bacteria infected food, too hot food and too cold food. Taking food quickly is harmful for health.

Quantity and Frequency of Food

In our *Dharmashastra* special attention has been paid on proper intake of food. More than required food intake affects our intestine, liver, and digestive canal. They become weak and diseased. Taking too less food than requirement decreases our energy, weight and shining of face. It also creates gastritis and loss of wisdom and sleep. We should take food in such a way that its two parts should be filled with food, one part with water and remaining one part as blank for circulation of air.

Taking food before digestion of previous meal is also very harmful for health. This behaviour influences our health negatively. In our traditions, children have been allowed to share meals frequently, adults thrice in a day and aged twice in a day. Small meal can be taken in between two meals.

Chewing Food

In our traditions great importance has been attached to chewing food for maintaining good health. If we take food without chewing, we are deprived of a number of health benefits. On following this behaviour, we are affected by loss of appetite. In this situation, our digestive canal has to perform the function of teeth. When we take food chewing properly, our digestive canal does not have to perform the function of teeth. Another benefit is that chewing food creates digestive juice which helps in proper digestion of food.

Food and Mental Happiness'

In our *Dharmashastra* emphasis has been placed upon such a method of food intake which can give us mental pleasure. We should follow food in take which can give us mental pleasure. We should take rice, pulse, vegetables, leafy vegetable as a boon given by God. This provides mental happiness related to health. When food is taken with sense of fear, anger and conflict, it creates poison in the body and makes us unhealthy. Food taken with satisfaction keeps us healthy and provides immortality. It is better to remain on fast to encounter the feeling of fear, anger and conflict.

Food and Purity

Our *Dharmashastra* attaches great importance to the purity of food to maintain good health. It has been told that food should be cooked, served and eaten at a pure place. Food should be protected from the touch of lizards, cockroach, ant, flies, insects and others. It should be protected from dust, sand, pebbles and pieces of stone. Before taking food hands, teeth and mouth should be washed properly. Food should be taken at pure place sitting on a small carpet. Food should be cooked after performing bath and wearing clean dressed. The food should also be served in clean dresses. Food eater and food service provider both should maintain purity. Our mouth should be towards north, east or west at the time of eating. It should not be in south direction. Before sharing food, some water is put on palm and poured around the plate containing food. The God is offered prayer with folded hands with whose grace we are getting food to eat. Thereafter, sharing of food should be started.

Aachaman (Washing Mouth and Hands)

In our sacred text, there is tradition of *Aachaman* (washing hand and mouth) properly. All food particles sticked to fingers, mouth, gum and teeth should be washed properly with pure water. Tongue is also cleaned properly. Now hands, mouth and face are drying with towels or *Gamachha.*

Time of Food

In our sacred texts and traditions great significance has been attached to time of food. It has been mentioned that timely intake of breakfast and meal keeps us healthy. Untimely intake of food creates a number of diseases and makes us unhealthy. The best time of food intake is morning and evening time. We should take light breakfast in between 7 to 8 a.m. We should take first meal between 12 noon to 1 p.m. We should take night meal (dinner) between 7 to 8 p.m. In-between two main meals some light meals should be taken. But in between two main meals and light meals, digestion of previous meal should be taken into consideration. Without proper digestion of first meal, second meal should not be taken. Before sleeping at night we should take a glass of gentle hot milk or water. We should not sleep empty stomach at night. In case of indigestion some liquid food should be taken. In order to bring stomach in order, we should remain on 12 hours or 24 hours fast.

The First Food Item

In our sacred text and traditions, we do not find mention of soup as appetizer. Rather emphasis has been placed on intake of ginger, lemon juice, green chili and black salt. These first food items make food more tasty and cleanse throat and tongue. We should not take banana, watermelon, papaya, guava, apple and cucumber along with main food. They should be taken half an hour before or after meal.

Sequence of Food Items

Intaking food, the sequence of food item is also taken into account. Our sacred texts and traditions teach us about the sequence of food items to be taken. According to traditions, pulse should be eaten first followed by bread, rice and vegetables. Curd should be taken in the last. Fruits should be taken in breakfast. Fruits should not be taken in the evening and night. A glass of gentle hot milk should be taken half an hour after evening or night meal. One who follows his sequence of food items remains always healthy and lead long life.

Intake of water

Water intake is essential for our health and healthy life. Our sacred texts and traditions confirm that we should not take water along with meal or break fast. We should take water half an hour before or after principal meal. In summer gentle cold water is required during sharing meals, it should be taken in less quantity.

Food and Water Taboo for Hungery and Thirsty

In our textual and oral traditions, it is a taboo to give too much food and water to a hungery and thirsty. When one takes water when he is hungry and takes food when he is thirsty, it creates a number of diseases. The thirst is quenched first slowly and then food items be given to eat. Similarly, hunger is satisfied first slowly then thirst is quenched.

Food Sharing Utensils

In our texts and traditions emphasis has been placed on utensils to share food items. A brief description about them are as follows:

- ***Gold utensils:*** Gold made utensils destroy harmful effects and increases eyesight. They are beneficial for health.
- ***Silver utensils:*** Silver made utensils destroy biles and increase eyesight and brain.
- ***Bronze utensils:*** Bronze utensils destroy biles and increase wisdom/
- ***Brass utensils:*** They destroy cough, cold and germs.
- ***Iron utensils:*** They are beneficial for destroying a number of diseases.
- ***Leaf utensils:*** They are pure and increase interest in food.
- ***Plastic utensils:*** Plastic utensils are not healthy.
- ***Water utensils:*** Water should be stored in brass, copper or earthen pots for drinking purposes. Iron and plastic utensils are not suitable from the health point of view.
- ***Milk utensils:*** For heating of and storing milk, iron or earthen pots are good from the health point of view.

Activities after Taking Food

In our *Dharmashastra* some activities have been prescribed, while some activities have been prohibited. These activities are as follows:

- After taking meals fingers and mouth should be washed properly. Both hands should be rubbed together for some time and then covered both eyes with both hands. This activity increases our eyesight.
- We should not urinate before sharing food. One should urinate after sharing meal.

- Fingers of hand should be rubbed gently over stomach for a number of times.
- After day meal we should take rest for a while, but after night meal we should walk for a while.
- After sharing food we should not run.
- After sharing meal we should sleep towards left side and then towards right side for some time. This increases our digestion.
- With folded hands we should thank to God to get the food digested properly for running energy in the body.

Method of Sleeping

In our *Dharmashastra,* method of sleeping has also been described. In textual traditions it has been mentioned that after sharing meal we should lay dorsally till eight breaths, 16 breaths towards right side and 32 breaths towards left side. The entire process should take 2-3 minutes. It is very beneficial for the process of digestion.

Taboos on Some Work after Sharing Meal

In our sacred textual traditions some activities have been prohibited. They are as follows:

- We should not sit just after sharing food.
- We should not sleep for more time after sharing day meal.
- We should not sit in hot sun after day meal.
- We should not walk fastly after sharing meals.
- We should never run after eating food.
- We should not do exercise after taking food.
- We should not swim after sharing food.
- We should not ride on horse after sharing meals.
- We should not do bath after sharing meals.

Intake of Fruits

In our *Dharmashastra,* special emphasis has been laid on intake of fruits for good health. Fruits have been our natural food. In the beginning, we were not grain eaters. We were fruit and meat eaters because they were profusely available in environment. We became grain producer in Neolithic period. But more and more intake of grains have created more and more diseases. In order to cure diseases, we have to share fruits and vegetables. Intake of fruit make us energetic, free from diseases, attractive and live long. We should take seasonal fruit daily. If possible, we should breakfast with fruits. During fast, fruit food is allowed. The bark of fruits has natural digestive power. Therefore, bark of fruits should not be removed. But their barks should be washed properly. Note that there are some fruits, whose barks are not eaten. For example coconut, papaya, orange, banana. We should take fruits in sufficient quantity.

Fresh Vegitables

In our textual traditions, special alterntion has been placed on following food items:

- Fresh and green vegitables
- Raddish and carrot
- Methi sag
- Bathua sag and curd
- Milk with dry fruits.

Food Prescribed in Stomach Ache

In our textual traditions, too much or over-eating is a taboo. But if anybody eats more food, then some treatment has also been prescribed. They are as follows:

- If a stomach ache is due to overeating of banana, then ilaichidana should be taken.
- If stomach ache is due to sugarcane juice, four plums should be eaten.
- If stomach ache is due to overeating of mango, we should take Jamun fruits.
- If stomach ache is due to overeating of watermelon, we should take some black salt.
- If stomach ache is due to overeating of grains, we should take black salt, lemon juice and loaf sugar.
- If stomach ache is due to overeating of meat, papaya and Hing should be taken.

Tabooed Food

In our sacred text, it has been prohibited to take some food items together.

They are as follows:

- Milk and Fish
- Milk and Ragi
- Milk and Meat
- Milk and Pickles
- Milk and Wine
- Milk and Lemon
- Milk and Pomegranate
- Milk and Amla
- Milk and Bel
- Milk and honey in equal amount
- Hot milk and Honey
- Fish and Honey
- Fish and loaf sugar
- Meat and Sattu
- Khir and Khichari
- Meat and Honey
- Honey and Hot water
- Ghee and Honey in equal amount
- Uncooked, semi-cooked, burnt and leftover food
- Water and water melon.

Identification of Poisonous Food

In our *Dharmashastra,* identification of poisonous food has been mentioned. It has been described that a part of food items should be offered to fire before serving to the people. It is termed as *Agnihotra.* Where green smokes and flames appear, it means that the food is poisonous. The another method of identification of poisonous food is offering food items to crows. This is termed as Kakbali. If crow or dog eats and die, it means, that the food is poisonous. In poisonous meat blue flame, in poisonous *ghee* water colour, in poisonous curd black colour, in poisonous honey green colour flames appear. In poisonous oil, red colour flames appear.

Fasting and Health

In our *Dharmashastra,* special attention has been paid on fasting to maintain health and remain healthy. As service doers require rest at week end, in the same way our digestive organs also require rest to function properly and energetically. In order to provide rest to digestive organs, we go on fasting time to time. Our digestive system purify itself on fasting and provide energy to intestine to function properly and efficiently. Toxins present in our body get liberated from the body on fasting. That is why special significance has been attached to fasting to remain healthy in our culture and civilization. Mahatma Gandhi used to remain on fasting on every Monday. He used to observe *Maunvrata* (Silence *Vrata),* too. In our culture people remain on fast on any one day of the week to observe *Vrata* like *Som Vrata, Mangal Vrata, Buddha Vrata, Vrihaspati Vrata, Shukra Vrata, Shani Vrata* and *Ravi Vrata.* Our people also observe *Vrata* on 1st, 11th, 13th, 14th and 15th day of Dark half or bright half of a month. We also observe fast on festive occasions, rituals and ceremonies. In some *Vrata,* water is also not taken. To keep our body healthy, we should observe fast in a week or in a month. In order to maintain health, fasting has been given religious, social and cultural value. In our *Dharmashastra* it has been written that, "*Ati Bhojan Rog Molam*". The meaning is that too much eating is the root of all diseases.

Our *Dharmashastra* mentions that:

Rogah Sarwami Mande Agnau Sutramuvaranichal
Agirnam Malinais Chaneh Jayate Malsanchayat

Its meaning is that all diseases in our body are born due to loss of appetite and accumulation of filth.

It has also been mentioned that:

Sarveshamev Roganam Nidanam Kupita Mala
Tatprakopasya Tu Proklam Vishihahit Sewanam

The meaning is that rotten filth is the root cause of all diseases. They are toxins. Toxins are created due to intake of harmful food and excess food.

It has been adviced to take lemon juice and water in fasting. This activity purifies our intestine and kidney and acidity of blood is removed. Fruits and milk should be taken in fasting. Special attention should also be paid on breaking fast. The fast should be broken by milk, sugar syrup and fruits so that our digestive organs could start function properly. Fasting is also a treatment of a number of diseases. Fasting forces the toxin to go out of body through excretory organs and our body becomes light.

Intake of Sattu (Fried Grains Flour)

In our sacred and folk traditions, the intake of *Sattu* has been described very important from the point of view of health. When grains like paddy, gram, pea, and oat are fried in earthen pot and crushed into powder in *Janta-chakki* or mill, the fried grains flour, thus, obtained is termed as sattu. *Sattu* forms the food of both the rich and the poor. It is carried to eat in journey, pilgrimage and at work place. It can be eaten with salt or sugar/loaf sugar. It can also be eaten with pickles, onion and green chili. It is also taken as syrup-salty or sweet. *Sattu* filled bread or *Litti* (ball of wheat flour filled with *sattu). Sattu-Roti* and *Litti* have become, not only Indian food, but also global food and we have global market of *Litti* and *Sattu. Sattu* is nutritious and can be taken in any season. Its nature is cold in summer and hot in winter. The *sattu* of grain and oat is regarded as very nutritious. It destroys *kafa* and *pitta.* Although *sattu* can be taken in any season, but the intake of sattu requires some observance of taboos. They are as follows:

- *Sattu* should not be eaten twice in a day.
- *Sattu* should not be served to any one twice in a day.
- Too much quantity of water should not be taken immediately after eating *sattu* as a meal.
- One should not eat only *sattu* at night.
- While eating, sattu should not be chewed.
- *Sattu* should not be eaten with meat and fish.
- *Sattu* should not be eaten immediately after tea or a meal.
- *Sattu* should not be eaten without mixing with water.
- Hot water should not be taken after eating *sattu.*
- The *sattu* of *Khesari, Kuathi, Kodo* and Peas should not be eaten.

Though *sattu* has, now, global trade and market, but some proverbs deny the so much significance of sattu. They are as follows:

Aant Sattu, Danta me Kalabattu.

The meaning of the above proverb is *sattu* in stomach, but betel in mouth.

An another proverb is as follows:

Pet Men Sattu, Mochha Par Ghee.

The meaning is that Sattu in stomach, but *ghee* on mustache.

A still another proverb is as follows:

Khane Ko Sattu. Ginane Ko Paise.

The meaning is saving money by eating *Sattu.* Such persons are termed as miser.

These proverbs are probably related to bad quality of *Sattu.*

Intake of Betel

In our sacred literature and folk traditions, the intake of Betel leaf has been regarded as valuable from the point of view of health. It is offered to Gods and Goddesses on the occasion of rituals and *Puja-Path.* It is also offered to guests as mouth purifier. It has been status of *Raja, Maharaja, Nawab* and *Zamindars* to take betel leaf after eating breakfast and food. When betel taken along with *Katha, Kasaili, Ilachi, Saunf* and lime, it is beneficial for the health. But when it is taken with *Jarda* and tobacco, it is very harmful for health. Betel is light, hot, appetizer and remover of dirty smell of mouth. It also purifies our tongue. It makes our body attractive and beautiful. It removes dirt of teeth. It also destroys all diseases of throat. But when taken with *Jarda,* it creates stomach, throat, tongue and mouth diseases.

New betel leaves have less quality than old betel leaf. The apex, middle and root parts of betel should be removed. The first two watery substance of chewing betel should be thrown. We should not sleep having betel in mouth.

Too much and frequent intake of betel creates diseases of eye, hair, teeth, mouth, throat, ear and stomach. This practice destroys our energy.

The Intake of Salt

In our *Dharmashastra* and folk tradition, great value has been attached to the intake of salt for remaining healthy. It makes our food tasty and increases our appetite. It is digestive, appetizer, bile destructor, fat destructor and increases eyesight. The salt is of three types:

- *Sendha* salt or *Lahori* salt
- *Kala* salt or *Sambhar* salt
- Sea water salt.

Of all varities of salt. *Sendha* salt or *Lahori* salt is valuable from the religious point of view. It is regarded as pure and beneficial. *Kala* salt is valuable from the digestive point of view. It is used as appetizer. The sea salt is most commonly used salt in our day to day life. It is very valuable for our health. But too much intake of salt is harmful for our health. Too much intake of salt creates blood pressure and kidney diseases. Whatever fruits, vegetables and leafy vegetables we take, our body gets mineral salt from them. Therefore, there is no need to take more salt. Salt and mustard oil we rub over gum and teeth to make gum and teeth healthy. When we add salt in hot water and do gargle, it is beneficial in curing toncoelitis and throat diseases. Salt mixed in hot water is also beneficial in swelling and body ache.

Intake of Turmeric

In our *Dharmashastras* and local folk tradition turmeric intake and application has occupied significant place. It has fortunous, beneficial, pious and beautification value. The value of ginger is an integral part of our Indian culture. It is a beautifying material of our body as well famous food material. The beautification of deities is done by mixing turmeric in *chandan.* It enhances the beauty of king and *Samrat* at the time of *Raj Tilak* ceremony. At the time of marriage, turmeric paste is applied over the body of bride and bridegroom to beautify them and make their look attractive. In Indian culture, turmeric has social, cultural, religious and hygienic value. On all auspicious occasion, turmeric is regarded. For example marriage, *vidai,* entrance in new house and worship, turmeric is required. Turmeric reduces effect of heat, destroys *kafa, pitta* and *vayu,* makes taste of food interesting, provides nutrition, kills germs and bacteria, purifies sperms and reduces pain.

Turmeric is used as a medicine to cure a number of diseases. They are as follows:

Cough and Cold

Turmeric is regarded as destroyer of cough and cold. When turmeric powder is mixed in a glass of hot water and taken at bed time, it cures cough and cold.

Soaring Throat

When turmeric powder is taken with cow's *ghee*, it destroys scorching throat.

Destructor of Asthma

The turmeric cures Asthma when its powder mixed in *ghee* of cow is taken at bed time and morning regularly.

Beautifying material

Turmeric paste is used as a beautifying material. Its constant use makes our body very attractive and handsome.

Pain-killer

When turmeric powder mixed in hot milk and loaf sugar is taken, it reduces body pain.

Swelling-killer

When gentle hot turmeric paste mixed with some time is applied over a broken or swollen part, it cures swelling and pain.

Wound Destroyer

The use of turmeric paste or power cures wounds. It is also beneficial in scabies.

Poison Remover

Turmeric paste is also beneficial in neutralising the effect of snake bite and scorpion bite.

Taste-maker

Ginger paste or powder increases the taste of vegetables.

Teethache Destroyer

The use of turmeric powder with mustard oil and salt over teeth reduces teethache.

Leprosy Remover

Regular application of turmeric paste over affected area reduces the leprosy.

Pile Curer

The turmeric paste acts as a pile curer.

Helpful in Blood Flow

The turmeric powder stops the blood flow in case of cut or hurt.

Useful in Hathi Paon

The intake of turmeric powder regularly cures the disease of *Hathi paon* (Elephant feet), or fileria.

Intake of Tea, Coffee and Cocacola

In our sacred texts and folk traditions, the intake of tea, coffee and cocacola has been prohibited and described as destructor of health. It is because their use creates heat in our body, makes our brain active, energizes our body, and takes out sweat and protects us in composite environment. But its more and more use regularly is not beneficial for our healthy life. Their constant use makes us addicted and habituated. They reduce sleep, we feel urination again and again, constipation is created, our appetite is reduced, and heart beating increases. That is why its more and more use has been prohibited. Children are strictly prohibited to use them. We can use them sometimes but not regularly.

The tea has tannin which creates loss of appetite. Those who are habitual tea taker, they take very low diets. They become patient of a number of diseases.

A famous proverb prevalent in Indian society regarding coffee is as follows:

> *Kafa Katan Vayu Haran Dhatutin Balchhin*
> *Lahoo Ko Pani Kare, Do Gun Awagun Tin*

Coffee has two merits and three demerits. It is beneficial in cough, cold and gases. But harmful because it makes our blood thin, it makes us weak and it destroys sperms.

Intake of Tobacco

In our sacred texts and traditions, the intake of tobacco has been described as harmful for the health. The intake of tobacco, biri, cigarettes, *Gutakha,*

Gur-Gura, Hukka invites a number of diseases to attack in our body. They cause non-curable disease like cancer. It causes mouth cancer, teeth cancer, throat cancer and lung cancer. The nicotine present in tobacco causes heart diseases. Carbon mono-oxide present in tobacco cause shortage of oxygen in our body.

Wine Intake

In our *Dharmashastra* taking wine has been prohibited. It has been described as destroyer of human lineage. Its intake is described as the greatest destructor of health, wealth and family. It destroys our wisdom. It causes harm to body organs like liver, heart and kidney. In a proverb, it has been rightly said that:

Sharab Pikar Log Sarakpar Karte Hain Tamasha
Lat Juta Khate Parte Aganit Tamachha.

The meaning of above proverb is that on taking wine people perform drama on road, but they are beaten with hands, feet, slippers and shoes.

Immortal speech of Lord Buddha regarding taking wine is as follows:

Tum Sinha Ke Samane Jane Men Mat Bhaya Bhit Hona
Wah Parakram Ki Pariksha Hai
Tum Talwar Ke Niche Sir Dene Se Bhaya Bhit Na Hona
Wah Balidan ki Kasauti Hai
Tum Badhati Hui Jwalaon Se Bhaya Bhit Na Hona
Wah Swarna Pariksha Hai
Par Sharab Se Sada Bhaya Bhit Rahna
Wah Pap Aur Anachar Ki Janani Hai

The meaning of above immortal speech of Lord Buddha is that one should not be fearful from facing a lion because that is examination of one's strength. One should not be fearful from putting neck on a sword because that is measure of one's sacrifice. One should not be fearful from making a jump from the top of a mountain because that is one's means of devotion. One should not be fearful from the flames of fire because that is one's golden trial. But one should always be fearful from taking wine because that is mother of all sins and immoral acts.

Intake of Air

In our *Dharmashastra,* air has been described as *Pran* (soul) and life. We cannot survive even for some time without air. Through the act of breathing we take air inside our body for use and we takeout used air from our body. That is why in our *Dharmashastra,* special attention has been paid to inhalation of pure air and exhalation of impure air. Breathing in fresh air is regarded as beneficial for our health. The air of impure places, slums, dirty drainage and street is impure. We should not breath in such places because breathing in such places creates a number of diseases. Our houses should be airy and have sufficient space to enter the sunrays. In our sacred texts covering mouth with cloth at the time of sleeping has been prohibited. In order to breath in fresh air, morning walk on the bank of river has been prescribed. Only breathing with nose has been prescribed. In our sacred texts, the importance of air has been realized. The air has been regarded as *Pran.*

Intake of Water

After air, the second most valuable base of our life is water. We can survive without foodgrains for several days. But without water we can survive only few days. In our sacred texts, emphasis has been placed on the intake of fresh and pure water. 70 per cent of our body is filled with water. Water from our body gets out through urine, sweating and defecation. In order to make a balance between intake and out take of water, we have to take water in our body. Water has special energy to clean our stomach. It is life base of all living beings.

In our country, rural people drink water of well, river, canal, tank, stream. Some of them also have own hand pumps. In rural areas people have to make own arrangement of drinking water. Now-a-days, our Government is also constructing wells and installing Chapakals for drinking water. But the source of drinking water should be clean. If source of drinking water is not clean, then we should drink boiled water. It is because polluted water has a number of germs and bacteria which create diseases in our body. Cholera, diarrhoea, stomach ache, intestine fever and many other diseases are caused by them. During the period of sharing meal, we should take little quantity of water. But full stomach water should be taken half an hour before or after eating meals. We should not take water soon after defecation and running. We should also not take much water in empty stomach. We should take boiled water in rainy and winter seasons. We should take cold water in summer season. Water takes out all toxins from our body. When urine is stopped for two days, our body becomes poisoned. Taking sufficient water, cures the disease of constipation. It also reduces the complaint of fat deposit.

Drinking the water in the morning kept in copper pot at night is beneficial in a number of diseases. In our *Dharmashastra,* taking water of Ganges and bathing in Ganges or at confluence place of Ganges with other rivers removes our physical, divinal and bodily troubles. That is why, bathing in Ganges and its confluence place is regarded so significant in our culture. In our culture, water has been regarded as the best medicine. The taking water and bathing in water both are important from the point of view of health.

Tulsi

In our *Dharmashastra,* the entire Tulsi plant is regarded as medicine for the health. It removes all types of mental, physical, bodily troubles and the incidence of ultimate death. Textual hymns regarding Tulsi plant in our *Dharmashastra* are as follows:

Akal Mrityu Haranam Sarwa Vyadhi Vinashanam
Maha Prasad Janani Sarva Saubhagya Vardhanam
Aadhi-Vyadhi Hare Nityam Tulsi Twam Namastute

The meaning of above *shloka* is that Tulsi removes untimely death incidence and all kinds of mental, physical, bodily and divinal troubles. It is mother of the great divinal blessing and giver of all kinds of fortunes. O such pious and virtuous Tulsi, I offer my *Pranam* to you.

Tulsi Gandhamaday Yatra Gachhanti Marutaù
Dishodishacha Puta Syurbhuta Gramash Chatur Vidhah

The hymn describes that the air carries the good smell of Tulsi in all directions and at all places. It purifies all those places by its fragrance.

Trikalam Vinita Putram Prashayam Tulsi Yadi
Vishi Shyate Kaya Suddhish Chandri Kam Shatan Bina.

The meaning of this shloka is as follows: O Son of Vinita, One who shares Tulsi in morning, noon and evening, his/her body is purified in the same way as is purified by hundred Chandrayan Vrata.

Tulsi Kanan Rajan Griha Yasyawatisthati
Tad Griham Tirtham Rupam, Nayanti Yam Kinkarah.

The meaning is that O King! the house which has Tulsi plants that house enjoys like heaven and messenger of Yama do not dare to enter there.

Shepnat palnat Sekat Darshana Sparsana Nrinam
Tulsi Dahyate Papam Wad manah Kaysanchitam.

The plantation, watering and rearing of Tulsi plant destroy all sins done by body, heart and speech of a person.

Thus, in our *Dharmashastra* special significance has been attached to Tulsi plant for maintaining peace, harmony and health. Every Hindu house has a plant of Tulsi which is nurtured, reared, protected and watered regularly and daily after performing bath.

In our *Dharmashastra,* a number of merits of Tulsi plant has been described. They are as follows:

Malaria

When tea of 20 Tulsi leaves and *5 kalimirch* (Golki) is prepared and served to the patient, the disease malaria is cured.

Cold

The patient suffering from cold when served the juice of 20 leaves of Tulsi three or fourth times in a day, the patient is cured.

Cough

Serving juice of Tulsi mixed in juice of *adarakh* (ginger) three-four times a day is beneficial in cough disease.

Killing worm

The juice of Tulsi and Pudina plants when served to the patient, worms present in stomach are killed.

Liver disease

The juice of Tulsi is also beneficial in liver disease.

Sugar control

When leaves of Tulsi are eaten empty stomach in the morning, it controls sugar.

Skin disease

The juice of Tulsi leaves is beneficial in skin diseases.

Snake bite

The root of Tulsi is beneficial in snake bite.

Impotency

Regular intake of Tulsi cures the disease of impotency.

Sun stroke

The juice of Tulsi leaves is also beneficial in sunstroke.

Ear pain

The juice of Tulsi also cures ear pain.

Gas

The juice of Tulsi leaves also cures gas.

Contagious disease

The juice of Tulsi cures contagious diseases.

Cholera and Diarrhoea

The juice of Tulsi leaves is also beneficial in Cholera and Diarrhoea.

Heart attack

Juice of Tulsi is also beneficial in heart attack.

Vomiting

Tulsi juice also controls vomiting.

Beautification

The application of Tulsi juice on face makes face very attractive.

Vein disease

Tulsi juice also removes vein diseases.

Tulsi beads

When hymns of Gods and Goddess are recited with the help of a garland containing 108 beads, physical, mental bodily and divinal troubles are removed.

Intake of Amla

In our *Dharmashastra,* the intake of Amla fruits have been regarded as beneficial to health. Amla is also known as *Dhatriphal.* It is produced in all parts of our country. Worship of Amla tree on Akshay Nawami (9th day of bright half of Kartik month) and donating grains, coins, ornaments removes all physical, divinal and bodily troubles and provide all kinds of happiness in life.

Merits of Amla

In our *Dharmashastra,* a number of merits of Amla has been described. They are as follows:

Sugar

The powder of dry *Amla* fruits and *Jamun* seeds are beneficial in diabetic disease.

Constipation

The powder of *Amla, Harra* and *Bahera* (known as *Trifala)* is useful in removing constipation.

Cold

The regular intake of Jam of *Amla* provides extra energy to fight the cold.

Cough

The regular intake of Jam of *Amla* is also beneficial in cough.

Sun stroke

Amla oil is beneficial in sun stroke.

Diarrhoea

Amal juice is also beneficial in Diarrhoea.

Headache

Amla oil reduces and cures headache.

Pile

The Juice of *Amla* is also beneficial in removing problem related to pile.

Jaundice

When *Amla* juice mixed with honey is taken, it cures the disease of Jaundice.

Epilepsy

When *Amla* Juice and *ghee* are served to an epilepsy patient, he/she is cured.

Bile disease

When Juice of *Amla* is taken with loaf sugar, it cures bile diseases.

Indigestion

The pickle of *Amla* is helpful in indigestion.

Appetizer

The salt mixed dry *Amla* is taken as appetizer.

Impotency

The regular intake of *Amla* Jam removes impotency.

Anaemia

The continuous use of *Amla* removes the disease of anaemia.

Peepal (Long Pepper and holy peepal)

In our *Dharmashastra* Peepal fruit is regarded as beneficial for our health. A hymn related to Peepal fruits in *Geeta* is as follows:

> *Ashwattha Sarva Vrikshanam. Devarshi Namche Naradah*
> *Gaadharwanaum Chitrarach Sidhanam Kapilo Mune.*

As Narda in Deo Rishis, Chitrarath in Gandharvas and Kapil Muni in perfection are the best, in the same way Peepal is the best among all trees. Peepal is known by several names. One among them is Brahma. As Lord Brahma is our creator, in the same way Peepal is progeny giver. It destroys impotency and provides full energy to reproduce handsome progeny. Fruit, bark, leaves and seeds are used as medicine. Its use cures the disease of infertility of women. It is so valuable that Peepal is worshipped in our society. People offer water to Peepal after bath and on festive and auspicious occasions. It is found in every village and at every sacred place.

In the vrata of Ekadashi, the root of Peepal is watered and an earthen lamp of *ghee* is lighted to get blessings of Lord Vishnu. To get blessings of Lord Shani, water is offered in the root of Peepal tree and earthen lamp of oil is lighted. Peepal tree is the only tree which emits *Pranvayu* (oxygen) twenty four hours.

Peepal has a number of health related merits. Because it is constipation destroyer, barrenness curer, impotence remover, potency provider and destroyer of toxins. That is why Peepal has great hygienic value and religious significance. The main merits of Peepal are as follows:

Vomiting

The bark of peepal when burnt and ash thus obtained dissolved in water and served to the patient suffering from vomiting, vomiting is controlled immediately.

Malaria

The ash of peepal bark is also beneficial in Malaria.

Cholera and Diarrhoea

The ash of peepal bark also controls diarrhoea and cholera.

Typhoid

The ash of peepal *chhal* is also beneficial for typhoid fever.

Tertiary fever

The stick of green peepal when chewed and taken inside intestine, the tertiary fever is cured. This fever repeats on every third day.

Sugar

The powder of dry peepal fruit is beneficial in sugar.

Leucorhoea

The powder of peepal fruit when taken with milk, it cures leucorhoea.

Impotency

Peepal fruit powder cures the disease of impotency when taken with milk at bed time.

Constipation

The use of peepal fruits powder with hot water removes constipation.

Appetizer

The powder of peepal fruit when taken with honey, it works as an appetizer.

Toothache

The regular brushing of tooth with brush of green peepal stick removes tooth ache and other diseases.

Heart disease

The juice of new peepal leaves is beneficial in removing blockage of heart. But it should be taken empty stomach.

Brain disease

The juice of new peepal leaves is also beneficial in curing brain disease. It cures eclepsy.

Eye disease

The milk of peepal when applied on eyelid, it cures eye disease.

Skin disease

The tea of peepal bark when applied on skin, it cures a number of skin diseases.

Sexual disease

The juice of peepal bark is also beneficial in sexual disease.

Jaundice

The disease of jaundice is also cured by the juice of new peepal leaves.

Asthma

The powder of peepal bark when mixed with honey served to patient, it cures asthma.

Snake bite

The juice of new peepal bark are also beneficial in snake bite. The thin green sticks of peepal are also inserted in ear to neutralize the effect of poison.

Conch

In our *Dharmashastra,* conch is the most pious symbols. In order to increase the age of a child, a small conch is tied with thread in the neck of child. At the time of journey and auspicious occasion conch is seen and it is played to create sound. In the worship of Lord Vishnu, conch is worshipped and played. Where there is conch, there is residence of Lord Vishnu and Goddess Lakshmi. The ash of conch removes a number of diseases. It removes swelling of eyes and stomach ache. It removes liver and spleen diseases and destroys acidity, indigestion, constipation.

Honey (Madhu)

According to our *Dharmashastra,* honey is regarded as natural immortal thing. It is one of pious things. It is offered to Gods and Goddesses at the time of rituals and worship. It is the most auspicious thing. It is beneficial for our health in a number of diseases. The main merits of honey are as follows:

Fever

The use of honey and peepal powder removes all kinds of fever.

Loss of Appetite

When honey with peepal powder is taken after washing mouth, it cures loss of appetite.

Obesity remover

The regular use of honey removes fat of our body. Thus, it is helpful in removing obesity.

Heart Blockage

The use of honey with juice of ginger and lemon removes heart blockage.

Beautification

Constant use of honey on our face makes our face handsome and attractive.

Nutrition

The honey has nutritious value, too. It is taken with bread and *paratha.*

Cold

Its use is beneficial in removing cold.

Acidity

Use of honey regularly reduces acidity.

Liver disease

The constant use of honey reduces liver disease.

Jaundice

The honey is also beneficial in Jaundice.

Diarrhoea

Honey is also beneficial in Diarrhoea.

Worm

The regular use of honey removes worm from the body.

Natural Nectar

Honey is regarded as natural nectar. It is useful in a number of diseases and maintaining good health.

Gur (Loaf sugar) Intake

In our *Dharmashastra Gur* is regarded as artificial nectar. It is also one of pious things. It is favouite offering for all Gods and Goddesses.

Gur is also taken as medicine in a number of diseases. They are as follows.

Destryoes of Kafa and Pitta

When a little quantity of *Gur* is taken at night before sleep without water, it destroys *Kafa* (cough) and *Pitta* (bile).

Acidity destroyer

The use of Gur in milk and curd destroys acidity.

Anaeia remover

The regular eating of *Gur* with bread cures the disease of anaemia.

Appetizer

The intake of *Gur* increases the appetite.

Indigestion

The intake of *Gur* with black salt is beneficial in indigestion.

Diarrhoea

The intake of *Gur* is also beneficial in the disease of Diarrhoea.

Milk (*Dudh)*

Milk is a whole nutritious diet. Its intake is regarded as the best food from the point of view of health. It is a nutritious diet of persons belonging to all age and sex groups. It is also a favourite offering of all deities. God Vishnu and Goddess Lakshmi resides in Kshir Sagar (Sea of milk). The milk of cow is a medicine for a number of diseases. It is also regarded as whole some diet. In our *Dharmashastra,* the milk of cow occupies important place after the milk of mother. The milk provides entire nutrition to the body. Butter, *ghee* and curd of cow milk are used as medicine. The intake of a glass of milk before sleeping makes us wise and strong. It is also beneficial for the patient of heart diseases. The curd of cow milk is also beneficial in heart diseases. Heart patient can take little quantity of cow's *ghee* in food. The *ghee* of cow cures cough and allergy. It is also beneficial in Asthma. The lamp of cow's *ghee* purifies the environment. The *ghee* of cow is also offered to deities as *Hawan* which purifies the environment.

Cow urine

In our *Dharmashastra* urine of cow is regarded as valuable from the point of health. It is used as a medicine in a number of diseases. It is taken as naturopathy in a number of diseases. The urine of cow is beneficial in following diseases:

Malaria

The intake of cow's urine cures malaria.

Gastric

The intake of urine of cow removes gas formation.

Stomach ache

The intake of cow's urine cures lever diseases.

Diabetes

The intake of cow's urine is also beneficial in diabetes.

Cholera

The intake of cow's urine cures cholera.

Pile

The use of cow's urine is also beneficial in pile disease.

Dry Cholera

The use of cow urine is very much beneficial in dry Cholera.

T.B.

The use of cow's urine also cures T.B.

Leprosy

The use of cow's urine is also beneficial in leprosy.

Worm

The use of cow's urine kills worms of intestine.

Obesity

The constant use of cow's urine removes fatness.

Scabies

The application and use of cows urine cures scabies.

Brahmacharya (Celebate Life)

In our *Dharmashastra,* the observance of *Brahmacharya* has been described as beneficial for energy, intelligence and health. In our *Dharmashastra,* the importance of *Brahmacharya* has been described in the following hymn:

> *Balena Prithavi Tisthati Balena Antariksham*
> *Viyameva Balam Balmeva Viryam*

The meaning of this hymn is that our earth is stable by force and sky is based on force. The force of our body is semen and semen is force. We loose force of our body by destroying it. Therefore, *Brahmacharya* is life. It is root key of our health and main pillar of our health. We should remain *Brahmachari* by heart, speech and act. We should keep sense organs under our control. Only then we can lead a disciplined life. We should maintain discipline in food, talking, work and health.

In our Veda, a hymn related to Gods and Goddesses is as follows:

Brahmacharyen Tapasa Deva
Mrityum Pughanat

The meaning of above hymn is that Gods and Goddesses have defeated the death on the basis of observing *Brahamacharya.* The observance of *Brahmacharya* increases our mental and physical power. We can serve our society and nation for a long time by maintaining our health through *Brahmacharya.* That is why the best way of controlling all diseases is observance of *Brahmacharya.*

In *Dharmashastra,* it has been mentioned that—"*Maranam Bindu Paten Jiwanan Bindu Dharnath*". The meaning is the fall of semens is death and holding semens is life.

Even today, the folk and rural people believe in observance of *Brahmacharya.* They eat simple food, wear simple dress, serve food to guest and have powers, fight with thieves and, lead collective life and maintain *Brahmacharya* by heart, speech and acts. The disease of impotency, quick fall, semen fall, indigestion and sleeplessness are almost absent in folk and rural society. But these diseases and a number of other diseases are very much prevalent in urban and metropolis society. The people of urban and metropolis society live in costly building, drink water of bottle, eat costly food, intake nutritious diet, sleep on costly bed, rest in air conditioned room and lead luxurious life. But they suffer from heart, kidney, sugar, liver, blood diseases. It is because they treat sex organ as organ of pleasure and consumption. They do not observe *Brahmacharaya Dharma* by heart, mind, speech and action.

Our semen is the extract of all six elements—Juice, blood, flesh, vein, bone and marrow. Semen is six times more valuable than blood. When all six elements are matured, semens are produced. Therefore, to destroy semens by using sex as an object of consumption is our greatest mistake.

Simple life

In order to lead *Brahmacharya* one has to lead a very simple life, but our thinking should be very high.

Virtuous food

We should take simple and virtuous food to maintain *Brahmacharya.* We should avoid exciting food. Because exciting food create trouble in maintaining life of *Brahmacharya.*

Devotion in God

In order to maintain *Brahmacharya Dharma* we should devote ourselves in Gods and Goddesses. Devotion in God and Goddesses helps us in observing *Brahmacharya Dharma.*

Regular life

Our regular daily routine from leaving bed to going to bed helps us in observing *Brahmacharya.*

Away from bad contact

We should keep ourselves away from the company of bad people. Because the company of bad people creates troubles in maintaining *Brahmacharya Dharma.*

Away from vulgar literature

We should keep ourselves away from vulgar literature. It is because vulgar literature creates excitement in our mind and body. We get deviated from the path of *Brahmacharya.* We should read holy books.

Away from vulgar cinema

We should also maintain a distance from vulgar show and cinema. It is because they create excitement in our body and mind. We forget our path of *Brahmacharya.*

Walking on foot

Walking on foot help us in maintaining *Brahmacharya.*

Strong determination

We should have our determination strong. Because strong determination helps in following the path of *Brahmacharya.*

In our sacred texts, two kinds of *Brahmacharya* has been mentioned. They are—(1) *Bal Brahmacharya* and (2) *Garhastha Brahmacharya.*

According to our textual traditions children engaged in study should observe *Brahmacharya* till his entire period of study. Those students who do not observe the *Bal Brahmacharya Dharma* are bound to face several troubles in their life. Another kind of *Brahmacharya* is *Garhastha Brahmacharya.* We should enter into *Garhastha Ashram* by getting married. Married couples are entitled to have sex relation for procreation of progeny. Although married couples are free to have sex relation, but they observe the *Dharma* of *Garhastha Brahmacharya.* They have to enter into sex relation according socio-cultural norms. They do not use sex as an object of consumption. Rather they use sex as a means of reproduction following discipline and sexual-cultural norms of the society. Married couples are strictly tabooed to have sex with other members of the community. Extra marital relationship is strictly tabooed. There is a proverb that—*Ek Nari Brahmachari.* The meaning is that having sex only with wife is *Garhastha Brahmacharya.*

In our sacred texts, a number of means have been mentioned to protect our *Brahmacharya.* They are as follows:

Great Ambition

According to our sacred texts, we can maintain our *Brahmacharya Dharma by* identifying some great ambitions. For example Service to Nation, Society, Community-Welfare work, development work, new researches, devotion to God, Self-achievement, Spirituality and Yoga.

Work engagement

We can observe the *Brahmacharya Dharma* by keeping ourselves engaged in food and welfare works.

Sleep

The main pillars of our health are food, sleep and *Brahmacharya.* In order to remain healthy, sleep is the demand of nature. Sleep is the chief means of our health. Sleep is natural and easy means of pacifying our fired mind and sex organs. Regarding the importance of sleep Maharshi Charak has written that *Nidrayatu Sukham*. The meaning is that our happiness depends upon our sleep. It is beneficial for all kinds of diseases. As our body gets energy from the food, similarly our mind and sense organs obtain freshness from the sleep.

In our *Dharmashastra,* the importance of sleep has been described in the following ways:

Nidyayantam Sukham Dukham Pusthih Kashyam Blabalam
Vrishatahh Clivanta Gyanan Gayanam Jiwito Nacha.

The meaning is that taking sleep in good time, good form and good quantity protects our energy, knowledge, intelligent, pleasure and life. But when we take sleep at bad place, in bad time and in bad quantity, it destroys our energy, knowledge, intelligent, happiness, potency and life.

Maharshi Charak has written further that

Prasangacha Na cha Nidra Nirshavite.
Sukhayushi Parakuryat Kalratri Shivapara.

The meaning is that person who wants pleasure in life should give up untimely sleep, more sleep and less sleep.

According to the law of nature, the night is meant for sleep and day is meant for work. An English proverb goes thus, 'Early to bed and early to rise' makes a man healthy, wealthy and wise. The persons who adopt behaviour against it become unhealthy. In order to live healthy, we should go to bed around 9 p.m. after sharing meal. We should get up before sunrise. Except in summer, we should not sleep in day time. Day time sleep increases cough, bile, heaviness, and persons on fast should sleep in day time.

For a healthy person, 7 hours sleep at night is beneficial. Farmers and labourers can sleep more hours. But intellectuals should sleep for less hours. The sleep is also related to age. In old age we do not have sound sleep.

In our *Dharmashastra,* method of sleeping has also been described. Sleeping towards left side at night and towards right side in day time is beneficial from the point of view of health. Sleeping ventrally and dorsally for a long time is not beneficial for the health. There is a proverb in Hindi which is as follow:

Jo Koi Bam Karvat Le Soi, Tako Kal Baith Ke Roi

The meaning of above proverb is that one who sleeps towards left side stomach remains always healthy and leads a long life.

According to our *Dharmashastra* the place of sleeping should be crowdless, lonely and airy. One should not wear tight cloth during sleep wood cot should be used. If not possible, the legs of iron cot should be covered with plastic or rubber. This does not allow the energy of the body to go in earth.

According to *Dharmashastra,* we should keep our head towards east or south at the time of sleeping. Keeping heads towards north and south is harmful from the point of view of health. Keeping head towards north at the time of sleeping creates eye diseases. The direction of head towards east brings all kind of happiness, towards south brings longevity, towards west brings tension and towards north brings death.

According to our *Dharmashastra* we should keep wooden slipper, shoe, stick, vessel of water, knife and torch near the bed. We should go to sleep after cleaning mouth properly. We should not sleep keeping betel in our mouth.

Sleeplessness

Today we are living in an age of machine. We are utilizing body as a machine. Machinization has created a number of diseases. Sleeplessness is one of them. Sleeplessness has emerged as a dangerous disease, now-a-days. Lakhs and lakhs of people complain about sleeplessness. They take medicine for sleep; the rich, industrialists, lawyers, doctors, politicians, intellectuals and administrators complain about sleeplessness and take medicine for sound sleep. It is because they have started leading unnatural life. They do not earn by virtuous means. That is only Goddess Nidra does not bless them.

In our *Dharmashastra,* some priceless laws of sound sleep has been described. They are as follows:

- Physical labour doers and exercise doers have sound sleep.
- Simple living and high thinking brings sound sleep.
- Those who lead regular life have a good sleep.
- We should keep night meal an hour before we go to sleep.
- Massage of mustard oil in head and feet brings good sleep.
- Devotion in Gods and Goddesses brings sound sleep.
- Happiness brings sound sleep.
- Satisfaction gives a good sleep.
- We should not take Wine, *Ganja, Bhang* and others for sleep.
- Too much eating does not bring sound sleep.
- Dirty and spicy food brings less sleep.
- Too much fear brings less sleep.
- Washing feet, hands and face before sleep brings sound sleep.
- A glass of light hot milk brings good sleep.
- Wrong ideas at the time of sleeping creates troubles in sleep.
- The prayer of God before sleep brings sound sleep.

Force Restriction

In our *Dharmashastra,* it has been mentioned that restricting thirteen kinds of forces are not good for the health. They should be released. Otherwise, they create a number of diseases. These forces are as follows:

Urine force

In order to lead healthy life we should not restrict our urine force. Rather urine force should be released immediately.

Defecation force

We should not control our defection force. Its restriction brings a number of diseases.

Semen force

For healthy life, we should not control our semen force.

Air force

For good health we should not control the air.

Vomiting force

We should not control the vomiting force for good health.

Sneezing force

For healthy life we should not prohibit sneezing force.

Hunger force

We should not control hunger force for healthy life.

Thirst force

We should not control our thirst force for our good health.

Tear force

We should not control our tear force for good health.

Sleep force

We should not control our sleep force for good health.

Breathing force

We should not control our breathing force to remain healthy.

Digestive force

We should not control our digestive force for our good health.

Tired force

We should not control our tired force.

Humour and Health

In our textual traditions being patient is taken as a crime. Disease is taken as fruit of sin. Man can achieve victory over death. Healthy life is real life. Unhealthy life is worst than death. Untimely death and long life are in the hand of man. But he should have strong will power. On the basis of strong will power, he can do what ever he likes. He can be what ever he likes. Man is a part of God. Being part of God, the disease does not like to go near him. But he invites diseases to come in his body. Thus, man himself is creator of pleasure, sorrow, health and disease. But he laughs in pleasure and weeps in sorrow.

The superhuman power which controls this mega universe is known as *Param Pita Parmeshwar.* One of his names is *Sachchidananda.* He is *Sat, Chita* and *Ananda.* His pleasure form created the universe. Man is master of animal kingdoms. In our sacred texts and traditions special emphasis has been placed on laughing for maintaining good health. *Param Brahma Parmeshwar* created man to enjoy the benefit of laughing on the earth. The God has send us to cause rains of pleasure, to distribute happiness among people and to enjoy the fruits of laughing. Laughing makes our mind pleasant. Man gets rid of all kinds of trouble at the time of laughing.

According to Ayurveda, laughing is the great medicine for all kinds of diseases. It has been taken as a divinal medicine. It is a boon for us given by God. It is the best means to make human life healthy and good. When one bathes in the current of laughing, he/she cleans all desire, anger, attraction, jealousy like waste things from heart and mind. The laughing does not only appear on lips, but it makes entire hairs of our body pleasant. The secret of our health is hidden in pleasure and laughing.

Some Sanskrit Hymns related to Gods and Goddesses

In our *Dharmashastra,* a number of hymns related to Gods and Goddesses have been created and whose regular recitation cures diseases, brings happiness and keeps us healthy. The recitations of hymn cures physical mental and material troubles. They are as follows:

Gayatri Mantra

> *Om Bhurbhuwah Swah Tatsavitur Varenyam*
> *Bhargo Devasya Dhimahi Dhiyo Yonah Prachodayat*

When a full garland recitation of Gayatri Mantra is done in the morning and evening regularly with clean body and heart, diseases do not dare to attack, magical effect becomes effectless and *Bhuta-Preta* go far away. The body remains always strengthful and healthy. Gayatri Mantra removes all kinds of mental distress. Gayatri Mantra is regarded as the most powerful mantra. Its daily and regular recitation, cures all kinds of miseries and provides all kinds of peace and prosperity in the family.

Mahamrityunjay Mantra

In our *Dharmashastra,* Lord Shiva is regarded as God of destruction. Mahamrityunjay Mantra is recited in order to get rid of any kind of destruction in the life of an individual or his family. Mahamrityunjay Mantra is as follows:

> *Om Trayambakam Yaja Mahe Sugandhim Pushti Vardhanam*
> *Urvarukmic Bandhanan Mrityormukshiya Mamritat*

The recitation of above Mahamrityunjay Mantra of a complete garland of Rudraksha containing 108 beads after being pured by bathing is beneficial in a number of deceases. It removes all kinds of fear leading to death.

Shani Mantra

Lord Shani is regarded as Lord of Justice. He provides justice on the basis of deeds of an individual. If deeds of an individual is according to justice, he/she is blessed by Lord Shani. But when his/her deeds are against justice Shani provides severe punishment. That is why in order to please Shani

Shani Mantra is recited on every Saturday with pure body, heart and mind. Shani Mantra is as follows:

Om Ravisutay Krishnamitay
Sam Shanishcharay Namah

One garland recitation of this Mantra on every Saturday pleases Lord Shani and he blesses the devotee.

Surya Mantra

Lord Sun is regarded as Lord of planets. For success in life and long life, the blessings of Sun God is a must. When Sun-God become angry he creates the disease of leprosy, and jaundice. That is why the blessings of Sun God is sought by reciting his Mantras. The Surya Mantra is as follows:

Om Suryay Namah, Bhaskaray Namah, Adityay Namah
Om Ghrini Suryay Namah

The recitation of one full garland containing 108 beads of Tulsi after offering water to Sun God is beneficial in a number of diseases. The blessings of Sun God is sought through this Mantra for long and healthy life.

Chandra Mantra

Chandra (Moon) also affects the life of an individual. The blessings of Moon God (Chandra) is sought by reciting his mantra regularly. The Chandra Mantra is as follows:

Om Som Somay Namah
Om Chandray Namah

One complete garland recitation of this Mantra brings happiness in the life.

Rahu Mantra

Rahu is regarded as harmful planet. He destroys peace and prosperity and causes a number of diseases to occur. That is why Rahu is pleased by reciting his Mantra. Rahu Mantra is as follows:

Om Rahu Rahwe Namah

When this Mantra is recited one full garland containing 108 beads, Lord Rahu's blessings and brings peace and prosperity in life.

Ketu Mantra

Ketu is regarded as dangerous planet. On being angry he destroys every peace and happiness of an individual and his family. Therefore, attempt is made to appease Ketu by reciting one full garland mantra. Ketu mantra is as follows:

Om Ketu Ketawe Namah

Devi Durga Mantra

In our sacred texts, Goddess Durga is regarded as Jagat Janani (Mother of Universe). She nourishes the entire world—river, mountain, earth, sky, sea, birds, animals and man. All are in existence by her grace. She provides good health to all living being because she is mother of the world. She removes their all troubles. The texts like *Durga Chalisa* and *Durga Saptashati* describe in detail the role and character of Goddess Durga as Jagat Janani. A number of hymns have been composed to offer prayer to mother Goddess Durga. Anybody recites her hymns regularly with pure body, mind and heart, his/her life becomes pleasureful and healthy. Devi Durga hymns are as follows:

Dehi Saubhagyamarogyam Dehi Men Parmam Sukham
Rupam Dehi Jayam Dehi yasho Dehi Dwirmo Jahi
Sharanagat-dinantam Paritran Parayane
Sarwa Syatir hare Devi Narayani Namastute
Jayanti Mangala Kali Bhadrakali Kapalini
Durga Kshama Shiva Dhatri Swaha Swadha Namastute.
Sarwa Mangal Mangalya Shive Sarwarth Sadhke
Sharanyam Trayambake Gauri Narayani Namastute
Sarwa Sarupe Sarwase Sarwa Shakti Smanete
Bhagebhya Strahino Devi Durga Devi Namastute
Sarwabadha Bini Muktyo Dhana Dhanyam Sutanwitah
Manshyo yat Prasaden Bhawishyasi Na Sanshayah

Lakshmi Mantra

Goddess Lakshmi is health, wealth and progeny giver. She blesses with good earning, good health and good progeny. When Lakshmi Mantra is recited regularly, all kinds of health and wealth troubles are removed. Lakshmi Mantra is as follows:

Om Aem Hrim Shrim Kamale Kamlay Prasid Prasid
Prasid Om Shree Maha Lakshaymai Namah

Ganapati Mantra

Shri Ganpati Maharaj is regarded as remover of all troubles. That is why he is regarded as Vighnaharankarta. Some hymns related to Ganapati Ji are as follows:

Om Gan Ganpate Namah
Om Ganeshay Namah
Om Lambodray Namah
Om Vighnahareshwaray Namah
Vighnoharan, Mangal karan shree Ganpate maharaj
Sada Kripalu Hoike Puran Kijiye mam kaj

Sri Hanumat Mantra

When Hanuman Chalisa and Hanumat Mantra are recited regularly, all physical, mental and divinal troubles are removed. Hanumat mantra is as follows:

Om Hanumate Namah
Om Markat Desh Mahotsah Surwa Shok Vinashani
Shatru Sanhar Ma Raksha Sriyam Dape Men Prabho
Anjani Garbha Sambhutam Kapindra Sachi Votam
Ramam Priya Namotubhyam Hanumat Raksh Sarvada

Some Taboos Related to Health

- Air coming from front side
- Sun rays coming from front side
- Sleep in dew
- To face storm
- Violent animal and snake
- Sleep in sunset, eat in sunset and stud in sunset
- Sleep below tree at night
- Smoke of Pyre
- Putting finger in nose

- Putting stick in ear
- Spitting here and there
- To drink water in standing position
- Sleeping in day time except summer
- Put out hairs of nose
- To sleep covering head with cloth.

Some Knowledgeable Matters Related to Health

- Health is real pleasure.
- Anxiety creates sadness.
- Sorrow destroys intelligence and energy.
- Fear makes our heart weak.
- Grains are the best means of energy.
- Water is the best drink.
- Exercise is the best way to keep fit.
- Milk and *ghee* destroy oldness.
- To live pleasant is beneficial for health.
- Satisfaction is the best nourishment.
- Greed is the root of all evils.
- Music removes mental disease.
- Pulling out the hairs of nose makes eye weak.
- Mistake in food intake is more dangerous.
- Laziness is like death.
- Our birth place provides a number of medicines to survive in a particular environment.
- Anxiety is more dangerous than pyre.
- Pure air creates energy and consciousness.
- Peace is the best beneficial thing.
- Devotion is the key of this visible and invisible world.

Some Matters for Healthy Life

- A number of diseases are created when we sleep in non-airy room.s
- When milk and fish are taken together, they create leprosy.
- Sleep destroys bile, massage destroys gastric diseases, vomiting destroys cough and fasting destroys fever.
- Protection of semen is the chief means of healthy living.
- We should not vex even insects.
- We should behave similarly in joys and sorrows.

- We should not develop hatred to see progress of others.
- We should not be jealousy in achieving result.
- Behave pleasantly according to his nature.
- Desire makes us poor.
- Satisfaction removes the difference between rich and poor.
- We should not allow our sense organs towards lust and passion.
- Always move with a stick at night.
- We should brush shoes before wearing.
- We should brush the bed before sleep.
- We should sneeze covering our nose and mouth.
- We should not urinate or defecate in front of Sun.
- Sun rays kills a number of germs and bacteria causing diseases.
- We should have satisfaction in women, wealth and food.
- One who does not use mind, speech and acts or who use more mind speech and acts become mad.
- Walking on green grasses in morning with barefooted is beneficial for health. This practice removes body ache, neck ache, old cough, eye disease etc.
- The persons who sleep towards left side of stomach, share meals two times, defecate two times, urinate six times and lead disciplined life, live long.
- Excess of *Tridosha—Kafa, Pitta* and *Vayu*—is disease and their balance is medicine.
- One who breathes through left nose at day and right nose at night lives long.
- Which is not to be occurred, will not occur and which is to be occurred, will occur. The view should be taken as medicine.
- Regularity in works makes a man diseaseless.

Simple Ways of Protecting Health

- To get up in early morning.
- To take water from copper glass kept at night in the morning.
- To use *Datun* (green stick brush) for washing teeth and gum.
- Walking in the morning.
- Performing regular exercise.
- Daily oil massage of body.
- Daily bathing.
- Regular study and devotion in God.
- Regular intake of milk.
- Not intake of tea and coffee.

- Distance from tobacco, *Ganja, Bhang,* drugs, wine and other intoxicants.
- Regular cutting and cleaning of nails.
- Not taking exciting food.
- Taking simple food.
- Wearing clean dresses.
- Taking balanced food.
- Do not stop velocity of urine and defecation.
- Maintaining *Brahmacharya.*
- Intake of Tulsi leaves regular in the morning.
- To take light food.

Some Folk Proverbs Related to Health Behaviour

A number of health behaviours are prevalent in folk proverbs. Some of them and their meaning in English are as follows:

Basi Pani Jo Piye Nit Utha Harre Khay
Taja Datun Jo Kare Ta Ghar Vaidya Na Jay

One who takes water left overnight and *Harre* powder in the morning and washes gum, teeth and tongue with fresh green stick (*Datun),* remains free from the service of *Vaidya* (Medicine man) because diseases do not dare to enter in his body.

Bai Karvat Jo Soye, Jal Bayen Swar Piw
Dahin Swar Bhojan Karo So Sukh Paw Jiw

The meaning of above proverb is that one who sleeps left side, takes water from left side of mouth and takes food from right side of mouth, he/she remains healthy and gets pleasure in life.

Sawan Sag Na Vado Mahi
Asin Dudh Na Kartik Dahi

The above proverb reveals food taboo to maintain good health. This proverb reveals that one should not take leafy vegetable in Sawan month, Mahi (curd water) in vado month milk in Ashin month and curd in Kartik month. It they are taken, they bring negative effect on health.

Brahma Muhurta men jo Uthe Jalda Rat Soy Jay
Sada Nirogi Bana Rahe Usa Manushya Ka Kay

The meaning is that one who gets up early in the morning and goes to sleep early at night, he/she remains always healthy.

Swastha Nar Sansarka Sarwa Sukh Hai Bhogata
Vyadhiyon Ki Andhiyon Ko Wah Hai Rokata.

This proverb indicates that a healthy person enjoys all pleasure of this world and he/she is able to stop the storm of diseases and troubles.

Swastha Khokar Biathana Hai Maha Ek Pap
Rogo Se Akrant Nar Mane Jate Abhisap

The meaning of above saying is that losing health is a great curse because diseased persons are treated as effect of curse.

Pratham Sukh Nirogi Kaya, Duja Sukh Ghar Men Ho Maya
Tisara Sukh Kulwanti Narri Chautha Sukh Sut Agyakari
Pahcham Sukh Bhai Balbira Chhatta Sukh Raj Men Sira
Saptam Sukh Ho Wash Suwasa Athawan Sukh Pandit Ho Pasa
Nawam Sukh Ho Mitra Dhanere Aise Nar Nahi Jag Bahutere

The meaning of above proverb is that there are nine kinds of pleasure. The first pleasure is diseaseless body, the second pleasure is beautiful women, third pleasure is faithful woman, fourth pleasure is obedient son, fifth pleasure is powerful brother, sixth pleasure is happiness in ruling, seventh pleasure is beautiful house, eighth pleasure is presence of learned man nearby and nineth pleasure is rich friend, but such type of persons are rare.

Adarakh ras Sang Shahad Ko Chatat Jo Nar Khay
Aruchi Nashta Ho Jat Hai Bhojan Ruchikar Hoy

The meaning of above proverb is that if any one takes ginger juice with honey, indigestion is destroyed and food becomes tasty and interesting.

Ek Dana lahasun Ko Nitya Sabera Khay
Dard Jakaran Us Nar Se Sada Ko Chali Jay

The meaning of above saying is that if any body uses garlic in the morning regularly, joint pain is removed.

Ankhe Pani Kane Tel
Kahe Vaidya Ki Rog Sab Gel

The above proverb reveals that washing eyes with water and putting oil drops in ears remove all eye and ear diseases.

Sada Bhojan Jo Kare Bhare Pet Tin Kon
Ajirna Aruchi Abhukh Rog Ho Jate Sab Gaun

The meaning of above proverb is that one who takes simple food up to three parts of body and keeps one part for water, he/she becomes free from indigestion, loss of appetite, and gastric.

Bel Ke Sarbat Jo Piye Aur Amjhora Khay
Take Andar Luk Lahar Kabhi Na Jat Samay

The meaning is that one who takes syrup of *bel* fruit and mango fruit during summer, he/she is protected from sunstroke.

Dal Roti Sang Jo Nitya Sag Ko Khay
Sare Rog Dekh Use Jat Dur Chale Jay

The meaning of this proverb is that one who takes leafy vegetable daily with pulse and bread, he/she becomes free from all kinds of diseases.

Pani Piye Chhan Ke
Bhojan Kare Jan Ke

The meaning of above proverb is that one should drink filtered water and take tested food.

Pratah Behraman Jo Kare Kadu Karaita Khay
Chiraita Pani Jo Piya Chinia Rog Chali Jay

The meaning of this proverb is that one who performs morning walk and takes water of chiraita, a kind of medicinal plant, she/she cures herself/himself from the diabetes.

Sahejan Ke Phool Phal Jo Nar Sahij Ke Khay
Man Hriday Vikar Sab Us Nar Se Chali Jay

The meaning of this proverb is that one who takes *Sahejan* (Munga or Suti) flowers, fruits and seeds regularly, his/her heart diseases are controlled and cured.

Garam Pani Jo Piye Aur Gargil Ko Lagay
Gale Sambandhi Sare Rog Us Nar Se chali Jay

One who drinks gentle hot water and does gargling all throats related diseases are cured.

Kala Namak Ajwaine Gur Agar Sewan Kiya Jai
Badhajami Ke Sare Rog us Narse Chali Jay

The meaning of above proverb is that if any body shares black salt powder mixed with *Ajawaine* and loaf sugar, all stomach related diseases are cured.

Datum Sang Tel Non Le Jo Nar Dant Ko Dhoy
Dant Sambandhi Sare Rog Us Nar Se Chali Jay

The meaning of above saying is that if any one washes gum and teeth with a green stick brush and mustard oil and salt paste, he/she becomes free from all kinds of gum and teeth related diseases.

Ras Pyaj Karu Tel men Achchha Se Milay
Khansi Khas-khas Jat Mit Jyohi Det Pilay

The above proverb saying meaning that if anybody takes onion juice with mustard oil, cough and cold disease are removed.

Kawar Karaita Chait Gur Vado Muli Khay
Paisa Jay Gansh Ka Rog Gale Par Jay

The meaning of above proverb is that one who takes *karaita* (a bitter vegetable) in *Kartik* month and loaf sugar (*Gur)* in Chait months, he/she is bound to suffer from a number of diseases and spent money on them.

Harre Bahera Amala Ghee Shakar Me Khay
Hathi Dabe Kankh Me Sath Kos Le Jay

The meaning of above proverb is that if anybody takes Harre, Amla and Bahera powder fried in *ghee* and sugar regularly, he becomes, so energetic and strong that he/she can pull miles and miles an elephant.

Sheet Bachay Sada jo Soye
Tako Dekh Rog Khub Roye

The meaning of above proverb is that one who sleeps away from dews, diseases starts weeping because they do not find place to attack.

Sonth Sohaga Sendha Kanghi
Sewat Jo Nar Goli Bandhi
Chausath vayu Chaurasi Sul
Kahe Dhanwanter Rahe Nahi Mul

The meaning of above proverb is that if any body takes pills made up of dry ginger (*Sontha), Sohaga* and *Sendha Namak,* all kinds of gas related pain diseases are cured from root.

Adarakh Lahsun Nimbu Ras Det Shahad Men Milay
Band Hriday Nas Jat Khul Nitya Sabero Jo Pilay.

The meaning of above proverbs is that when juice of ginger, garlic and lemon is mixed with honey and served to a heart patient, the blockage gets removed.

Haldi Chuna Garma Kar Jo Sujan Par Lagay
Do Tin Din Aisa Kare Sab Dard Chali Jay

The meaning is that is that if a paste of turmeric and lime is made and heated gently to apply over swollen parts, two times daily for three days, swelling and pains are removed for ever.

Brahmacharya Hi Jiwan Ka Mul Palo Ise Sambhal
Jo Nar Pale Na Ise Hot Jat Kangal

The meaning is that *Brahmacharya* is the root of healthy life. We should observe *Brahmacharya* in mind, speech and act. Those who do not obey it are bound to loose every thing for healthy and long life.

Madira Sewan Jo Kare Tamas Bhojan Roj
Bhog Wah Kya Karega, Ho Ga Usaka Bhoj

The meaning of above proverb is that one who takes wine and takes exciting food everyday, people will enjoy with his/her death feast.

Nitya Vyayam Jo Kare Sharir Mal Mal Ke Nahay
Sada Swasth Nar Wo Dikhe Thora Thora Jo Khay

The meaning of above proverb is that one who does exercise daily, takes bath by rubing body and takes light food frequently, he/she is bound to live long and be healthy.

Tan Man Dhan Ki Suddhata Rakhe Hame Arogya
Sukarma Safalata Sadoguno Ko Banaye Hame Yogya

The meaning of above proverb is than the purity of body, mind and wealth keeps us able to maintain good work, success and virtues.

Swastha Viruddha Acharan Aur Sakal Vyavhar
Pahunchata us Vyakti Ko Pahale Kal Ke Dwar

The meaning of above proverb is that total behaviours against our health lead us towards the gate of death (*Kal).*

Swastha Rahkar Lo Sada Jiwan Ka Anand
Rog Grasit Ho Kar Tum Jio Jaise Matimand.

The meaning of this saying is that we can enjoy pleasure only when we are healthy. Otherwise, we are bound to become mad and diseased.

Swastha hi is Dhartika Sakal Anand Ki Khan
Jite Hai Sau Varsh O Jo Jate Ise Jan

The meaning of above proverb is that health is treasure of all pleasure on this world. Those who knows about it survives for hundred years.

Swastha Gaya To Sab Gaya Kutum Pariwar Aur Dhan
Kuchha Bhi Kam Na Ayaga Reh Jayaga Sab Han

The above proverb indicates that when we looses health, he/she looses all relatives, family, friend and wealth. They all will do not help you.

Kare Acharan Viruddha Jo Swastha Hit Batlay
Samay Se Pahale O Manushya Kal Men Jat Samay

The meaning of above proverb reveals that if one adopts such habits which are against healthy life, he/she is bound to go in the mouth of Kal (death).

Aham Kabhi Mat Kijiye Nashwar Yah Sharir
Aham Pal Upar Gaye Kai-Kai Veer

The meaning of above proverb is that we should never rear ego, because a number of ego rearing heroes went in the mouth of Kal (death) before time.

Rukha Sukha Khaike Thanda Pani Piv
Dekh Virani Chupari Mat Lalchao Jiv

The above proverb indicates that one should lead simple life of sharing. Simple food and fresh water and we should not become greedy to see others' costly food and lifestyle.

Jioge To Bhogoge Is Dharati Ka Sukh
Nahi To Jiwan Katega Bhogte Bhogate Dukh

The above proverb reveals that if you are healthy you will enjoy all pleasures of this earth. But without health you will lead life in trouble.

Jo Nahi Jina Chahate Karate Safa Safai
Samay se pahale Us Nar Ko Ho Jata Hai Vidai

The above proverb reveals that those who want to survive log without sanitation, they will leave for heaven soon.

Ek Nari Brahmachari Dui Nari Ghar Bigari
Tin Nari Swastha Ujari, Char Nari Swarg Sidhari

The meaning of above proverb is that having one wife is like a *Brahmachari,* Two wives destroys house, three wives destroy health and four wives sends a man in heaven.

Kal Jan Jo Sangrah Karai
Kahe Nath Kahe Nahi Marai

The meaning of above proverb is that if one takes poison knowing that it will kill him/her, why will he/she not die. Therefore, we should not take poisonous food or heavy food which are like poison.

Khana Banaye Aur Khilaye Use Do Saman
Tumbhi Nashta Ho Jaoge Kar Usaka Apman

The meaning is that those who cooks and serve food to us, we should pay always proper respect to him/her. But if we abuse them, we are bound to be destroyed.

Jagat Janani Ke Dhyan Rakh Mukh Me Kawar Dal
Bhojan Pachakar Ras Bane Ho Joa Tum Lal

The meaning of above proverb is that we should share our breakfast and meals after offering worship to Goddess Jagat Janani. This will cause our food to digest easily and completely and we will become healthy.

Swastha Hai Hamara Ishwor Ka Vardan
Ishwar Ko Samman Do Nahi To Jao Viran

The meaning of this is that health is a boon granted to us by God. Therefore, we should pay every respect to God, otherwise we are bound to became barren.

Sachche Hak Kamai se Karo Lalan Palan
Nahi To Sab Chal Jayaga Kitana Bhi Lalan

The meaning of above proverb is that we should rear our body and family members with true and honest works. Otherwise all will be destroyed whatsoever we earn.

Sawastha Gaya To Sab Gaya Kitana Bhi Dhanwan
Swastha Ko Hi Palate Gyani Aur Vidwan

When we loose our health we loose everything in spite of huge wealth. That is why wise and learned man rear only health not wealth.

Swastha Se Hi Jura Hai Bal Aur Dhan Ka Bhog
Dhan Rahate Nahi Bhogat Jise Pakarata Rog

The above proverb reveals that healthy persons are able to enjoy the pleasure of energy and wealth. Unhealthy persons do not enjoy the pleasure of wealth.

Alaukik Shakti Ko Dhyan Dhar Jio Niyamit Jiwan
Rog To Pas Na Ayaga Dur Bhagega Maran

The meaning of above proverb is that we should lead regular and disciplined life under the grace of God. This will expel disease far away and will not allow death to come.

Rog Khud Nahi Ata Hai Tum Usako Bulay
Galat Adat Vyavahar Kar Beta Gale Lagay

The meaning of above proverb is that the diseases do not come to us. Rather we invite them to come by our bad habits and behaviour.

Similarly, a number of health related folk proverbs are prevalent in every language community. These folk proverb reveal folk knowledge of people regarding their health behaviour. They indicate clearly that what we should do and what we should not do to remain healthy and long life.

5
Magical Concepts, Diseases and Treatment

In our society a number of beliefs and practices are prevalent related to the magical effects upon our health. People believe that they loose their health and ultimately meet death due to magical acts performed by a magician. According to our belief system, there are some persons who possess spirits. They keep spirit under their control. They direct the possessed spirit to cause harm to a person. As the spirit remains under their possession, that is why they have to work according to the guidance of the person who possesses them. The persons who possess control over spirits are termed as magician. The magicians are divided in to two categories:

- Black magician
- White magician.

Black Magician

The black magicians are those occult practitioners who possess spirits and direct them to cause harm to a person. Since these magicians are concerned with causing harm to a person including death, they are termed as black magician. For example witch craft.

White Magician

White magicians are such persons who possess spirit but they direct the spirit to counter the effect of black magician. Thus, they are not concerned with causing harm to a person. Rather they are concerned with curing diseases and providing relief from witchcrafts. For example—*Ojha, Guni, Bhaktin, Bhakta, Baba* etc.

Besides these two types of magicians, there are some other persons responsible for creating diseases in the family and community. They are:

- Evil-eyed person,
- Evil- tongued person, and
- Evil mouthed person.

Evil-eyed Person

According to belief system, some persons of the community possess evil eye. They are known as evil-eyed person. When they see children, suckling cow, pregnant women, good crops and other thing, a misery is bound to occur in the family. Children fall ill, lactating women loose their milk, pregnant women meet abortion, green tree dries, good crops turned into diseased crops. In this way, evil-eyed persons cause harm to community members.

Evil-tongued Person

According to belief some members of community have evil-tongue. They have black tongue. They are not taken as good for the society. If they curse anybody, a number of miseries are bound to come including death. Community members do not want to quarrel with them or even talk to them. Thus, evil tongued persons are also responsible for causing harm, diseases and death.

Evil-mouthed Person

According to belief system, some persons of the community possess evil mouth. The evil mouthed person's speech become true. Whatever they say, that becomes true. That is why people try to avoid them. Nobody wants to displease them. Whatever they abuse and curse that happen to be true.

The beliefs related to witchcraft, evil eye, evil tongue and evil mouth and *Ojha, Guni, Bhakta* and *Bhaktin* present before us sufficient folk ground that health is a magical concept. Our health may fall and we may meet death due to magical performances. The magical performances are also encountered. The ill health caused by magician can be encountered and neutralized by another magician. Therefore, people take help of *Ojha, Guni, Bhakta* and *Bhaktin* to encounter and neutralize the effect of a black magician.

The effects of evil eye, evil tongue and evil mouth are also neutralized by the help of *Ojha, Guni, Bhakta* and *Bhaktin* and also by performing *Totaka* himself/herself.

Witchcraft and Diseases

Witchcraft is associated with black magic. The black magician called as witch causes a number of diseases and death in families of enemy. This concept is based on faith and it has not any scientific base. This belief is based on two kinds of principles:

- Like Produces Like, and
- Once in contact always in contact.

According to like produce like principle, the witch performs some experiment for causing harm to an enemy and his/her family members. She makes an image of enemy concerned and inserts pin in its heart and chest. She repeats this experiment time and again at lonely place till the enemy does not fall ill seriously, or meet a death. Witch attached person starts loosing health day by day. Medicines do not bring positive result. All efforts start becoming unsuccessful. If a treatment by witch doctor is not done, the person gradually meets death. Thus, by performing magic with photos or effigies or images of person concerned, the black magician attempts to cause harm to health and wealth.

According to 'once in contact always in contact' principle, the witch collects hairs, combs, shoes, clothes and ornaments used by a person and performs experiment with those things. It is believed that the things thrown after use have always relation with the person concerned. That is why witch collects things used by a person to perform experiments related to black magic.

The witch can bring following types of misfortunes by her black magical experiments:

- Barrenness
- Impotency
- Abortion
- Birth of dead child
- Death of baby soon after delivery
- Child mortality
- Mother mortality
- Husband's death
- No flow of milk in lactating mother
- Breast cancer
- Continuous weeping of baby without suckling milk
- Dryness of child's body

- Stoppage of urine of child
- Flow of blood through urine
- Snake bite
- Scorpion bite
- Dog bite
- Jackal bite
- Widowhood
- Widowerhood
- Disability
- Death of working members
- Death of cattle wealth
- Breakout of fire
- Destroy of tree wealth
- Destroy of crops
- Fire in thrashing field
- Fire in house
- Non-curable diseases
- Eye diseases
- Skin disease
- Kidney diseases
- Liver diseases
- Attack of evil spirits.

From the observations of above misfortunes brought in a family through black magical experiments (sorcery), it is quite clear that very tearful and sorrowful beliefs are associated with witchcraft (black magician, *Dain).* That is why people get frightened to hear the name of witch. Acts after acts have been enacted and implemented, but it has not been possible to curb the practice of witchcraft. It has not been possible to prevent the exploitation and oppression of womenfolk in the name of witch, witchery and witchcraft. It is because beliefs associated with witchcraft are so deep rooted that any adverse occurrence in family are taken as a result of black magical experiments performed by a witch. The folk people do not want to know the reality of an event or scientific causes of an incidence. But they believe in blaming their neighbours in the name of witchcraft. Conflict and quarrel are true for the society. Enmity leads towards belief in witchcraft. Enemies are blamed as witches and witches can bring any kind of misfortunes in a family. Sorcery is mostly performed by an individual at late night in a lonely place. The performance of black magical experiments requires following things:

- *Tantra* (System or method)
- *Mantra* (Hymns or *shloka)*
- *Yantra* (Materials).

Tantra

The black magical experiments are performed systematically. In its experiment, series of methods are followed one after the other. If experiments are not performed systematically, the experiment will not bring positive result. Rather it will bring adverse result. That is why special emphasis is placed on Tantra in performance of black magical experiments.

Mantra

Special Mantras or hymns or *shlokas* are recited at the time of performance of black magical experiments. They are uttered in a special manner with an angry facial expressions. Emphasis is placed on correct pronunciation in correct method. *Mantras* are recited in the name of Goddess to please her and bring positive result.

Yantra (Materials)

The black magical experiments are performed by *Yantra.* The *Yantra* are in the form of materials such mustard, pulse, earthen pot, mustard seeds and oil, effigy or photo of person concerned, his/her hairs, slippers, shoes, clothes worn, nails, black clothes, broom, human skull, bones, crow feathers, sunfried rice and so on.

When *Tantra, Mantra* and *Yantra* are integrated systematically at the time of performing black magical experiments, a woman performs such systematic black magical experiment without an expert. Therefore, an expert is not required for the performance of black magic. It is believed that a witch acquired witchery from an expert who may be a male or a female. Expert is required at the time of learning.

Treatment of Diseases by White Magician

According to folk belief system, in order to make the effect of sorcery ineffective, white magical experiments are performed. The white magical experiments neutralize the effect of black magical experiments. The white magicians are regarded in the society. As they are supposed to have power to null the effect of black magical experiments. White magicians are known as *Pujari Ji, Panda Ji, Baa, Bhagat, Bhagatin.* They cure following types of diseases:

- Impotency
- Barrenness
- Abortion
- Live birth
- Unsuccessful delivery
- Disease of lactating mother
- Breast cancer
- Mother mortality
- Child mortality
- Weeping of baby
- Baby disease
- Child diseases
- Urine diseases
- Stomach diseases
- Liver diseases
- High fever
- Skin diseases
- Protection of husband
- Protection of wife
- Protection of house
- Protection of health
- Protection of cattle wealth
- Protection of crops
- Neutralize black magic
- Encounter evil eyes
- Encounter evil mouth
- Neutralize evil tongue
- Neutralize effects of *Bhut-Preta*
- Remedies of all evil spirits
- Not suiting medicines in the body
- Disease caused by Bhuta-Preta.

White Magical Experiments

White magicians cure health, protect wealth and property by performing white magical experiments. Like black magicians, they also perform experiments, but their experiments are not related to causing harm to anybody. Rather their experiments are related to cure of diseases and welfare of community members. Like black magicians, white magicians also believe in two principles, which include—

- Once in contact always in contact
- Like produces like.

According to the principle of 'once in contact always in contact', the white magicians also believe that contact of object remains always with the persons who used them. That is why the white magicians also tell to bring used clothes touched rice, pulse, mustard, salt for the treatment, if the person is unable to visit to the place of white magician. With those used or touched materials the white magician is able to know the power of witch or *Bhut-Preta* inside the body of patient.

According to the principle of 'like produces like', the white magicians attack on the body of patient that beating will cause witch power, evil spirit or *Bhuta-Preta* to leave the body.

In performance of white magical experiments they also like black magician take help of following:

- *Tantra* (method or system)
- *Mantra* (enchantment of hymns)
- *Yantra* (materials).

Tantra

At the time of performing white magical experiments, the white magician follows systems or methods, which is termed as *Tantra* in local parlance. He/she performs white magical experiments systematically in a sequence, not in haphazard manner. If experiments are not performed systematically following step after step methods, they do not bring positive result. The experiments can fail. They do not bring desired result. They are performed again. The failure of black magic brings adverse impact on the performer. But the failure of white magic does not bring adverse effect. They are repeated to get success.

Mantra

The white magician also pronounce or recite *mantra* or hymns to please the Devi Kamakhya. He/she also offers wine, meat, sacrifice, *prasad, dhup, gugul, agarbati,* sunfried rice, flower pulses and other things to make Goddess pleased for curing a patient and protect different kinds of wealth.

Yantra

Like black magician white magician also uses *yantra* to cure patient and protect the wealth. He/she provides *Tabij* (amulets) to wear in arm, waist, hand and neck. He/she provides bark and root of some plants to tie in cloth and hang at the door of house or at the door of bedroom.

Using *Tantra, Mantra* and *Yantra,* the white magicians cure the patient and protect wealth and property. This method of treatment of diseases and protection of property is known as *Jhar-phuk* method about which a detail description has been furnished hereinafter.

Jhar-phuk Method

This is very popular method of curing diseases and encountering the effects of witch, spirit, *Bhut-Preta,* evil-eyed, evil-mouthed and evil-tongued persons. White magicians are also known as *Jhar-phuk* doctor, witch doctor or experts of driving away the evil spirits. They are known as *Baba, Sain, Fakir, Ojha, Guni, Bhakta, Bhaktin, Sadhu, Achari,* or *Acharya* and so on. They do the work of treating with *Jhar-phuk* method from morning to late night. On special request they do the work of *Jhar-phuk* at anytime of day or night. Some *Jhar-phuk* doers visit from door to door in villages and do the work of *Jhar-phuk* to cure patients suffering from various kinds of diseases. They do *Jhar-phuk* of a patient with the help of a broom of peacock or owl or crow feathers. They enchant *mantra,* spray water or ash or rice or pulse on him and her and blow air from their mouth in the ears of patient and utter sound like *Phu-Phu-Phu*....They repeat this process several times. At the last they provide *Tabij* to wear in arm, neck, waist or hand. For this work He/she gets payment in cash and kind.

But there are some such *Jhar-phuk* doers who do not visit from door to door for curing patient by *Jhar-phuk* method. Rather they occupy seat in front of their house and patients or their parents or guardians pay a visit there for *Jhar-pukh.* Those who do not bring patients, have to bring sunfried rice, pulse, mustard or salt touched by the patient or sufferer. The *Jhar-phuk* doer reads sunfried rice, pulse, mustard seed or salt touched by patient to know the power of spirit and the way by which it will leave the body.

Knowing the strength of the evil spirit or witch, the *Jhar-phuk* doer starts treatment. If the case is not serious he/she returns patient or guardian along with read rice, pulse, mustard seeds and salt. The rice, pulse and salt are served to patient along with food and mustard seeds are sprayed in every part of the house. The *Jhar-phuk* doers also provide some herbal medicine to be eaten or applied and a *Tabij* to hold in arm, neck or waist.

When the case is serious, the *Jhar-phuk* doers call the patient along with wine, sacrificial birds like cock or egg and *Dhup-Agarbatti.* Some sunfried rice, pulse, oil and salt are also asked to bring along with patient. The *Jhar-phuk* doers do worship to Goddess first. Then offering of cock, egg, rice, pulse, oil, salt is made in his name amidst enchanting *mantras.* While enchanting *Mantra,* the *Jhar-phuk* doers sound like *phu-phu-phu*... in the ears of the patient. He/she strikes with the broom of crow, owl or peacock feathers around the head of the patient first and them on the entire body. After repeating this process, he/she declares that the patient is now free from the attack of witch or evil spirits. He/she provides the *Tabij* to hold and sacrificial meat, rice pulse and salt to be taken by the patient as *Prasad.*

Now let us describe the practice of *Jhar-phuk* treatment related to some diseases.

Jhar-phuk Treatment of Bhuta-Preta Attack

According to folk belief system, *Bhuta-Preta* are dissatisfied souls of dead persons who have met unnatural and untime death. As they have met premature death, therefore, their souls wander from place to place as dissatisfied souls. They make their shelter on old tree, house, old garden, bushes, river bank, old buildings, bridges and other lonely places. When they find a child, woman, pregnant lady, lactating lady alone, they make an attack on them. They enter inside the body and the person concerned starts behaving like an abnormal being. He/she sometimes laughs, sometimes weeps. He/she becomes sometimes aggressive and sometimes submissive. Sometimes he/she does not eat and sometimes eats food of several people. Seeing such abnormal behaviour family members took him/her before a white magician, may be *Baba, Bhagat, Bhagatin, Sai, Fakir.* The white magician asks the guardian of the patient suffering from the attack of *Bhuta-Preta* to bring *gugul* and *lohban* for burning. He/she starts doing *Jhar-phuk* with the help of a broom of cock, owl, or crow feathers and some human bones. At the time of doing *Jhar-phuk,* he/she also recites *mantra* and beat the body of the patient with special broom and asks the soul to leave the body for ever. He/she makes request to run away again and again. He/she offers smoke of *Lohban* and *gugul* near the nose of the patient. When the soul is not ready to leave the body, the *Jhar-phuk* doer beats the patient with shoes or stick. He/she puts a stick in both ears of the patient. In place of wood, turmeric is also put in ears. When patient starts saying that, now, I am going out of body and will not come back again. The soul asks to have water, sweets or fruits before running away from the body. The *Jhar-*

phuk doer offer water and fruits or sweets in the mouth of the patient. When the patient starts behaving in a normal way, the *Jhar-phuk* expert gives a *Tabij* to be held in arm, neck or waist. The *Jhar-phuk* experts do not demand anything but they accept gladly whatever the guardian of patient pays.

Jhar-phuk Treatment of Witch Attack

According to folk and peasant belief system, a witch makes an attack on pregnant woman, lactating mother, infant and child, bride, bridegroom, young wife and young husband. Witches are possessed by spirits and they make an attack with the help of them. The witch attack is encountered by the *Jhar-phuk* method. The *Jhar-phuk* experts are also known as witch doctors. The patients suffering from witch attack are brought before the *Jhar-phuk* doers or *Jhar-phuk* experts or witch doctors. If patient is not in a position to go the place of *Jhar-phuk* doers, any member of patient's family go there with mustard seed, sunfried rice, and salt after getting them touched with the hands of the patient. *Gugul* and *Loban* are also brought for burning. Black cloth is brought to tie the *Tabij.* The *Jhar-phuk* experts do *Jhar-phuk* with the help of a broom of peacock feathers or owl feathers or crow feathers. They burn *Loban* and *Gugul,* enchant *mantra* and broom the entire body of the patients attacked by witch. While reciting *mantra,* they make sound with mouth like *Chu-Chu-Chu* and blow air towards the eye and head of the patient. The smoke of burning *Gugul* and *Loban* is brought near the nose and eyes of the patient. The *Jhar-phuk* doer does *Jhar-phuk* of a patient for nearly half an hour. Then he returns rice and salt after making them powerful through reciting *mantras.* They are served to the patient for 21 days. The *Jhar-phuk* doers also provide *Tabij* (amulet) to be held in neck, arm or waist of the patient. The powerful mustard seeds are spread in all rooms and courtyards of the house. After *Jhar-phuk* treatment, the evil effects of a witch goes out from the patient for ever. Now he/she feels well and protected.

Toothache Treatment by *Jhar-phuk*

In folk and peasant society, there is a belief that toothache is generally caused by black magic, evil-spirits; evil-eyed and evil-mouthed. Therefore, people take help of *Jhar-phuk* treatment for the cure of toothache. The patient suffering from tooth ache visits the *Jhar-phuk* doers for *Jhar-phuk* treatment. The *Jhar-phuk* doers do the *Jhar-phuk* with the help of *Tantra*, *Mantra* and *Yantra.* It is believed that when tooth ache is caused by black magic or occult power, even powerful allopathic medicines do not bring positive result. Therefore, people visit the *Jhar-phuk* doer to make allopathic medicine effective and to neutralize the effect of black magic and evil spirit. The Jharphuk doer does Jharphuk with the help of Tantra, Mantra and Yantra. He/she also provides *Tabij* to be held in neck or arm. Some *Jari-booti*es are also provided. The patient feels relief by *Jhar-phuk* treatment.

Jhar-phuk Treatment of Headache

In folk and peasant society, the headache is cured by *Jhar-phuk* treatment. According to their belief, back magicians, witches, evil eyed, evil mouthed and evil spirits cause head ache to put a person under physical trouble. If the allopathic medicines do not work on patient caused by black magic, witch, and evil spirits. In folk society only way left is to visit *Jhar-phuk* doers. The *Jhar-phuk* doers do the *Jhar-phuk* treatment with his/her *Tantra-Mantra-Yantra.* He/she also provides oil made powerful through recitation of hymns for applying on forehead and head. A *Tabij* is also given for holding in arm or neck. The *Jhar-phuk* doers drive out the evil spirits from the head and patient feels good. The allopathic medicine also starts working positively.

Jhar-phuk Treatment of Bodyache

Black magicians and evil spirits cause a person to suffer continuously from bodyache. The allopathic medicines also do not bring relief result. The option left before people is to visit the *Jhar-phuk* expert who cures the body ache of patient by his/her *Jhar-phuk* treatment. The patient suffering from continuous body pain visit the house of *Jhar-phuk* expert with sunfried rice, salt and mustard oil. The *Jhar-phuk* expert attempts to know the power of spirit causing continuous body ache through reciting hymns taking sunfried rice, salt, turmeric and oil. Then he/she starts doing *Jhar-phuk* with his/her *Tantra*, *Mantra* and *Yantra*. When the *Jhar-phuk* treatment is over, the expert returns rice, salt and turmeric to the patient for sharing 21 days with daily food. He/she returns oil to be applied over the body. He/she also provides his own oil, pulse *Jari-booti* for applying on body. Finally an amulet is given to be held in neck or arm. After *Jhar-phuk* treatment the patient starts feeling relief and allopathic medicines also begins to bring positive result.

Jhar-phuk Treatment of Knee-ache

In folk and peasant society people believe that continuous knee-ache is caused by the attack of black magician, witch, and evil spirits. Their attack brings such a severe pain in knee that the person concerned becomes unable to stand up and walk. Allopathic treatment also brings no result. When allopathic medicine does not bring positive result, the belief in attack of black magician and evil spirits become strong. The patients visit the *Jhar-phuk* expert treatment. They bring oil, turmeric powder, salt and sunfried rice to be studied by the expert. The expert makes study of rice, oil salt and turmeric touched by the patient for knowing the strength of the evil spirits and black magic. Only then he/she starts *Jhar-phuk* of knee pain by *Tantra Mantra* and *Yantra.* At the time of doing *Jhar-phuk* the expert enchants *mantra* and makes a symbolic attack on affected part with his/her feathers' broom. He/she cries *Chhu-Chhu-Chhu.* The *Jhar-phuk* treatment is over. The expert returns rice, turmeric, oil and salt to the patient for sharing in daily food for 21 days. He/she provides his/her own prepared oil to be applied over the affected area. Finally, a *Tabij* is also given to be worn in neck or arm.

Jhar-phuk Treatment of Waistache and Backboneache

The *Jhar-phuk* treatment of waist and backbone ache is also done. People believe that waist and backbone ache are caused by the black magic and evil spirits. When allopathic treatment does not bring positive result, their belief in black magic becomes more and more strong. Now, they visit the *Jhar-phuk* doer for treatment of waist and backbone ache and to make allopathic medicine effective. The person suffering from waistache and backbone ache visits to *Jhar-phuk* doer with oil, salt, turmeric, red chilli and sunfried rice to be read by expert. By reading the settings, the expert attempts to know the power and magnitude of the black magic and evil spirit. Knowing power and magnitude, the expert starts *Jhar-phuk* by *Tantra, Mantra* and *Yantra.* The expert recites *mantras* after *mantra* and make sound like *Chhu-Chhu-Chhu* with his/her mouth near the affected area. Then he/she makes symbolic attack on the affected area with his/her white magical feathers broom amidst recitation of *Mantras.* The white magical brooms drives away the evil spirits from the body and the patient feels well. The *Jhar-phuk* treatment continues for an hour or even more. At the end of *Jhar-phuk*, the expert provides a *Tabij* to be held in neck or arms or waist. The expert returns oil, salt, rice, red chilli and turmeric to patient for sharing with daily food for a weak or so.

***Jhar-phuk* of Stomachache**

In folk and peasant society, stomachache is also cured by *Jhar-phuk* treatment. When stomach pains continues even after allopathic treatment, the belief of people becomes strong that it has been caused by black magic and some malevolent spirits. Now, people visit the house or place of *Jhar-phuk* expert along with rice, salt, oil, turmeric and red chilli. The *Jhar-phuk* expert recites *mantra* and touches all things with his/her hands observing seriously. He/she tries to know the power of black magic and evil spirits knowing the power, he/she starts *Jhar-phuk* by his white magical feathers' broom. He/she burns *Lohban* and *Gugul* in a pot and brings the smoke nearby the face of the patient. He/she reads mantra after mantra. Now after some time, he/she makes symbolic attack on the affected area with his/her magical brooms pronouncing sound like *Chhu-Chhu-Chhu*, *Ja-Ja-Ja*. This process is repeated several time till the patient says that he/she is well now. It is believed, now, that the evil spirit has left the body and the patient is all right. The expert returns rice, salt, turmeric, oil, red chilli to the patient to be shared in daily food for one or three weeks. The expert also provides *Jari-booti* to eat and a *Tabij* to wear in waist or arm.

***Jhar-phuk* Treatment of Eye Diseases**

The folk people has a belief that eye diseases are caused by black magic and evil spirits. That is why, they visit the *Jhar-phuk* experts for the treatment of eye diseases. The evil spirit and black magician may cause a person not to see even during day time. The eye becomes red. Wound appears on eyelid. The eye gets infected. When such diseases attacks a person, he/she visit the *Jhar-phuk* expert for the cure. The patient has to go to the expert with oil, salt, turmeric, rice and dry red chilly. The experts makes study of these things to know the nature and power of the black magic and evil spirits. Knowing the power of the black magic and evil spirits, it becomes easy to do *Jhar-phuk* treatment. The expert keeps Lohban and Gugul burning in an earthen pot. He/she reads Mantras, adds Lohban and Gugul and brings the smoke nearby the eyes of the patient. Now, he/she makes his white magical broom powerful by enchanting *mantras*. He/she makes symbolic attack on eyes with the broom amidst uttering mantras and pronouncing sounds like *Chhu-Chhu-Chhu-Ja, Ja Ja*... etc. By this process evil spirit is driven out from the body. Now the patient feels well. The expert returns rice, salt, oil, turmeric, chilli to the patient to be eaten in daily food. He/she gives a *Tabij* to be held in arm or neck.

Jhar-phuk Treatment of Nose Disease

According to folk belief system, nose diseases are caused by black magic, witch and evil spirits. When they make an attack on nose of a person, his or her nose starts suffering from diseases. Being vexed by trouble and pains, the patient goes to doctor, but the medicine of doctor does not work. The patient does not recover in spite of allopathic treatment. Being disappointed the patient visit to *Jhar-phuk* doer with sunfried rice, turmeric, salt, oil and mustard seeds. The *Jhar-phuk* doer reads all things brought by patient one by one with the help of enchanting mantras. By this process the *Jhar-phuk* doer attempts to know the strength of black magic and evil spirits. Now he/she brings smoke of *Lohban* and *Gugul* in front of nose of the patient. When the patient starts feeling suffocation, the pot containing *Lohban* and *Gugul* is removed. Now the process of *Jhar-phuk* starts. The *Jhar-phuk* doer enchants mantras taking magical feathers broom in hand and moving round the head of the patient. Time to time he makes symbolic attack on the nose of the patient with magical broom. The expert makes sound like *Chhu-Chhu-Chhu-Ja-Ja-Ja*, *Bhag-Bhag-Bhag*. The expert asks patients to take water time to time. When the patient starts saying that going-going-going, never come back, never come back, never come back. On hearing such sounds from the mouth of the patient, the expert gets confirmed that evil spirit is going out of the body. The expert stops doing *Jhar-phuk*. He/she asks patient to take rest. The expert returns the rice, salt, oil and mustard seeds to the patient for sharing along with food for 21 days. The expert provides an amulet to be held in arm and or neck of the patient.

Jhar-phuk treatment of Throat-Disease

The folk people believe that black magic, witch and evil spirits cause throat infection by making attack on the patient. The belief of patient in attack by black magic, witch and evil spirit is confirmed when infection continues even after allopathic treatment and the patient feels no relief. Now they visit to *Jhar-phuk* expert with rice, salt, turmeric oil and mustard seeds. The patient has to wait because expert remains busy in doing *Jhar-phuk* of other patients. The expert do *Jhar-phuk* with *Tantra, Mantra* and *Yantra*. First of all he/she reads mantras and observe seriously the things brought by the patient. This is known as *chawal,* salt, turmeric, oil and mustard *se Padhana* (Reading). By reading the things brought from the patient, the expert attempts to know the strength of the black magician, witch and evil spirits. Knowing the strength, the *Jhar-phuk* doer starts the *Jhar-phuk* work. First of all *Lohban* and *Gugul* are burnt in a pot kept for this purpose. The smoke of the *Lohban* and *Gugul* is brought before the face of the patient enchanting mantras. This is known as driving evil spirits by the smoke. It is also known as smoke therapy. After this magical broom of feathers is brought and empowered by offering some drops of wine, an egg or some pieces of meat by reading special *mantras.* The expert brings the powerful magical broom and starts enchanting *mantra.* He/she moves the broom around the head of the patient. The patient is asked to close his/her eyes. The expert makes symbolic attack on the throat with white magical brooms several times amidst enchanting mantras. He/she also strikes the broom on earth and then attack on throat. He/she speaks *Chhu-Chhu-Chhu-Bhag-Bhag-Bhag* and *Ja, Ja and Ja*. The expert continues this *Jhar-phuk* process till the patient does not start crying that do not beat, do not beat, do not beat, I am going, I am going, I am going. But give me a glass of water and some drops of wine. Water and wine is served to the patient. The patient feels well. The expert thanks the deity for removing such powerful spirit from the body of the patient. He/she returns rice, salt, oil, mustard oil and seeds to the patient for sharing along with daily food for 21 days continuously. The expert also provides the patient with a *Tabij* to be held in arm or neck.

Jhar-phuk Treatment of Ear Disease

According to folk and peasant belief system, the disease of ear is caused by black magician, witch and evil spirit. They cause continuous pain in ear and ultimately make a person deaf. Witch or evil spirit affected person does not get relief and cure even after treatment by allopathic ear specialist. The witch or evil spirit makes all medicine ineffective. Being disappointed with allopathic treatment the patient decides to visit *Jhar-phuk* specialist. The *Jhar-phuk* doers have their own identity in the folk and peasant society. The people know them by name and village. The also know that a patient is required to bring rice, oil, salt, mustard seed and red dry chilli for *Jhar-phuk* treatment. This practice is known to everybody. Some cases demanded to make the deity of *Jhar-phuk* pleased in next visit.

As usual practice of *Jhar-phuk* treatment the *Jhar-phuk* doer starts *Jhar-phuk* by observing the things brought by the patient from his/her house. While observing the things, the expert recites *mantras* in the name of white magic deity. With the help of recitation of *Mantras* and observation of things touched by the patient, the *Jhar-phuk* doer attempts to identify the spirit or witch and their strength. After identification of spirit and recognition of power, it becomes easy for the *Jhar-phuk* doer to do *Jhar-phuk* treatment and drive out the evil spirit from the affected part of the body.

After identification, the first process to be followed is burning *Loban* and *Gugul* in a pot for this purpose. The smoke of burning *Gugul* and *Loban* is brought before the eye, ear, mouth, nose and face of the patient. The patient is left for some time to inhale the smoke and feel suffocated so that the spirit may also feel suffocation. This is known as *Dhuan Dikhana* (showing smoke). After *Dhuau Dikhana,* the *Jhar-phuk* by white magical feathers' broom is done. The broom is purified and made powerful by reciting hymns by the expert and moving the broom in both hands, around smoke, and striking the broom on earth. After this the expert moves towards the face of the patient. He/she recites hymns loudly and fastly rubbing the body of the patient by broom. He/she creates sound like *Chhu-Chhu-Chhu-Ja-Ja-Ja*, *Bhag-Bhag-Bhag*, otherwise be ready to bear beating more and more. The expert makes symbolic attack with broom on the affected area. He/she repeats this *Jhar-phuk* process, till the patient does not tell that he/she is going to leave the body. The patient may demand water, sweet, loaf sugar and even wine to leave the body. The *Jhar-phuk* doer tells that it is not patient the evil spirit inside the body is telling and demanding like. When the patient speaks, after taking water, sweets, loaf sugar or wine to go for ever, the expert asks him/her not to come back again, otherwise, a severe beating is threatened. The spirit through speech of patient assures the expert not to come back again. After hearing this, the expert announces that *Jhar-phuk* process is over. He/she returns rice, oil, turmeric, salt, mustard seeds, red chilli to the patient to be consumed in daily food for three weeks or more. He/she also provides a *Tabij* for which the patient has to pay something in cash. The *Tabij* given by the expert is held in arm or neck or waist.

Jhar-phuk Treatment of Big Wounds

In folk and peasant society, people visit to *Jhar-phuk* doer for the treatment of wounds. They believe that wounds are caused by black magic witch and evil spirits to bring a person or an enemy under trouble of different kinds. The *Jhar-phuk* treatment not only drives out spirit causing wounds but makes the use of allopathic medicine more effective. The patients suffering from wound visit to the place of *Jhar-phuk* expert. The expert attempts to know the effect and strength of the black magician, witch or evil spirits. The entire *Jhar-phuk* process is based on this method. Once the strength is known, the effect of black magic can be neutralized. Now expert burns *Loban* and *Gugul* brings near he face of the patient. He/she allows some to enter in nose, eyes, and ears of the patient. The smoke sends the message to the spirit that be ready to go out of body or die for ever. After some therapy, the patient is asked to be ready to face magical broom therapy. Symbolic attack on affected area is made by magical broom made up of feathers of crow, eagle, owl and peacock. While making attack *Jhar-phuk* doer makes his/her face angry and radish. He/she shouts sounds like *Ja-Ja-Ja Bhag, Bhag, Bhag, Mat Lautana-Matlautana-Mat-Lautanas*, etc. He/she repeats this process, till the patient do not start saying that I am leaving, will never come back again. But please give me some water, food and wine to share. *Jhar-phuk* doer provides water, loaf sugar and some wine. Now the body of patient is free from the evil spirit or witch or black magic. The *Jhar-phuk* doer returns the purified and hymned read rice, salt, oil, mustard and red chilli to the patient for sharing 21 days as medicine along with other food items. A *Tabij* is also given to hold in arm or neck or waist. *Jari-booti* is also provided to apply over the wound. Thus, folk people attempt to cure big wounds with *Jhar-phuk* treatment which remains spirit causing. The patient feels well. Now, allopathic medicine also suits to him/her (Patient).

Jhar-phuk Treatment of Leprosy and other Skin Diseases

Significantly, folks and peasant people believe in cure of leprosy and other skin diseases by *Jhar-phuk* treatment. The patient suffering from leprosy and other skin diseases visits to *Jhar-phuk* expert for the treatment of leprosy and other diseases. Folk and peasant people believe that leprosy and other serious skin diseases are caused by the attack of evil spirits which enters inside the body and cause serious diseases. The patient suffering from skin diseases visit to the *Jhar-phuk* doers or expert along with some rice, salt, pulse, oil mustard seed, and dry red chilli for treatment of disease. The expert attempts to study these materials by taking them in own hands, observing seriously and enchanting spirit identifying hymns. The *Jhar-phuk* doer believes that food-grains and spices touched by the patient provide significant clue regarding the type and strength of the evil spirit. After verifying through hymns and reading, they are returned to the patient to be taken for three weeks along with other food items as medicine. In this case also, the *Jhar-phuk* treatment is started with showing smoke of *Loban* and *Gugul*. The smoke forces the evil spirit to feel suffocated and make up its mind to leave the body and go somewhere else. After some therapy, the white magical broom therapy is given. In this therapy, the white magical broom of feathers of peacock, owl, and eagle is used. First of all the power of magical broom is awaken by reciting the deity and hymns for some time. The broom is brought near the affected part. Symbolic attack on the affected part is made with the help of broom. This process is repeated several times. In the meantime hymns are uttered along with sounds like *Chhu-Chhu-*

Chhu, Ja-Ja Ja, Nahin to Markha. The *Jhar-phuk* doer strike the broom on earth, too. The *Jhar-phuk* treatment continues till the hidden spirit in body of the patient does not accept to leave for ever. The spirit demands water, loaf sugar and wine before leaving the body. The demand is fulfilled and after the fulfillment of the demand, the spirit leaves the body. The patient feel well. The *Jhar-phuk* doer returns the read and spiritualized oil and *Jari-booti* is also provided to the patient for taking and applying over the effected part of body regularly. In this way *Jhar-phuk* treatment is provided to the patient to be cured.

***Jhar-phuk* Treatment of Jaundice**

Jaundice is a kind of disease related to liver. The liver becomes hot and needs rest for some days. The patient suffering from Jaundice yield yellow urine. The body and eyes become yellow. The bed sheet used for sleeping also becomes yellow. The folk and peasant people also believe that jaundice is caused by the attack of evil spirit, witch and *Bhuta-Preta.* Their attack can be neutralised by *Jhar-phuk* treatment. The *Jhar-phuk* treatment is done by professional expert on two fixed days of a week. For example Sunday and Tuesday. In other days of week, they perform their own work. But for two days, they do welfare work. The process adopted in this treatment is also similar. First of spirit identification therapy is given to the patient. For this purpose, rice, pulse, mustard, salt, oil and chilli brought by the patient is observed and read by the benevolent spirit of the *Jhar-phuk* doer. The expert with his own benevolent spirit is able to know the strength, and type of evil spirit and how it will go out of the body. By reciting a number of hymns all grains and things brought by the patient is also powered. Now they possess special curative power. They are returned to the patient to be shared with daily food for 21 days without any break.

After this, *Jhar-phuk* treatment by magical broom is done. This broom possesses a special benevolent spirit. But it has to be awoken by reciting hymns and recalling the white magic deity again and again. When the strength of the magical broom is empowered by reciting hymns, the *Jhar-phuk* doer makes an attack on the part of liver with the broom and request the evil spirit to go out of the body of the person and never come back. The *Jhar-phuk* doer not only makes symbolic attack on the liver of the patient, but he also recites hymns and creates sound like *Chhu-Chhu-Chhu, Ja-Ja-Ja, Kabhi Na Aa-Kabhi Na Aa*. This process is repeated till the bad spirit through the mouth of the patient does not tell that I am going and will not come back again. The evil spirit also makes a demand of water, loaf sugar or wine. The demand is fulfilled. The spirit goes out of body forever, at last some herb is provided to the patient for taking regularly. A *Tabij* is also given which has protective function. The spirit of the *Tabij* protects the patient from next attach of witches. The *Jhar-phuk* doer also provides some *Jari-booti* to take regularly. The *Jari-booti* has preventive and curative function.

Jhar-phuk Treatment of Barrenness (Interfertility)

In folk and peasant society, there is a belief that women suffer from the diseases of barrenness due to attack of witch, evil spirit and other negative power. That is why such women visit to the place of *Jhar-phuk* doer. It is believed that evil spirits and negative powers make the treatment of allopathic doctor in vain. In order to make allopathic treatment effective, barren women also visit to a *Jhar-phuk* doer. The *Jhar-phuk* doer makes the attack of evil spirit and negative power ineffective by *Jhar-phuk* treatment. He/she drives the evil spirits or negative powers out of the body of the patient. The patient feels well and allopathic medicines also suits to her. Ultimately she is blessed with an offspring.

In this case also *Jhar-phuk* treatment is completed by Tantra, Mantra and *Yantra*. As usual practice, the patient visits to a *Jhar-phuk* doer with some rice, mustard seed, oil, salt and turmeric powder. The *Jhar-phuk* doer observe's these things taking in own hands and reciting *Mantras*. Through recitation of *Mantra,* the *Jhar-phuk* doer attempts to know the strength of evil spirit and negative power. He/she also makes those things full of spiritual power by his/her observation and recitation of hymns. The *Jhar-phuk* doer returns enchanted rice, salt, oil, mustard, chilli, turmeric powder to be eaten by the patient with daily food for 21 days, when the *Jhar-phuk* treatment is over.

Now, the *Jhar-phuk* doer starts *Jhar-phuk* treatment by burning *Loban* and *Gugul* and taking the smoke before eyes, nose and face of the patient. The smoke makes the patient to feel suffocated. The face and eyes of patient becomes red. By this method, the evil spirit or negative power is awaken to be ready to leave the body of patient. In next step, the *Jhar-phuk* doer brings his brooms of feathers of owl, eagle, black crow, and peacock. He/she makes the broom empowered by reciting *mantras.* The spiritualized broom is now used to drive out the negative power. The *Jhar-phuk* doer makes a symbolic attack on the entire body of the patient amidst reciting *Mantras* and sounding like *Chhu-Chhu-Chhu, Bhag-Bhag-Bhag, Bol-Bol-Bol, Kya lega, Kya lega* or *markhayaga, markhayga* etc. The *Jhar-phuk* done till patient not start saying that going, going, going but give me water, wine, sweet, egg or cock. The *Jhar-phuk* doer offers these things to the spirit and the spirit goes out of body of the patient with a promise not to return again. Now, the patient is free from the attack of evil spirits and negative powers. A *Tabij* and some *Jari-booti* is also given to the patient. She is asked to continue her allopathic treatment. Thus, the *Jhar-phuk* doer does not stop the allopathic treatment but he/she drives out the negative powers from the body of patient for the success of the treatment.

Jhar-phuk Treatment of Frequent Abortion

According to folk and peasant belief system, frequent abortion to a woman is caused by witch, evil spirits and negative powers. As a result, a woman is not in a position to become mother. She is conceived but meets abortion. The evil or negative powers prohibit her to become mother. That is why such a woman takes help of *Jhar-phuk* treatment, besides allopathic and other treatments. The process adopted in *Jhar-phuk* treatments is same. Here, too, *Tantra, Mantra* and *Yantra* method is applied one after another to drive out the evil or negative powers from the body of patient and to inculcate positive power in her body to face the situation and achieve success.

The woman, who meetes frequent abortion and does not become mother, approach the *Jhar-phuk* doer for treatment along with some rice, pulse, oil, salt, mustard seed, red chilli and turmeric powder. The *Jhar-phuk* doer spiritualizes these edible things by taking in own hands and reciting *Mantras* again and again. The spiritualization process makes the edible things blessed with positive power to drive out negative power from the body. The *Jhar-phuk* doer returns all rice, pulse, salt, oil, mustard seeds and chilli to the patient for sharing along with daily meals for at least 21 days, when the *Jhar-phuk* treatment is over. After empowering the things brought by the patient through spiritualization process, the *Jhar-phuk* treatment begins with showing smoke of *Gugual* and *Lohban* to the patient is which burnt in an earthen pot. The pot along with burning smoke of *Gugul* and *Lohban* is brought near the face of the patient. The smoke makes the patient to feel suffocated. The suffocation makes the evil spirit inside the body to become ready to go out of the body. Now, the *Jhar-phuk* treatment is done with white magical broom of feathers containing feathers of owl, crow, eagle and peacock. First of all the positive magical power of the broom is awoken by reciting hymns and striking the earth with broom. Then the body of the patient is beaten with broom amidst recitation of hymns and pronunciation of sounds like *Chu-Chu, Chhu*, *Bhag-Bhag-Bhag*, *Aur markha*, *Aur Markha*. Through symbolic beating on entire body from head to feet and reciting hymns and threatening words, the *Jhar-phuk* doer forces the evil spirit to go out of body. The *Jhar-phuk* treatment continues till the patient does not start sounding like going-going-going, but give me water, sweet, wine and cock before leaving. The *Jhar-phuk* doer fulfils the demands of evil spirit. Then evil spirit leaves the body forever. The *Jhar-phuk* doer provides a *Tabij* to hold in arm or waist or neck. He/she also provides a *Tabij* to hold in arm or waist or neck. He/she also provides some *Jari-booti* and advices the patient to follow instructions of doctor which will be more effective now.

Jhar-phuk Treatment for Live Birth and Prevent Mother Mortality

In folk and peasant society, there is a belief that evil spirits and negative powers cause death of mother and child in womb. Therefore, for live birth and successful delivery, folk and peasant people take help of *Jhar-phuk* treatment. The *Jhar-phuk* treatment prevents death of mother and child during delivery. This does not mean that they avoid allopathic treatment completely. They take help of allopathic treatment along with *Jhar-phuk* treatment. The *Jhar-phuk* treatment has preventive function. According to their belief system, the *Jhar-phuk* treatment prevents prenatal death and mother mortality.

The *Jhar-phuk* treatment adopted in this case is also same as in case of *Jhar-phuk* treatment of other cases. It also follows, the system of *Tantra*, *Mantra* and *Yantra*. When a woman becomes pregnant, the evil spirits, witches and negative cause harm. That is why she goes under the treatment of a *Jhar-phuk* doer. The *Jhar-phuk* doer spiritualizes the rice, pulse, oil, salt, mustard seeds and red chilli and returns them to pregnant women for sharing along with daily meals till the successful delivery. He/she provides a *Tabij* to be held in arm, waist, or neck. The *Jhar-phuk* doer drives out the evil spirits and negative powers from the body of woman with his/her white magical broom made up of feathers of owl, crow, peacock and eagle. He/she asks guardian of pregnant women to remain in his/her touch, if the pregnant woman faces any kind of problem.

Jhar-phuk Treatment of Lactating Mother

According to folk and peasant belief system, the evil spirits, witches, and negative powers cause a number of problems to a lactating mother. They stop the flow of milk in her breast or may cause disease called Thanail in her breast. After occurence of this disease the milk flow in breast is stopped. In order to prevent such diseases, the woman folk visit to the *Jhar-phuk* doer for treatment. The *Jhar-phuk* doer adopts the same process of *Jhar-*

phuk in this case, too. He/she employs *Tantra, Mantra* and *Yantra* system to cure or prevent the diseases related to lactation. Lactating woman has to visit the *Jhar-phuk* doer along with rice, pulse, salt, oil, mustard, chilli or a guardian of the lactating woman goes to the *Jhar-phuk* doers along with these food materials after touch of patient concerned. The *Jhar-phuk* doer observes reads and spiritualizes them through reciting *mantras*. He/she returns them to the patient or his guardian with an advice to share them atleast for a month along with daily food. This removes the negative energy of the body and generate positive energy for flow of milk and cure of disease. The *Jhar-phuk* doer also does *Jhar-phuk* of the clothes of the lactating mother with white magical broom of feathers. He/she also provides a tabij filled with positive energy to be worn in arm, neck or waist. He/she tells the patient or her guardian not to stop allopathic medicine, if any she was taking.

Jhar-phuk Treatment of Infant and Child Diseases

The infancy and childhood period is full of diseases such as diarrhoea, cough, cold, fever, not suckling, weeping continuously, jaundice, stomach ache, becoming lean day by day, *Najar-Gojar* (attack of evil spirit) and others. In order to cure such diseases and attack of evil spirits, the folk and peasant people take help of *Jhar-phuk* treatment, besides treatment of doctors. The mother or guardian brings the child to the place of *Jhar-phuk* doctor along with mustard seeds, oil and red dry chilli. If child is not brought, his/her dress is brought along will red dry chilli, mustard seeds and oil. The *Jhar-phuk* doctor observes, reads and spiritualizes the dress, oil, mustard seeds and chilly through enchanting hymns. They drive out the negative powers and prevent their re-entry in the body. The *Jhar-phuk* doctor also provides a *Tabij* to be held in arm, neck or waist of the infant or child. According to their belief system, the *Jhar-phuk* treatment has preventive, curative and rehabilitative function.

Jhar-phuk Treatment of Impotency

This is a disease of males related to erectile dysfunction. According to belief system of folk and peasant people, this disease is caused by evil spirits, witches and negative powers. The impotent persons are not in a position to reproduce children and are bound to lead childless life. Therefore, patient visits to *Jhar-phuk* doctors, though they are also under the treatment of allopathic doctor. The *Jhar-phuk* doctor employs *Tantra, Mantra* and *Yantra* system to cure and rehabilitate the patient sexually. The patient visits the *Jhar-phuk* doctor with some rice, pulse, oil, salt turmeric and red dry chilly. The *Jhar-phuk* doctor observes, reads and spritualizes the materials brought by the patient through hymns or mantras. Now, they are full of positive energy. The *Jhar-phuk* doctor gives them to the patient to be shared along with daily meals for a month. The *Jhar-phuk* doctor, now, sweeps the body of patient with a broom made up of feathers of owl, crow, peacock and eagle. This is known as *Jharrna* (sweeping). This broom has positive spirit or benevolent spirit. The spirit is awoken with the help of recitation of *Mantras* and beating the broom on ground for some time. In this way, broom is charged with positive power to drive out the negative power. Now this positive power charged broom is used for sweeping the entire body of the patient. While sweeping the body, the *Jhar-phuk* doctor recites *mantras* and pronounciates sound like *Chhu-Chhu-Chhu, Ja, Ja, Ja, Nahi to Markhha* in the ears of the patient. The *Jhar-phuk* doctor repeats this till the patient does not start saying that going-going-going, do not beat me, do not beat me. But serve me a glass of water, wine, sweet, egg or cock. The *Jhar-phuk* doctor fulfils the demand of the evil spirit. The evil spirit leaves the body for ever. The *Jhar-phuk* doctor allows the patient to take rest for sometime. He/she gives a *Tabij* full of positive power to be worn in arm, neck or waist. He also gives some *Jari-booti*, to the patient and asks the patient to continue allopathic treatment.

Jhar-phuk Treatment of Snake Bite

In folk and peasant communities, the incidence of snake bite is very frequent and common. It is believed that snake bite is caused by evil spirit and witches. They force the spirit of snake to have an attack on the person concerned so that the person may meet an end. There are *Jhar-phuk* doctor of snake bite in folk and peasant communities. They attempt to cure the patient suffering from snake bite. The snake bite doctor attempts to know whether the sanke is poisonous or non-poisonous before starting the *Jhar-phuk* treatment. For this purpose, they take a brass or bronze plate. They rub some dust or ash on the back of the patient. They put brass or bronze plate on the back of patient and sprinkle some pieces of soil collected from the abode of mouse. If the plate remains attached to back, it symbolizes that the snake is poisonous. But when the snake is non-poisonous, the plate does not remain attached to the back of the patient.

An another method of identifying the poisonous and non-poisonous snake is chewing *Golmircha.* If the taste of *Golmircha* is not bitter, it means that the snake is poisonous. But when the patient feels bitter taste of *Golmircha,* it means that snake is non-poisonous.

Thus assessing the poisonous nature of the snake, the *Jhar-phuk* treatment is started. The *Jhar-phuk* doctor enchants hymns and reads mustard seeds. He sprinkles the read and spiritualized mustard seeds over heads of the patient and requests the spirit of snake to get poison down on the affected part. He sweeps the body of the patient with magical broom to get the poison down to the affected point. He asks the patient not to sleep. In order to keep the patient awaken, he tells someone to pour water over the head of the patient continuously slowly and slowly. When poison comes down, the *Jhar-phuk* doer cuts the affected part of bite with a thorn and allow the blood to flow on the ground for some time. Then he brings *Jari-booti* and applies over the wound. He goes on enchanting *mantras* for the whole night and keeps the patient awaken. Next day, he provides a *Tabij* to hold in arm or waist or neck. This magical *Tabij* keeps the spirit of snake away from the body of the patient. The *Jhar-phuk* expert does not demand anything from the patient as pre-condition. He does social welfare work and leaves on the family of patient to pay in cash or kind as they like to pay. Generally member of *sapera* community performs this work of *Jhar-phuk* as treatment of snake bite. Now-a-days, people visit to an allopathic hospital for the treatment of snake bite. Now, there is an opinion among the people, that the bite of a poisonous snake cannot be cured by a *Jhar-phuk* by snake bite doctor. The bite of poisonous snake can only be cured by the allopathic treatment.

Jhar-phuk **Treatment of Scorpion Bite**

In folk and peasant society, the incidence of scorpion bite is very common. The people cure scorpion bite by *Jhar-phuk* treatment. Few persons of the village community know the *Jhar-phuk* treatment of scorpion bite. First poisonous and non-poisonous nature of scorpion bite is found out by brass or bronze plate and soil from mouse hole. They are spread over the back of the patient. The plate of brass or bonze is placed over the back. Some pieces of soil are thrown over the plate amidst enchanting *mantras.* When the plate falls down, it means that scorpion is non-poisonous. But when plate remains attached to the body, it means that the nature of scorpion bite is poisonous. An another method to know the poisonous or non-poisonous nature of scorpion bite is to give *Golmirch* in the mouth of the patient to chew. If the taste is bitter, it indicates non-poisonous nature. But if the taste is not bitter, it means that the nature is poisonous. After knowing the poisonous and non-poisonous nature of scorpion bite, the *Jhar-phuk* treatment is started. The *Jhar-phuk* doer, takes mustard seeds from the hand of the patient. He reads mustard seeds and spiritualizes them for getting the poison of scorpion bite slowly down up to the point of attack. He sprinkles and reads and spritualized mustard over the head and shoulder of the patient amidst enchantment of mantras and pronounciation of sound like *Chhu-Chhu-Chhu* at the end of each recitation of hymn. The poison of the scorpion starts coming down from the head slowly. It gradually comes down at the point of bite. The patient feels coming down of poison. When the poison comes down at the point of attack, the *Jhar-phuk* doer stops the *Jhar-phuk* treatment. He provides some *Jari-booti* (herbs) to the patient to apply over the point of bite. The *Jari-booti* absorbs all poison and the patient becomes well in few hours. Now a days, the people are taking help of modern treatment in case of scorpion bite.

Jhar-phuk Treatment of Dog Bite

In folk and peasant communities, the incidence of dog bite takes place frequently. Incidence of dog bite can take place with a man, or a domestic animals like cow, buffalo, goat etc. The folk and peasant people visit to a dog-bite *Jhar-phuk* doer for the treatment of dog bite. The incidence of dog bite is taken very serious because it can cause death. First of all, attempt is made to know whether the dog was mad or not. It is because only mad dog bite might cause death. If a dog survives for 14 days after bite, it means that the dog is not mad. But when dog dies within 14 days of bite, it means that the dog was mad and poisonous. Now the *Jhar-pukh* treatment is required to save the patient. The *Jhar-phuk* doer asks the guardian of the patient to do some *totaka* (protective remedies). The patient is advised to see his face in 21 wells or ponds. He/she is asked to take water of 21 wells, ponds and rivers. The patient has to drink the mixed water of 21 wells. After performing these *Totaka*, the patient is asked to come for *Jhar-phuk treatment* on any Sunday or Tuesday or any day told by the *Jhar-phuk* doer. The *Jhar-phuk* doer burns *Gugul* and *Lohban* and brings the smoke near the face of the patient. The patient has to inhale the smoke for some minutes till he does not feel suffocated. Thereafter, the *Jhar-phuk* doer enchants some *mantras* and sweeps the body of the patient especially the bite part with magical broom of feathers. He repeats the *Jhar-phuk* treatment several times. After some time, he speaks in the ear of the patient like *Chhu-Chhu-Chhu* and declares that the body of the patient has become poison-free. Now he provides some *Jari-booti* to the patient for eating for three days continuously. The *Jari-booti* is taken with empty stomach each day an hour before taking meal.

Like man, the *Jhar-phuk* treatment of dog bite of domestic animals like cow, ox, buffalo and goat is also followed. Now-a-days, besides *Jhar-phuk* treatment, the injection is also taken to avoid the risk of death.

Jhar-phuk **Treatment of Jackal bite**

In folk and peasant areas, the incidence of jackal bite is also very common. In order to avoid the death risk from jackal bite, folk and peasant-people take help of *Jhar-phuk* treatment. The *Jhar-phuk* procedure of jackal bite is same as that of dog bite. Generally the *Jhar-phuk* doer of both dog bite and jackal bite is same person. Hence repetition of procedure is not being done.

Jhar-phuk **Treatment of Barren Cow and Buffalo**

According to folk and peasant belief system, witch and evil spirits make cow and buffalo barren. That is why to save cow and buffalo from barrenness, the help of *Jhar-phuk* treatment is taken. When a cow and buffalo does not get fertilized timely, it is believed that some witches and evil spirits have made attack to make her barren. The owner of cow or buffalo brings the affected cow or buffalo to *Jhar-phuk* doer. The *Jhar-phuk* doer makes *Jhar-phuk* treatment in the same way as he/she makes *Jhar-phuk* treatment of a barren woman. For detail please read *Jhar-phuk* treatment of a woman in the same chapter.

Jhar-phuk **Treatment of a Lactating Cow and Buffalo**

According to folk and peasant belief system, lactating cow and buffalo are attacked by witches and evil spirits. When they make an attack the flow of milk gets stopped. The cow or buffalo does not give milk. In order to cure this disease people take help of *Jhar-phuk* treatment. The *Jhar-phuk* treatment of lactating cow or buffalo is same as that of lactating woman. Hence, entire *Jhar-phuk* treatment is not being repeated.

Jhar-phuk **Treatment of Cattle Fever**

The domestic animals like cow, ox, goat and buffalo sometimes fall seriously ill. They suffer from high fever with foot and mouth diseases. The folk and peasant visit *Jhar-phuk* doer for their treatment. The *Jhar-phuk* doer does *Jhar-phuk* treatment of cattle fever and other diseases in the same way as that of *Jhar-phuk* treatment of a man suffering from high fever.

Jhar-phuk Treatment of Snake bite and Dog bite to animal

The folk and rural folk also take help of *Jhar-phuk* treatment in case of snake bite and dog bite of animals in the same way as they take help in case of snake bite and dog bite of man.

Totaka (Protective Magic)

Totaka is a protective white magic which is performed to avoid the attack of evil spirits, witches, evil eyed and evil tonged persons. It is a protective measure or remedies. *Totaka* encounters the black magic and attack of evil spirits. In *totaka* following remedial acts are performed:

- Black cloth is tied to pregnant and lactating woman.
- Black thread is tied on hands and feet of newly delivered children.
- Black thread is tied in hands of bride and bridegroom.
- Black thread is tied in neck of pregnant and lactating cow, buffalo, goat etc.
- Black ointment (kajal) is applied on forehead of infants.
- Black ointment is applied in eye-brow of the bride and bridegroom.
- Black ointment is applied in the neck of lactating woman and pregnant woman.
- To avoid the effect of *Najar-Gojar* (evil eye and evil mouth) red dry chillies are burnt.
- A broom or winnowing tray is tied in front of house to stop entrance of evil spirits.
- Black shoe or slipper is tied over the roof to avoid diseases in the family.
- An earthen pot containing black and white spots is placed in the field of vegetables to protect fruits. It is also done in case of other crops.
- *Ajawain, Lawang, Kapoor, Lohban and Gugul* are burnt in house daily to encounter the attack of evil spirit, witches and black magic.
- *Tabij* of sacred places are held to avoid attack of witches and evil spirits.
- Swastik sign with black ointment is made at the gate of house to avoid effect of black magic and witches in house and family members.
- White onion is kept in pocket to avoid the impact of storm.
- Garland of garlic is made and worn to neutralize high cold fever.

6

Religious Concepts, Diseases and Treatment

According to popular folk and peasant belief system, Gods and Goddesses also cause diseases, when they become displeased with the behaviour of a person. They make a person to suffer from serious diseases. Thus, diseases are caused due to anguish of deities. Hence, in order to cure diseases and remain healthy, Gods are worshipped and their hymns are recited. Special worships are also performed when the patient become quite well. The worship of Gods and Goddesses is taken as a treatment for the cure of diseases.

As per the folk belief system, health is a divinal boon and disease is a divinal curse. That is why in our *Dharmashastra,* emphasis has been placed on attainment of *purushartha* (*Dharma, Artha, Kama* and *Moksha)* through accepting the supremacy of Gods and Goddesses. We must always follow good path shown by deities. We should lead simple life with high thinking. The God has sent us on this earth to enjoy the pleasure of heaven by good acts, good food, and good health. We should lead regular and law abiding life. In the proud of wealth and strength, we forget that our health is divinal gift. We start doing acts against path shown by deities of societies. We start using our body as machine and creating pathological conditions in the society. Being displeased, God makes us patient by creating diseases. There are a number of diseases which are taken as curse of Gods and Goddesses. For example, Cholera, diarrhoea, jaundice, pox, leprosy, heart disease, liver disease and non-curable diseases.

In folk and peasant society, there is a tradition of worshipping and appeasing deities in order to remain healthy. In every folk and peasant communities, there are some places dedicated in the name of Gods and Goddesses with their symbols. These symbols may be of wood pole, bamboo pole, big tree, tree root, mud hill, bushes and temple like structures. These religious places are known as sacred centres. On these places worships are performed, which are known as sacred performances. There are priests or specialists who medicate between folk and peasant people and the deities. They are known as sacred specialists. In order to cure disease, special worship is promised to Gods and Goddesses. After wish fulfilment, a special worship is performed. Deities become pleased with worship and removes all types of troubles—physical, divinal and bodily. Devotion, worship, deities, sacred centres, sacred specialists and sacred performances all are part and parcel of religious belief system. Following this belief system, people go in the shelter of deities for cure of diseases.

Now, a description of some diseases and their treatment by worship of deities is being presented one by one for the purpose of study.

Pox

According to folk and peasant belief system, the disease of pox is caused by the mother Goddess Bhagvati. When mother Goddess becomes displeased, she causes the disease of pox in the body of a person that is why, it is known as mother disease. This is of two types *Chhoti Mata* (small pox) and *Bari Mata* (big pox). The disease of small pox is not so dangerous. But the disease of big pox is very dangerous. This is taken as contagious disease. Big pox is very dangerous. This is taken as contagious disease. It spreads through contact of patient. Thus, a patient spreads it in the society from one person to another. That is why, a patient is separated from the other family members. The care taker of the patient maintains cleanliness. He/she takes special care on the bed, bed sheet, and other clothes of patient as well as his/her own cleanliness.

According to prevalent tradition, the best means to cure this disease is to get blessing of mother Goddess Bhagvati. A family member of the patient visits in the temple place of mother Goddess and seek special pardon to cure the disease. He/she also makes promise to Goddess Bhagvati to offter special worship after the cure of the patient. He/she offters some money to be spent on the worship of the Goddesses after cure. He/she brings Bhabhut (ash of *Dhup, Gugul, Lohban)* from the place of Bhagvati as a blessing material and puts near the patient. *Lohban, Gugul* and *Dhup* are burnt in the room of patient. A lamp is kept always burning with *ghee*. This process is repeated till the patient does not become cured. When the disease starts becoming cure, it is meant that the Goddess Bhagvati has cured the patient. When the patient is fully recovered, all rooms and courtyard of the house are washed property with cow dung, soil and water. All clothes are washed with surf. A special worship is offered to Goddess Bhagvati for accepting the prayer and curing the patient. Special worship in temple of Goddess Bhagvati is performed with the help of priest. The ritual of

Hawana is done with *dhup, gugul, ghee,* sunfried rice, black til, jaggary and sweets. The ritual of *Hawana* marks the completion of the worship offered to Devi Bhagvati. Belief in Goddess Bhagvati is so deep that without making a promise to offer special worship after cure, people do not take any kind of medicine.

Cholera (Haija)

It is taken as very dangerous disease. It spreads through contact from one person to another and in entire community. It is regarded contagious and killer disease, an epidemic. The person suffering from this disease meets vomiting and loose motion frequently. As a result the water of body gets lost and the patient results in death, if proper treatment is not done. According to prevalent folk and peasant belief system, cholera is caused when mother Goddess Bhagvati becomes angry on the behaviour of people. Being angry, she sends the disease of cholera in the community. When people becomes aware of spread of cholera in the community, they rush towards the place of Goodess Bhagvati, bow down head to the feet of image of Bhagvati to pray to cure the people and promise to offer a special worship soon after the cure of the disease from the community. Before starting modern treatment, the blessing of the Goddess is sought by prayer and offering of coins for performing special worship after cure. The promise is fulfilled immediately. People still have deep faith in the worship of Goddess Bhagvati for the cure of disease of cholera. People offer sacrifice of goat as a part of special worship and do *Havana* in which *ghee, oat*, black *til,* loaf sugar, curd, sweets, coconut and other *prasads* are sacrified in fire in a fire tank made for this purpose. After special worship people start leading normal life in the village community.

Plague

Plague is very serious contagious killing disease. The folk and peasant people leave their community when they hear that the disease of plague has spread. It is believed that this disease spread when the vehicle of Lord Ganesha (rats) becomes angry. Mouse when becomes angry, the disease of plague spreads. The folk and peasant people worship Lord Ganesha to control the mouse. When Lord Ganesha is pleased, he asks his vehicle mouse to stop the disease immediately. When people heard the spread of plague, they run towards the temple of Lord Ganesha to make promise to offer special worship, when the disease is cured. The people fulfils the promise made to Lord Ganesha immediately after the cure and control of the disease of plague.

Leprosy

According to folk and peasant belief system, the disease of Leprosy is caused by curse of Sun-God. When Sun-God becomes displeased with the behaviour of a person, he curses him/her thus causing leprosy. The scientific concept associated with occurring the disease of leprosy does not coincide with religious concept of Hindu folk and peasant. The members of folk and peasant society still have deep religious faith in Sun-God as cursing an individual with the disease of leprosy. The members of folk and peasant community never want to displease the Sun-God knowingly and unknowingly. Because Sun-God is only visible God who never gives pardon to a person for wrong deeds. In order to please Sun-God people offter water to Sun God daily in the morning after bathing. They observe fast on Sunday or do not take salt on Sunday. People perform *Chhath Vrata* which is held in four days during Kartik and Chait months of our Hindu national calendar. People have faith that the worship of Sun-God provides relief and cure of the disease of leprosy. The persons suffering from leprosy are found sitting nearby the temple of Sun-God and mother Goddess Bhawani. They are found begging money, food and clothes. Mother Goddess and Sun-God cure the disease of Leprosy by gracing the patients good and attractive body. Hearing *Surya Purana* in sun-temple is also very beneficial.

Jaundice

According to folk and peasant belief system, the disease of Jaundice is caused by curse of Sun-God. When Sun-God becomes angry with a person by his/her behaviour, he causes the disease of jaundice in his/her body as punishment. But when Sun-God is offered a special worship, the disease of Jaundice is cured for ever. With such belief in mind folk and peasant people offer a special worship to Sun-God for curing jaundice. They observe Sunday fast, offering of water to Sun-God daily in the morning after bathing, *Chhath Vrata* in the month of Kartik and Chait and offer worship to Sun-God in Sun temples. Hearing *Surya Purana* and performing rituals in Sun-temple is very beneficial for the cure of Jaundice disease.

Cure of Impotency Disease

According to folk and peasant belief system, the disease of impotency occurs due to curse of Sun-God. When the behaviour of an individual is against the norms established by Gods and deities, Sun-God punishes an individual by causing impotency. But when an individual makes correction in his behaviour and starts offering a special worship, the disease of impotency is cured by the Sun-God. The Sun-God removes the disease of impotency and provides good health to him. That is why impotent individual visits the temple of Sun-God to perform special worship and hear *Surya Purana.*

Cure of Barrenness Disease

According to folk and peasant belief system, Sun-God is giver of progeny. He blesses children to a barren couple. When a woman is not blessed by a son or daughter after four or five years of marriage, she is treated as suffering from barrenness. As per belief system, barrenness is taken as cure of Sun-God, who is giver of progeny. Such women and their husbands start worshipping Sun-God in different ways to make him pleased to provide progeny. They offer regularly water to Sun-God in the morning, observe Sun-day fast, visit Sun-temples, offers special worship, performs rituals, and *Chhath Vrata* and hear *Surya Purana* and *Harvansh Purana.* Such religious performances please Sun-God and mother *Chhathi.* They bless the couple with child.

Cure of Eye Disease

According to prevalent belief system of folk and peasant communities, the disease of eye is caused by the curse of mother Shitla. When mother Shitla becomes angry by the behaviour of an individual, she causes eye disease as curse. But when she pleases with the changed behaviour as per norms established by God and deities, she cures the eye diseases. Due to prevalence of such belief, folk and peasant communities do not forget to offer worship to mother Shitla in Srawan, Ashwin and Chait months of our national calendar. They offer a special worship for the cure of eye diseases of a person.

Religious Protection of Untimely Death

Untimely death is taken as curse for the individual and his/her family. Untimely death occurs when the God becomes displeased. The God and deity sends signals to make a change in behaiovur time to time. But the individual concerned does not pay attention and make no change in his/her behaviour and untimely death occurs. People visit the temple of Lord Shiva, performs worship and Rudrabhishek and Mahamrityunjay Jap. Performing

Mahamrityunjay Jap protects an individual from untimely death.

Religious Activity for Increasing Longevity

In order to achieve longevity, folk and peasant people take blessings of Gods and deity daily in the morning and before sleeping. People visit temple, offer prayers, and seek blessing in the early morning. They also offer prayer in the evening. Morning and evening prayers to God and deities increase our longevity.

Worship of Village Deity

In folk and peasant villages one finds abodes of different Gods and Goddesses. They are known as village deity. They control the behaviour of village dwellers and provide good harvest, good health and longevity. The annual or time to time worship by village dwellers provide good harvest, Good health and longevity. Their annual or time to time worship by village dwellers brings good health, wealth and longevity. That is why, the worship of village deity is done regularly at family level and village level.

Worship of Town Deity

Each town has its own Gods and Goddesses. They are known as town deity. They are worshipped by town dwellers at family level and community level. Their worship provides good health, wealth, progeny and longevity to town dwellers. Town deity protect health, wealth and property. The deity blesses the town dwellers with all types of prosperity including health.

Cure of Disease by Lunar Vrat

The folk and peasant communities take help of Vrat for good health and cure of diseases. The women-folk observe the *Vrat* on *Chauth* to please Moon-God. They remain fast for the whole day. In night they offer *Arghya* to Moon-God with water, milk, fruits and *pakwan* (*Prasad)* cooked for this purpose. At the end of *Vrata,* they perform the ritual of *Hawan* in which items of *Prasad,* dry coconut covered in red cloth, *ghee,* oat, rice and black til are offered to Fire-God Agni. The observance of this *vrata,* cures all kinds of diseases, brings all kinds of peace and prosperity and provides longevity of family members.

Cure of Disease by Jitia Vrata

The women-folk and peasant community observe the *Vrata* of Jitia in the month of Ashwin. They remain on fast without water. In the evening, they hear the story of *Jitia Vrata* and perform worship to Jitvahan God (Sun-God) with fruits and *Pakwan* (cooked *Prasad* in *ghee* and gur), but they do not breakfast. They breakfast in next morning by offering worship and *Hawana* to Jit-Vahan Deo (Sun-God). This *Vrata* is observed by all mothers for good health, cure of diseases and longevity of their children. Jitvahan Deo provides good health to children, cures all diseases to children and brings longevity to children. He remains always with children to protect them and pull them out from miseries.

Cure of Disease by Tij Vrata

The Bhado Tij *vrata* is observed on 3rd day of bright half of Bhado month by married women for good health and diseaseless body of husbands and for all kinds of prosperity in the family. Married women observe a fast of 24 hours and do not take even water. They prepare varieties of *pakwan* and offer worship to Moon God with fruits and *Prasad.* They hear story of Lord Shiva, Parvati and Ganesha. They do Rat-jaga (not sleeping at night) by singing prayer songs. *Geet* and *Bhajan* are sung to seek blessing of Moon-God, Lord Shiva, mother Parvati and Lord Ganesha for long healthy and prosperous life of husbands and alround development of family.

Cure of Disease by Chauth Vrata

The *vrata* of *chauth* is performed in the month of Bhado on fourth day of bright half of Bhado month by married woman for long and diseaseless life of husband. Married women observe fast on this day. In the evening, when moon rises, they offer *Arghya* to Lord Moon with fruits and *pakwan.* They see the mouth and face of their husbands through a sieve after performing bath next morning. Then, they breakfast. The observance of this *vrata* keeps husbands free from any kind of accident and attack of evil spirits. This *vrata* has preventive and curative health functions. This *vrata* is repeated each year.

Bhai Duj Vrata

The *vrata* of Bhai Duj is performed in the month of Kartik on second day of bright half. This *Vrata* is observed by sisters for long and healthy life of brothers. The performance of this *vrata* keeps brothers physically and mentally fit. This *vrata* is performed each year.

Ram Navami Vrata

The *vrata of* Ram Navami is performed on the 9th day of bright half of Chaitra month by the people of all age and sex group belonging to Hindu Communities. The people remains on fast and offer worship to Lord Rama, Janaki, Lakshman and Lord Hanumana. The observance of *Vrata* keep people fit physically, mentally and economically.

Janmastami Vrata

The *vrata* of Janmastami is performed in the month of Bhado on 8th day of dark half. This *Vrata* is performed by children, men and women of Hindu community. The people observe fast and offer worship to Lord Krishna and Radha. They breakfast next morning. The performance of *vrata* cures diseases and keep people fit physically, mentally and economically. It removes all kinds of bodily, divinal and physical griefs.

Durga Puja Vrata

The *vrata* of Durga Puja is observed in the month of Ashwin from 1st day to 9th day of bright half. The devotees observe fast, food taboos and physical purity for nine days. They perform bath and clean their body. They offer worship to Goddess Durga and then share milk, fruit and sweet dishes. They do not take onion and garlic. On 9th day they do *Hawan.* The performance of *Hawana* marks the end of the *Vrata.* The observance of this *Vrata* brings good health, good wealth and peace in the family. This *Vrata* is observed each year by one family member.

Lakshmi Puja Vrata

The *Vrata* of Lakshmi Puja is observed on the full dark night of Kartik month for good health, wealth and all kinds of peace in the family by the women head of the family. She observes fast and performs worship to Goddess Lakshmi with sweets, fruits and *khir* (rice and loaf sugar cooked in milk) in the evening. She does the worship of Goddess Lakshmi again at midnight. The Goddess Lakshmi becomes pleased with worship and *Vrata. She* provides good wealth, health and peace in the family and blesses the family with alround development.

Chhath Vrata

The *Chhath Vrata* is performed in the month of Kartik and Chaitra on 4th to 7th day of bright half. The *Vrata* is completed in a period of four days from *Tithi* fourth to seventh in both months. This is a very pious *Vrata* and is performed with great devotion, piousness and purity. The first day of *Vrata* is known as *Asnan-Khan,* second day is known as *Kharana* or *Lohara,* third day is called *upavas* and the fourth or final day is termed as *Paran.* This *Vrata* is performed by males and females both. In the first day, the body is cleaned and light meal of sunfried rice, green pulse and vegetable of pumpkin is taken. After eating meal at night, the body and mouth is cleaned properly. On the second day the devotee observes fast. In the evening devotees perform bath and cook *Prasad* of *kharana* which consists of *Khir,* and *puri.* Devotees offer worship to Sun-God and share the *Prasad* of *kharana.* Then the *Prasad* of *Kharana* is distributed among all family members, friends and relatives. Devotees observe fast on third day and in the evening offer *Arghya* to setting Sun-God with fruits and *pakwan* kept in a new winnowing tray. Next morning Araghya is again offered to Lord rising Sun. At the end, *Hawana* ritual is done and fast is broken. The performance of this *Vrata* brings good health, happiness, wealth, peace, prosperity, and alround development of family and family members

Ananta Chaturdashi Vrata

The Ananta Chaturdashi vrata is observed on 14th day of bright half of Bhado month. On this day, devotees observe fast and afternoon offer worship to Lord Krishna, who is also known as Ananta Bhagwan, with milk, *gur,* sweets, curd, fruits and *Khir-Puri.* The Ananta Vrata Katha is heard with great devotion. The observance of this *Vrata* brings good health, harvest, happiness and all types of satisfaction and development.

Trayodashi Vrata

The Trayodashi Vrata is observed on 13th day of bright half of Baishakh and Phalgun months in which one day fasting is observed. The worship of Lord Shiva and his family members is offered in the evening with singing *Bhajan* and *Kirtan.* The observance of this *Vrata* and worship of Lord Shiva and his family members bring good health, harvest, happiness and alround development in the family.

Basant Panchami Vrata

The Vrata of Basant Panchami is observed on the 5th day of bright half of Magh month. Devotees observe fast and offer worship to Goddess Saraswati, Lakshmi, Kali, Lord Shiva and his entire family members. The observance of this *Vrata* brings good health, cure of diseases, happiness and alround development.

Mai Puja

The worship of Devi Mai is done in the month of Chait, Sawan and Ashwin month on 7th to 9th day of bright half at family level. On this occasion Goddess Bhagwati (Devi Mai) is worshipped with fruits, flowers and *pakwan.* Devotees observe fast and breakfast after worship. The worship of Devi Mai brings good health, wealth, progeny and alround development of family members. This puja is done each year as preventive and corrective and curative measures for goal health, wealth and progeny.

Nag Panchami Puja

This *puja* is clebrated in the month of Shravan on 5th bright half day in which people offer worship to images of Lord Nag Baba (Snake God) with *Lava,* and milk. The worship is offered Snake God which prevents death due to snake bite in the family.

Kul Devi-Devata Puja

Kul Devi-Devta Puja is offered to family deity each year in the month of Sawan on 7th or 9th day of bright half. On this day, the *malik* and *malkin* observe fast, prepare and cook *pakwan* and offer worship to family deity whose place remains in a wall of a room of house. This room is termed as Kul Devi-Devta room. The worship of family deity is done each year. The worship of family deity brings good health, harvest, harmony, peace and development in the family.

Ekadashi Vrata

The Vrata of Ekadashi is observed on 11th day of dark and bright half of all twelve months of a year. The devotee observe fast, offer water to Sun-God, *Peepal* tree and *Tulsi* plant. They offer worship to Lord Vishnu. After offering worship, they break fast with sweet dishes or salty dishes cooked in

Sendha Namak (pure white salt). The observance of this *vrata* brings good health, wealth, progeny and all kinds of good development in the family. It also provides *Moksha* after death.

Ravivar Vrata

Ravivar (Sunday) is observed on each Sunday continuously for a period of 4, 8, 12, 15, or 18 sundays. The devotee observes fast and shares saltless meal after offering worship to Sun-God and Tulsi plant. The performance of this *Vrata* bring good health, wealth, progeny and prosperity in the family. The Katha of Ravivar Vrata is also heard.

Somvar Vrata

The Vrata of Somvar is observed on each Monday at least for 16 Mondays continuously. The devotee observes fast, offer worship to Lord Shiva and his family members with fruits, *Prasad* and *dhup, ghee, agarvati.* He/she also hears the *Katha* (story) of Somvar Vrata by a specialist. This *Vrata* is also performed for good health, wealth, progeny, peace and prosperity in family. At the end *Havana* is done and food materials are offered to *Brahmans.*

Mangalvar Vrata

The Vrata of Mangalvar is performed on each Tuesday at least for 16 Tuesdays without break. The devotee observes fast and offers worship to Goddess Bhagvati and Lord Hanumana wearing red clothes and offering red sweets, flowers and fruits. He/she hears the story of Mangalvar Vrata. Then the fast is broken. At the end of *Vrata, Hawana* is performed. Food materials and red clothes are given to the priest of temple or *Brahmans.* The observance of this *Vrata* brings good health, wealth, peace, prosperity and all kinds of success in the family.

Buddhavar Vrata

The Vrata of Buddhavar is performed on each Wednesday continuously for 16 Wednesdays without break. The devotee observes fast and offers worship to Lord Ganesha with *Dub* grasses yellow flowers, fruits and *Prasad.* He/she hears the Katha of Buddhavar Vrata. At the end of the worship, *Hawana* is performed. Food materials, clothes and rupees are offered to the temple priests. Observance of *vrata* brings good health, wealth progeny and prosperity.

Vrihaspativar Vrata

The Vrata of Vrihaspativar is observed on each Thursday continuously for a period of 16 Thursdays without any fail. The devotee observes fast, wears yellow dresses and offers worship with yellow flowers to Lord Vishnu. He/she hears the story of Vrihaspativar Vrata katha. On final Vrihaspativar Vrata, *Dan-Dakshina* is given to the *Brahman* priest. The observance of this *Vrata* brings good health, wealth, peace, prosperity and all kinds of success in family.

Shukravar Vrata

The Vrata of Shukravar is observed on each Friday continuously for 16 Friday without any break. The devotee observes fast and offers worship to Goddess Lakshmi, Parvati, Ganesh and Santoshi Mata. He/she offers white *Prasad,* flowers and wears yellow dress. The story of Shukravar Vrata is heard. On the 16th Friday, final worship is offered. After worship, *Havana* is done. Feast is served to *Brahmans* and unmarried boys and girls. The observance of *Vrata* brings good health, long life, wealth, peace, prosperity and success of all kinds. On final day, *Dan-Dakshina* is given to the priest.

Shanivar Vrata

The Vrata of Shanivar is performed on each Saturday continuously for 16 Saturdays. The devotee observes fast, visits temple of Shani Dev, wears black dress and offers mustard oil, black cloth, *kala til,* black umbrella and iron knife to Shani Dev. The observance of Shanivar Vrata brings good health, wealth, prosperity, peace and success of all kinds. On the final day of worship, *Dan-Dakshina* is given to the priest *Brahmans.* The Sudarshan hymns is recited one lakh times in a week. At least, two expert Brahamans are required for this purpose. One the last day, the ritual of *Hawan* is made and *Dan-Dakshina* is given to the *Brahmans.* The recitation of this *path* is beneficial in recovering good health, wealth, peace, prosperity and different kinds of success in life of an individual.

Sunderkand Path

In order to get good health and recovery from various kinds of health problems besides mental and physical recovery, the reading or hearing the path of Sunderkanda of *Ramayana* is regarded as very much beneficial religiously. The persons suffering from health problems and different kinds of grief read or hear Sundarkanda path regularly for one and quarter month.

This religious practice removes all mental, physical, bodily and divinal griefs.

Hanuman Chalisa Path

Reading, or hearing or reciting Hanuman Chalisa is regarded beneficial religiously to get rid of bodily, physical, mental and divinal griefs. Persons suffering from such agonies visit the temple of Lord Hanumana, offer red cloth, red flowers and water, hear or read Hanuman Chalisa after performing bath daily in the morning. The daily practice of Hanumn Chalisa path cures physical, mental and divinal agonies of a devotee.

Devi Durga Path

Reading or hearing of Devi Durga Path during Navratra of Chait and Ashwin months is regarded as beneficial religiously for cure of various kinds of trouble such as physical, mental and divinal. Those who are literates read Durga Path. But those who are not literate hear Durga Path continuously for nine days from Ist to 9th day of bright half of Chait month and Ashwin month. Reading and hearing Durga Chalisa and *path* brings good health, wealth, progeny, educational and occupational benefits in family.

Satya Narayan Swami Katha

The hearing of Satya Narayan Swami Katha on full bright night of each months continuously for a year is regarded as very much beneficial to get rid of all types of troubles—physical, mental and divinal. Satya Narayan Swami, Lord Vishnu, is regarded as giver of physical, mental and divinal pleasures. People enjoy all kinds of pleasure by his blessing and grace. In order to get his grace and pleasure people hear Satya Narayan Swami Katha in his house of each night of Purnima (Full bright day) continuously for a year. The devotee observes fast, prepares pakwan, purchases fruits, dhup, *ghee, agarbati,* milk, curd, *Tulsi* leaves and betel leaves to be offered to Lord Satya Narayan Swami. The *Brahman* priest is called to get the *puja* performed. *Nai* (barber) is called to invite the community members to hear Satya Narayan Swami Katha. The Brahman recites the Katha of Swami Satya Narayan in Sanskrit and Hindi after establishing Gauri Ganesh, *Kalash, Nawagraha* and Satya Narayan Swami at proper place and sites. The priest plays conch at the end of each chapter of Satya Narayan Katha. At the end, *Hawan* ritual is done. Prayer songs are sung to obtain grace of Lord Satya Narayan Swami. *Prasad* is distributed among all present there and houses of the community. This religious practice helps in getting good health, wealth, progeny, property and success of various kinds.

Thus, from above account, it is quite clear that members of folk, peasant and even urban communities observe religious practices and traditions to get rid of bodily, physical, mental and divinal griefs.

Mahamrityunjai Jaap

One lakh and twenty five thousand times recitation of Mahamrityunjai mantra by specialist Brahmans is regarded as beneficial for curing diseases and saving the life of a person concerned. This is a costly religious means for cure of disease and improvement of pitiable condition of a person. This *Jap* (recitation) is done with the help of a Rudraksh bead containing 108 Rudraksha. This preventive and curative religious health practice is costly and requires expert *Pandit* to get the recitation of Mahamrityunjai hymns done successfully. If not done properly, it can bring adverse effect. It takes at least a week, but it can be completed in two, four and five weeks. Its completion depends upon the number of *pandits* employed for this purpose. On the last day, the ritual of *Hawan* is done and *Dan-Dakshina* is given to Brahman priest. This *jap* is done in a famous Shiva temples.

Rahu-Ketu Jap

In this *Jap,* the hymns to please the planet—Rahu and Ketu, is recited one lakh and twenty five thousand times with the help a green bead containing 108 grains. This *Jap* is done to please Rahu and Ketu for good health, wealth, peace, prosperity and all kinds of success in life. This *Jap* is done in a famous temple dedicated to Lord Shiva, Vishnu, Hanuman or Devi Mai. Expert Brahmans are required to do and complete the *Jap* of Rahu Ketu Mantra. It can take a week to five weeks time in completion depending upon the number of Brahamins employed for this purpose. This is done for cure of serious diseases and adverse physical condition. The *Jap* of this *mantra* improves the health and other physical conditions of the person for whom *Jap* is recited. On the final day *Hawan* is done and *Dan-Dakshina* to Brahman priest is made.

Sat Sudarshan Jap

This *Jap* is done in order to please Lord Vishnu for removing physical and mental griefs of various kind. This *Jap* is completed in a week. Hymns of Lord Vishnu is recited with the help of expert. It is completed in a week. At the last day *Hawana* ritual is done and *Dan-Dakshina* is made to Brahmans priest.

7

Scientific Concepts of Disease and Treatment

In preceding chapters, discussion on magical and religious practices related to disease and treatment prevalent among people have been discussed. In this chapter, discussion is being made on scientific causes of diseases, their treatment and scientific methods of treatment practiced by the people.

There is no doubt that today we are living in an era of science and technology. It is quite natural that this era has influenced our thinking related to occurrence of diseases and their treatment through modern scientific methods. But it cannot be said safely that we are not practicing magical and religious beliefs and practices pertaining to diseases and their treatment. It is also a fact that scientific method of identifying diseases and their treatments have attained popularity among the people due to scientific knowledge and researches in medical sciences. We have been able to know the diseases of each parts of the body. For better diagnosis and treatment we have been able to establish separate departments under different medical specialists. We have been able to discover medicines of different types of diseases. Now, we have been able to treat killer diseases like T.B., AIDS, Cancer, Ebola and others. All these have become possible due to scientific inventions and discoveries in medical science. The medical sciences have developed scientific concept of pregnancy, delivery, rearing and caring children, lactation period, space between two births, sexually transmitted diseases, communicable diseases, nutrition, health and sanitation and killer disease. A number of allopathic medicines have become integral part of primary treatment of disease even among folk and rural masses.

Now, it is fitness of the thing to present here the scientific concepts of disease, health and treatment one by one. These are as follows:

- Children caring responsibility.
- Some important scientific information related to women and child health.

- Proper time of child birth.
- Safe maternity.
- Breast feeding.
- Development of children.
- Vaccination.
- Diarrhoea.
- Cough and cold (Pneumonia).
- Health and sanitation.
- Malaria.
- AIDS
- T.B.
- Leprosy
- Cancer.

Children Rearing and Caring Responsibility

According to traditional health concept, the responsibility of rearing and caring children lies in the hands of women. But according to modern concept, the responsibility of rearing and caring also lies in the hands of males. It has been found that women have to share majority of agricultural and domestic work in developing countries. They do domesting chores, like cleaning, rooms, courtyard and house, cleaning cooking utensils, serving food utensils and water storing utensils, bringing water from water sources and cooking and serving meals to children and other family members. Besides these household chroes, they also do work related to agriculture and domestication of animals. They also do marketing of essential commodities in local *Haat (*bazaar). They take care of ill family members. Besides performing such work, they have to deliver children and rear and care them. Thus, majority of burden of society is shared by women in developing countries like India. According to modern health concepts, women also have equal right to keep themselves healthy and physically fit. But women cannot enjoy this equal right without cooperation of their male counterparts. Therefore, males should also share responsibility of rearing and caring children so that female counterparts could also keep themselves healthy and physically fit.

Some Important Scientific Informations Related to Women and Children Health

It is proper to present here some important scientific information related to women and children health. They are as follows:

- In our society the health condition of women and children can be made better by maintaining a gap of two to three years between births of two children, not making a woman pregnant before eighteen (18) years of age and not producing more than two or three children from a woman.
- During the period of pregnancy, a pregnant woman must consult health workers for tests related to pregnancy and other problems.
- The delivery must take place under the supervision of a trained *dai* or health workers.
- For a period of first six months only breast feeding should be provided. Other kinds of feed should be avoided.
- After an age of six months, the child should be served supplementary food such as cow milk and soft boilded food materials.
- Children below the age of three should be served meals five to six times in a day. Their meal should contain some *ghee* and boiled vegetables.
- The children suffering from Diarrhoea should be served liquid food like milk, pulse water, starch and ORS to avoid loss of water in body. On serious condition of dehydration, health workers should be consulted.
- The vaccination course should be followed strictly.
- The pregnant woman should also take injection of tetanus.
- On continuation of cough and cold, health worker should be consulted.
- Pregnant women and lactating women should use lavatory essentially.
- After defecation, women should wash hands with soap.
- Before and after sharing meal, women should use soap for washing hands.
- If drinking water is not safe, boiled water should be taken.
- After illness, children should be served some extra food to get recovered quickly and to get health loss compensated.
- The weight of children should be taken continuously. In first year, the weight should be taken in each month, but in second and third years, weight should be measured in every two months. When there is no increase in weight for two months, then it is possible that the child is suffering from some problems.

Proper Time of Child Birth

It is also fitness of the thing to deal here with proper scientific time of child birth as it is directly related to health of women and children. All mothers and women of our society should know that for better health of mother and children, there should be a gap of two to three years between births of two children. They should not bear more and more children. Frequent births of children result in untimely death of mother and children. Some scientific informations related to proper timing of child birth are as follows:

- The birth of a child before 18 years and after 35 years of age of a woman increases the risk of life of both child and mother.
- Less than two years of gap between two children increases 50 per cent of death risks of child.
- More than three pregnancies increases the child and mother death risk. This risk increases more in fourth time pregnancy.
- In order to maintain gap between two births and avoid more than two pregnancy family welfare measures should be adopted.
- The family having two children take proper care in rearing of children.

Some Extra Scientific Information

Some extra scientific informations regarding children and mother health are as follows:

- In each year nearly one lakh and twenty five thousand pregnant women die in our country due to complexities during delivery.
- Nearly one and half lakh children become motherless due to mother mortality in delivery.
- By providing proper scientific informations the death of mother during pregnancy and delivery can be prevented.
- From the point of view of health, a girl must avoid pregnancy before 18 years of age.
- A child born before 18 years of age of mother has low weight and suffer from death risk during very first year of age.
- All girls must be provided occasion to become mother only after 18 years of age.
- The communities having the custom of child marriage should avoid it or should adopt family welfare measures and should produce child after 18 years of age.
- The pregnancy after 35 years creates life risks of both mother and children.
- Father and mother should maintain a gap of at least two years between birth of two children.

- Couple should avoid unwanted birth by employing family welfare measure.
- A gap less than two years between birth of two children creates physical and mental risk for the child. Non-observance of this gap also creates the problem of abortion. If such child is delivered, it is quite possible that the child will meet death during very first year.
- Becoming pregnant after three deliveries is very risky for the life of woman.
- Majority of health centres have useful means of family welfare means. To avoid unwanted births or untimely birth, family welfare measures should be used.

Scientific Concept of Safe Maternity

In our country, nearly more than 400 women die everyday during pregnancy and at the time of delivery. Therefore, it is fitness of the thing to present here the scientific concept of safe maternity for the people. Some important information in this regard is as follows:

- The health risk during pregnancy and delivery can be controlled with the help of trained *Dai* or other health worker.
- Family members of pregnant woman should know the health risk during pregnancy and delivery. They should extend full cooperation to pregnant and expectant woman in treatment at right time.
- The pregnant and expectant woman needs more diet during pregnancy and expectancy. They should take light meal after regular intervals.
- The pregnant and expectant woman needs more rest. Therefore, other family members should cooperate such woman.
- A gap of two to three years should be maintained between births of two children.
- A woman should not meet pregnancy before 18 years and after 35 years of age.
- The unhealthy adolescent girls have to face more health problem during pregnancy.

Some More Scientific Information Related to Safe Maternity

For safe delivery and safe maternity, our health workers perform following functions:

- To send pregnant and expectant women to hospital when they face health trouble during pregnancy and expectancy.
- Regular check-up of blood pressure because it is harmful for expectant mother and child both.
- Supply of iron tablets on anaemic condition of pregnant women.
- To provide two injections of tetnus which protects expectant mother and child both.
- Regular check-up of child growth during expectancy.
- To provide tablets of malaria, if required.
- To prepare expectant mother for delivery of child.
- To tell child feeding and rearing methods.
- To advice for maintaining a gap of two to three years between births of two children.
- To advice to call trained *Dai* at the time of delivery pain because the trained *Dai* knows to caring patient to hospital after 12 hours of suffering from pregnancy pain.
- The advice for sanitation at the time of delivery so that infection could be avoided.
- To clean navel and cut it scientifically to avoid infections.
- To advice to carry hospital immediately when the child is in opposite direction.
- To advice means for preventing extra bleeding.
- To call senior doctors for help during emergency.
- To tell to what to do when the child does not start breathing soon after birth.
- To tell the time of starting breast feeding after birth.
- To clean cloths of the child properly.
- To advice mother to prevent unwanted birth by adopting family welfare methods.
- To make family members aware of risks related to pregnancy and delivery.

Pre-pregnancy Warning Signs

The followings are prepregnancy warning signs:

- A gap of less than two years between birth of two children.
- Less than 18 years and more than 35 years of age of mother.
- To deliver three or more than three children by a mother.
- To become the weight of previous delivered child less than 2 kg.
- Premature delivery of previous child.

- Previous time abortion or delivery of dead child.
- Less than 35 kg prepregnancy weight of a woman.
- Less than 145 c.m. pre-pregnancy stature of a woman.

Warning Signs During Pregnancy

The following are the warning signs during pregnancy:

- No increase in weight of a pregnant woman.
- An increase of 10 kg of weight during pregnancy is a good health sign.
- Appearing of yellowish sign under eyelid is a danger sign for a pregnant woman. It should be rosy colour.
- Appearance of swollen signs on legs, hands or face of a pregnant woman is a danger sign.

Danger Signs which Require Immediate Assistance

The four danger signs which require immediate assistance of health workers are as follows:

- Bleeding during pregnancy.
- High headache (Blood pressure).
- More and more vomiting.
- High fever.

Safety Measures During Pregnancy

- The family members of a pregnant woman should know to provide the special food during pregnancy.
- Family members should know to provide milk, vegetable, fruit and leafy vegetable during pregnancy.
- Family members should bring pregnant woman to health centre for recording weight regularly in each month. The weight of woman should increase each month. By the birth of child, her weight should record an increase of 10 to 12 k.g.
- No intake of wine, tobacco and other intoxicating materials or medicines.
- No intake of medicine without doctor's prescription.
- Planning of proper timing and spacing of births.
- No pregnancy before 18 years of age and after 35 years of age.

- Not to think to produce more than three children.
- Not help of illegal abortion.
- Not abortion by untrained persons.
- Abortion only by expert doctor.
- Attention on proper health of adolescent girls.

Breast Feeding

In our culture and tradition, a number of beliefs and traditions are prevalent pertaining to breast feedings. Mother's milk has attained high value in all cultures. But the first milk from the breast of mother is thrown on the ground with a belief that it is not clean and does harm to the child. But according to recent scientific researches, the first milk or framing milk of a mother contains a number of nutrients and is beneficial for the child to fight against infections. Therefore, it should not be thrown, rather it should be served to the newly born child. Breast feeding is very pious work and every member of society should extend cooperation to a mother for breast feeding.

Important Scientific Information Related to Breast Feeding

- The milk of mother is the best feed for a baby for four to six months.
- The mother should start breast feeding to the baby as early as possible after the birth.
- In general situation, every mother can breastfeed her baby.
- In order to get more and more milk for breast feeding, the baby should be breast fed again and again.
- Bottle feeding creates infection in baby which increases the risk of a number of diseases leading to the death of baby.
- The mother should breastfeed her baby for a period of two years.

Some More Information Related to Breast feeding

- Only milk of mother is the best feed for the baby till six months. The milk of cow, goat, camel and sheep is not substitute of mother's milk. Such milk can be served as extra-feed after six months.
- The mother's milk is sufficient to quench the thirst of baby during summer season till six months. Therefore, water should not be served. Mother milk is sufficient.

- The milk of mother save the baby from cough, cold, fever, diarrhoea and a number child diseases.
- If milk of mother is served for six months, the baby develops energy to fight against a number of diseases.
- The baby needs water and extra food after six months, but breast feeding should be continued for two years.
- The breast feeding is also beneficial in preventing next conception.
- Breast feeding frequently is a useful natural means for family welfare.
- A mother should start breast feeding within an hour of birth of baby.
- To allow more and proper flow of milk in breast, the practice of breast feeding should be started frequently.
- In our country, there is a belief that first milk of mother which is yellow and thick should not be served to the baby. But this practice is bad in the interest of health of mother and baby. This first milk contains a number nutrients which develop immune system of baby to fight against a number of diseases. Therefore, the first milk of mother should be served essentially. It should not be destroyed.
- The first time mother should take advantage of other experienced mother of the community in breast feeding.
- Nearly all breast feeding mothers should follow two types of practices:
    - Breast feeding should be done both in day and night.
    - The child should hold nipple properly in mouth.
- The baby should be in proper position at the time of breast feeding. If the position of baby is not proper at the time of breast feeding, it causes disease in nipple and breast.
- The proper position of a baby at the time of breast feeding is as follows:
    - The entire body of baby should be towards mother.
    - The child shows interest in breast feeding.
    - The mother does not feel pain in nipple at the time of breast feeding.
    - The child feels pleasure.
- The weeping of child does not always mean that the child is hungry and needs feeding. Sometimes, the baby weeps for rest in mother's lap.
- If essential, only then bottle feeding should be done. But the bottle and nipple should be cleaned properly with hot water and milk should be prepared in hot water.

- Where breast feeding is not possible, the milk of cow should be served with spoon. Spoon feeding is better than bottle feeding because it is easy to clean and wash.

Growth of Children

In our country malnutrition is a big problem which creates hindrance in mental and physical growth of millions of children. Therefore, for proper growth, the children should be given proper nutrition. Some important scientific information regarding proper growth of children are as follows:

- The weight of children should be taken in each month till one year of age. In second and third year, the weight should be taken at each three months. If there is not increase in weight of child for two months, then it is possible that the child is suffering from some health problem.
- For proper growth, the children need extra-food after six months.
- The children below three years of age need food five or six times in each day.
- The children below three years of age should be served some pulse, bread, rice, vegetable and *ghee* each day in their food.
- The children need extra-food after cure from illness to recover their health.
- All children need some nutritious food with vitamins.
- For proper mental and physical health of children, it is necessary to love and play with them.

Some Important Information Regarding Growth of Children

Some important informations regarding growth of children are as follows:

- One of the signs of growth of children is continuous increase in weight. If not, then it is not a good sign for the growth of children. In first year, the weight should be taken each month. If there is no weight increase in two months, health workers should be consulted.
- Vaccination helps children in recovering weight loss.
- Till six month of age, the milk of mother provides all kinds of nutrition to the children and it is very necessary for the growth of child.
- After six months, extra meals are given to children. They include

cow milk, goat milk, water, pulse water, leafy vegetable soup, and others. But they also create infections in children. Therefore, extra meals should be served after breast feeding.

- The breast feeding should be continued till two years of age besides extra food.
- After two years of age, the children should be served bread, rice, pulse, milk, fruit, *ghee* and home made food. They should be served five times in a day in between morning to going to sleep at night.
- The food of children should not be left open because they may be contaminated by germs and bacteria and become dirty. They cause a number of diseases and hamper the proper growth of children.
- Growing age of children requires extra energy. The extra energy can be provided by green fruits, dry fruits, vegetables, oil, *ghee* and milk.
- To avoid sight-loss leafy vegetables should be served to children along with meals. The leafy vegetable is important source of Vitamin A which controls the disease of blindness. Mother's milk, orange and yellow fruits, vegetables, papaya, mango, banana provide Vitamin A to children.
- The loss of appetite also creates problem in proper child growth. In case of loss of appetite, the children should be served sweet, salts and sour meals so that they could develop interest in sharing food and regain appetite.
- Illness creates uninterest in sharing food and regain appetite, therefore some extra food materials should be given to the child to compensate illness related loss.
- For proper growth of children, efforts should be made to keep child illness free. If child falls ill, doctor or health worker should be consulted immediately.
- In order to keep child illness free, only mother milk should be served for six months, thereafter extra food should be served in liquid form, all vaccination should be given in time, lavatory should be used, hands, mouth and kitchen should be kept quite clean.

Mental Growth of Children

Along with physical growth, mental growth of children is also essential. The proper mental growth of children can be maintained by following practices:

- The child should have emotional attachment with those involved in rearing and caring.
- From the very first day of birth, the infant starts giving and taking emotional attachment. Emotional attachment is very essential for internal growth of infant. He/she feels secure in the lap of mother and father. Gradually, he/she develops emotional attachment with grandfather, grandmother, brother, sister, uncle, aunt, and so on.
- Loving kins and cooperation among family members develop safety in the mind of children.
- Use of abusive words and quarrel among family members develop sense of insecurity in the minds of children.
- Mental health of children also depends on help extended by family members.
- For proper growth, children require love, affection, play and conversation in mother tongue.
- The children should be allowed to play and communicate with children and other community members.
- No talk, no play and no question answer with children make him sad and unhappy which is very harmful for mental growth of children.
- The child acquires social virtues and qualities with community members. Through acquiring process, he/she gradually becomes adolescent, young and finally adult. Therefore, children should be allowed to play, and communicate with community members.
- The children should be allowed to play with new kinds of toys as playing with toys also develops mental health of children.
- The children should be allowed to take own decision and solve problems in their own ways.
- The children should be allowed to learn drawing and painting which develop mental health of children.
- The children should be allowed to listen poems, stories and riddles; such practices enhance the mental ability and creativity.
- The children should be rewarded time to time because this helps in developing mental health of children.

Vaccination

Vaccination is very important scientific means for immunization to certain diseases to save infants and children from a number of life-taking diseases such as pneumonia, T.B., Polio, diphtheria, tetanus and *khasara* (measles).

Important Scientific Informations Related to Vaccination

Some important scientific informations related to vaccination are as follows:

- With the help of vaccination, children can be saved from a number of dangerous diseases like T.B., cough and cold, black cough, pneumonia, polio, tetanus, diphtheria and others.
- Vaccination is also helpful in saving child from malnutrition, disability and death.
- All primary injections should be given within one year of age.
- Children suffering from illness can be given life saving vaccination.
- All women between 15 to 44 years of age should take vaccination.

Some more Scientific Information Related to Vaccination

Some more scientific information related to vaccination are as follows:

- Vaccination saves children from a number of life taking diseases. Vaccination is taken with injection or oral drop. These injections increases the immunity of the children.
- If a child falls ill before injection, it means that injection has not been given timely.
- The child without vaccination has more death risk due to cough, cold, pneumonia, diphtheria, Tetanus and T.B.
- If children survives without these vaccinations, they become victims of malnutrition and other diseases.
- Blindness is caused by malnutrition.
- The children, who are not served polio drops, become victim of polio.
- The germs of tetanus develop in open wounds. If a child is not given tetanus injection, the child may die of tetanus.
- Mother's milk is a natural immunity which saves children from killing diseases.
- The children get immunity from the milk of mother to fight from killer diseases.
- Colostrums, the first milk, has more immunity to fight against life taking diseases.
- It is important that all basic injections should be given within a year.
- It is important to take all vaccinations in due course otherwise,

they do not bring desired positive result.

- Some vaccinations are given only one time, while others are repeated three times. Two doses must have a minimum gap of two month.

The Programme of Child Vaccination

Age	Vaccination	Name of Disease
Birth	B.C.G.	T.B.
1.5 month	DPT, Polio	Diphtheria, Black cough, Tetanus, Polio
2.5 month	DPT, Polio	Diphtheria, Black cough, Tetanus, Polio
3.5	DPT, Polio, Khasara	Diphtheria, Black cough, Tetanus, Polio
9 months	Khasara	Khasara
1.5 year	DPT, Polio	Diphtheria, Black cough, Tetanus, Polio
5 year	D.T.	Diphtheria, Tetanus

Some Important Information

If the child is ill, even then the vaccination table should be followed:

- To save the child from black cough, khasara, tetanus, Diphtheria and T.B., vaccination and follow-up of vaccination table is a must.
- Vaccination results in fever and swelling, but there is nothing to become restless. Rather the child should be served feeding properly like a healthy child. But when fever continues for three days, health workers should be contacted.
- The B.C.G. injection causes wound which is cured naturally. It does not need any treatment.
- In our country, some mothers deliver child in unhealthy condition. In this situation, mother and child both can become victim of Tetanus. Such mothers should take injection of tetanus.
- When the navel of child is cut with dirty knife or blade, it causes Tetanus. Navel should always be cut with a new blade or knife washed in boiled water.
- Tetanus injection during pregnancy save mother and child both from tetanus.
- All women in reproductive age should take Tetanus vaccination.
- All infants should be given three injection of Tetanus in very first year of age. It is included in D.P.T. The booster dose should be given in the age of five.

Diarrhoea

Diarrhoea is a killer disease for infants and child. In this disease the water of infants or child body goes out in the form of loose motion. This causes water loss or dehydration in the body. The disease causes death of nearly 10 lakh children every year. It is also one of the causes of malnutrition.

Some Important Scientific Information Related to Diarrhoea

Some important scientific information related to diarrhoea are as follows:

- The disease of diarrhoea causes water loss in the body of children and ultimately results in death. Therefore, children should be served sufficient liquid food so that loss of water in body could be compensated.
- If the child of lactating woman is suffering from diarrhoea, she should continue breast feeding to compensate water loss.
- The Diarrhoea suffering children should also be served liquid food.
- When the situation becomes serious, the child should be brought to a health worker.
- The children recovered from the Diarrhoea should be given more food than general at least for a week.
- Medicine should not be given without consulting a doctor.

For preventive measures against Diarrhoea following steps should be taken:

- ➢ Continuation of breast feeding.
- ➢ Vaccination of Khasara to all children.
- ➢ Use of lavatory.
- ➢ Use of clean water and food.
- ➢ Cleaning hands with soap before and after touching meals.

Some other Important Information Related to Diarrhoea

Some other important informations related to Diarrhoea are as follows:

- It is very serious disease causing death to children.
- The cause of death is flow of water from the body as thin loose motion.
- The children suffering from Diarrhoea should be given sufficient liquid drink materials.

- Giving liquid food or drink material helps in compensation of water loss.
- Mother's milk, water of pulse, water taken out from *khichari* and churned curd should be given as the liquid food.
- ORS should be given which is available in all medicine shops village shop, quack houses, health sub-centres and health centres.
- The ORS powder should be dissolved in clean water before giving to children suffering from Diarrhoea.
- ORS powder should not be dissolved in milk, soup or lemon soda.

Signs of Water Loss in Body

The main signs of water loss in body are as follows:

- Deepen eyes.
- More and more thirst.
- Not blow of tears from eyes on weeping.
- Fever.
- Loss of appetite.
- No desire of meal and water.
- A number of loose motions in an hour.
- Blood in loose motion/stool.

Healthy Steps for Cure of Diarrhoea

- When above signs appear in child, he/she should be brought in hospital.
- Medicine should be given according to prescription of a doctor.
- After cure from Diarrhoea, the child should be served some extra food.
- Severing extra food helps the child to compensate health loss due to Diarrhoea.
- The child can be taken as fully cured only when he/she starts playing and gaining weight as before.
- The frequency of breast feeding should be increased.

Measures to Prevent Diarrhoea

The following measures can be adopted to prevent Diarrhoea:

- The germs of Diarrhoea are found in loose motion. They enter inside body through mouth with the help of water, food, hands, utensils, flies, and nails of hands and feet. Therefore, every care should be taken to prevent such germs in the mouth of child.

- A number of families in our country are poor and do not have fresh drinking water and lavatory. Therefore, their children become victim of Diarrhoea easily. They should take some such steps as mentioned in points below to prevent the disease of Diarrhoea.
- Only mothers milk should be served for six months.
- After six months children should be given clean extra home-made liquid meals.
- Bottle feeding should be avoided and spoon feeding should be continued.
- Fresh drinking water should be used.
- The water of well, tank, stream, river should be used after boiling and cooling.
- Lavatory should be used.
- Night soil of children should also be dropped in lavatory.
- After defecation, hand should be washed with soap.
- Food materials should be preserved in utensils having lids.
- Fresh and immediately cooked food should be served as far as possible.
- Clean dresses, bed sheet, and bed cover should be used.
- Child should be washed in light hot water.

Health and Sanitation

All people should know that the cause of most of the diseases are germs and bacteria. They enter inside mouth through food and water and reach inside body. Now they start causing a number of diseases. Germs and bacteria can be prevented from entering mouth. It has been observed that communities lacking fresh and clean water sources, latrine facility and airy houses become more victim of diseases. There is a need to create awareness towards health and sanitation in such communities. The Government should support them with materials to erect latrine, urinal, drainage and airy houses. They should be trained for their participation in such sanitation and health related programmes.

Some Important Scientific Informations Related to Health and Sanitation

Some important scientific informations about health and sanitation are as follows:

- We should wash our hands with soap properly before touching food and after defecation.
- The use of latrine for defecation can prevent a number of diseases.
- Diseases can be prevented by use of safe and clean freshwater.
- If water sources are not safe, boiled water should be used after cooling.
- Diseases can be prevented by preserving food materials in utensils covered with lid.
- Disease can be prevented by burning or burying dirty things in a pit.

Some Other Informations Related to Health and Sanitation

Some other information related to health and sanitation are as follows:

- Our hands and nails are carrier of germs and bacteria in our mouth when we touch food and water, they inter inside our mouth. But when we wash our hands with soap and cut our nails with blades properly, germs and bacteria do not get a chance to enter the mouth. Therefore, we should keep our hands and nails clean before touching food and water.
- All members of family should inculcate the habit of washing hands with soap before touching food and after defecation.
- All members should cut nails regularly and clean them properly.
- All members should wash hand properly after cleaning children at the time of defecation.
- The hands of children should also be cleaned properly because children put fingers in mouth again and again.
- The face and body of children should be washed properly at least twice a day.
- All family members should dispose of knight soil of children properly in latrine.
- All members should use lavatory with sufficient water.
- Defecation should never be done near by the water sources if there is no latrine in house.
- In case defecation in open field, night soil should be covered with soil powder.
- Children should also be allowed to use latrine, because their night soil also contains a number of germs and bacteria.
- Latrine should be washed properly after each use.
- Cattle dung and urine should be kept away from water sources.

- The use of safe drinking water of hand pump and boring suffer less from diseases.
- Families having no safe drinking water facility, should use boiled water.
- Water storing utensils should be kept quite clean.
- Animals should be kept away from water sources.
- We should not throw shoes and slippers in water sources.
- Food materials should be preserved properly.
- Meal should be cooked properly before eating.
- Meals should be consumed immediately after cooking.
- Leftover foods should not be taken.
- Unused cooked food should be taken after heating gently.
- Meals should always be kept in utensils covered with lids.
- Domestic waste should be burnt or buried in a pit.

Malaria

Malaria is disease which is caused by mosquito bite. It is also killer disease of children and others. It kills thousands of children each year. Crores of people become victim of malarial disease. Now-a-days we have diseases like cerebral malaria, dengue, and chickengunia which are caused by mosquito bite. Therefore, it is fitness of the thing to present here the scientific concept related to malaria.

Some Important Scientific Information Related to Malaria

Some important scientific informations about malaria are as follows:

- We should save our children and ourselves from the mosquito-bite.
- We should use mosquito net during night.
- We should destroy larva of mosquitoes which develop in dirty water in storage nearby our houses.
- In malaria infected areas, pregnant women should be served tablets of malaria during whole pregnancy period.
- For treatment of material fever, patient should be brought immediately in health centres or hospitals.
- Persons suffering from malaria should be given full course of medicine.
- Persons suffering from malaria should be kept also at place which is not every hot or not very cold.

- After control of material fever, extra food materials or meals should be given to the patient.

Some other Information Related to Malaria

Some other information about malaria are as follows:

- It is well known fact that malaria is caused by mosquito bite. Hence in order to prevent malaria, we should use mosquito net, mosquito quiet, mosquito net on window and spray of mosquito killing liquid.
- All members of the community should adopt safety measure for preventing mosquito bite.
- Mosquitoes spread malaria from one person to another.
- Mosquitoes are born in water of drains, pit, tanks, cooler tanks, open jars. The water from these places should be allowed to become dry. Kerosene oil should be sprayed at these places. Kerosene oil kills the larva of mosquito.
- Streets and neighbourhood should be kept quite clean.
- The pregnant women have double chance of suffering from malaria.
- Malarial fever during pregnancy is more dangerous.
- The attack of material fever causes lack of blood in pregnant woman and they become anaemic
- As blood of pregnant women becomes thin, the chances of abortion becomes more.
- Such pregnant women may deliver premature child or child having less weight.
- Such women may deliver dead child too.
- The pregnant women can save themselves from the malaria and its adverse impact on health and child to be delivered by taking malarial tablets regularly during the period of pregnancy.
- Malarial preventive medicines are available in all medicine shops, village soaps and at health sub-centres and centres.
- All pregnant women should be allowed for test of malaria.
- When malaria is confirmed after test, full course of medicine should be taken.
- The malarial preventive medicine course is 1day to 10 days.
- The small children should be served syrup of anti-malarial medicine.
- If malarial fever gets down, even then full course should be followed.

- If malarial fever is very high, the following steps should be taken:
  - Use of paracetomol.
  - Washing body with a cloth wet and dried in cold water.
  - Very less clothes on the body of children.
  - Cover the body with sheet at the time of very high fever.
- The persons or children suffering from malaria should be served food and water on their demands. This can prevent malnutrition and loss of water.

Cough and Cold

The cough and cold when not treated properly, they turn into pneumonia. Nearly six lakh children in our country die each year from pneumonia. Therefore, all members of the community should have scientific information about the cure of cough and cold, when cough and cold become pneumonia and when to consult a doctor for treatment of pneumonia.

Some Important Scientific Informations Related to Cough and Cold

Some important scientific informations related to cough and cold are as follows:

- If a child is suffering from cough and cold and his/her heart rate is more than normal, then it is a danger sign for the health of child. The child should be brought immediately to hospital or health centre.
- By breast feeding the child for a period of six months from the birth, mother can save her child from pneumonia.
- Pneumonia can also be prevented by following the child vaccination table.
- The child suffering from the cough and cold should be served sufficient liquid foods.
- The child suffering from cough and cold should be covered with clothes properly.
- The child should be kept in clean and smokless place so that he/she can breath in fresh air.
- Generally cough and cold is cured naturally, but sometimes it turns into pneumonia. Pneumonia is very dangerous disease. It results in death, if not treated properly.
- When cough and cold turn in to pneumonia, the child should be brought to a doctor for the treatment.

- The main sign of pneumonia is fast rate of breathing, i.e. 50 times in a minute and not showing interest in breast feeding by the child.
- The breast feeding child suffer less from pneumonia than bottle or spoon feeding child.
- Vitamin A protects child from pneumonia and Vitamin A is available in orange and yellow fruits, vegetables and green leafy vegetables.
- Till the age of one year, all vaccination courses should be completed. The vaccination prevents infection.
- Cough and cold is a contagious disease, therefore, leaving breastfed children, other children should be allowed to sleep separately.
- The nose of child should be cleaned again and again.
- The child living in places having smoke, has more chance of suffering from pneumonia.
- The persons suffering from cough and cold should maintain distance from the children.
- Cough and cold can be treated at home. But following care should be taken:
    - The child should be breastfed frequently.
    - Big children should be served meals frequently.
    - More food should be served after cure of the child.
    - This should be continued till the child does not start playing as before.

AIDS

The disease of AIDS is a global health problem. All countries of the globe are facing problem related to this disease. This is a non-curable and communicable disease. This disease is caused by AIDS virus. Crores of people in the world are suffering from this disease. An AIDS patient becomes very weak. As a result, the patient is not in a position to fight against this disease. Till now, effective medicine has not been available to treat this disease. The patient has to die ultimately. Now-a-days, AIDS virus is found even in children. Millions of children may become orphan due to this disease in near future. Therefore, members of the community should have proper scientific informations regarding disease of AIDS and proper means of treatment.

Important Scientific Information about AIDS

Important scientific informations about AIDS are as follows:

- AIDS is a non-curable disease.
- This disease spreads due to unsafe sex relation, donation of infectious blood to another person or use of infected needle or blood.
- This disease spreads from infected mother to child in womb or newborn.
- The spread of AIDS can be prevented by safe sex relation.
- The safe sex relation means husband and wife not suffering from AIDS. Both should not have extra marital relation. In case of doubt, Condom or Nirodh should be used.
- Unsterlized injection may prove dangerous.
- The woman suffering from AIDS should not conceive.
- Parents should tell their young children about the AIDS, its spread and preventive measures.

Some Other Scientific Informations Related to AIDS

Some other scientific informations related to AIDS are as follows:

- AIDS spreads from such a virus (known as HIV) which damages the immune system of the body.
- Patients suffering from AIDS die because their poor immune system does not prevent disease to spread.
- It is not necessary that persons having HIV are suffering from AIDS. But persons suffering from AIDS can infect other persons.
- There is no specific sign which identify that person has AIDS virus. The persons having AIDS virus looks quite normal and healthy.
- If a person has doubt of AIDS virus, he/she should visit health centres or hospitals for test.
- The persons having AIDS disease should learn and take proper advice as to how he/she can contribute in non-spread of this disease to other.
- AIDS virus can reach from one person to another through some limited means. These are as follows:
  - The infected persons have AIDS virus in their sperms or limbs, blood, and liquid secretion of reproductive organs.

These viruses reach in other persons through sex relation. Thus, the disease of AIDS can spread through unsafe sex relation.

- AIDS virus can reach from male to female, female to male, male to male and female to female through sex relation.
- AIDS viruses spread through the use of unsterilized needles or syringe.
- AIDS also spread through transfusion of blood, if donor is suffering from AIDS.
- AIDS viruses spread from infected mother to child in womb or newly delivered.
- The used razor, blade, brush, tooth brush also causes spread of AIDS virus from one person to another.
- The use of unsterilized needle for ear boring, tattooing, making figures on face and for acupuncture may lead to spread of AIDS virus from one person to another.
- The mother having AIDS virus can breast feed to their children. But it can spread when the child makes a bite in breast or breast has any cut scar.
- Bottle feeding has more chance of spread of AIDS viruses than breast feeding.
- Going, talking, touching, sneezing shaking hands, meeting shoulder to shoulder to a person having AIDS virus do not cause spread of AIDS disease.
- The use of latrine, urinal, plate, spoon, cup, glass, towels, bed sheet and common place by a person having AIDS virus does not cause spread of AIDS disease.
- Vaccination through sterilized injection does not cause AIDS viruses to spread from one person to another.
- Oral doze does not cause spread of AIDS viruses.
- Vaccination should always be taken from a health centre or hospital under a trained workers.
- In order to save ourselves from AIDS, we should follow the direction and rule of safe sex relation.
- The couple should remain faithful to each other in sex relation. On having doubt, they should use Nirodh or Condom.
- Anal sex, oral sex, bleeding sex, sex with male or female prostitutes and sex with persons taking intoxicants are more dangerous.
- Young generation people should be taught about the AIDS, its causes and preventions.

Tuberculosis

The disease of tuberculosis is generally known as T.B. This disease spreads through germ or bacteria. That is why this disease is known as a contagious and communicable disease. When a T.B. patient coughs, spits and breathes nearby another person, the germs of T.B. get entered inside his/her body. Thus, the germs of T.B. disease reach from one person to another. T.B. is a major health problem in our country. This disease can occur to individuals belonging to any sex and age group. In our country nearly one lakh children in every five years become victim of T.B. disease. Therefore, it is necessary to present here the scientific causes, informations and remedies for the community members. Every young member of the community should know what T.B. disease is?, how it spreads and how it can be prevented? Here all scientific informations related to the disease of T.B. are being presented one by one for the members of community.

Main Scientific Informations about T.B.

Main scientific informations about T.B. are as follows:

- T.B. is such a disease which is above age group and sex group.
- If T.B. is not treated properly, it becomes fatal.
- It is possible to save ourselves from the disease of T.B.
- This disease attacks more on children below five years of age.
- The vaccination of B.C.G. can save the children from the disease of T.B. Injection should be given soon after birth.
- The children having nutritious diet can fight this disease in better way.
- When young and aged T.B. patients cough, spit and breath, the germs of T.B. get inside the body of child through mouth. Thus, it is a contagious disease.
- Children should be kept away from T.B. patients.
- T.B. patients should be brought in hospitals for proper treatment.
- T.B. patients should not cough, spit and breath before children and other persons.
- The most dangerous form of T.B. is meningitis (brain T.B.). In this disease, death is sure to occur. If any one survives, he/she becomes mentally invalid.
- T.B. affects lungs, bones and swellings badly.
- The disease of T.B. can be cured.
- If proper treatment be given, T.B. is not dangerous and can be cured.

Some Other Scientific Informations Related to T.B.

Some other scientific informations related to T.B. are as follows:

- T.B. is one of life-taking diseases in our country.
- T.B. spreads in villages as well as in towns.
- T.B. spreads generally at such places which lack cleanliness and sanitation.
- This disease spreads more in such a place where population density is high.
- When patients of T.B. cough and spit, the germs spread in air and get inside the body of another persons and make them infected. Thus, it is a contagious disease.
- If a person is suffering from cough since a month, he/she should go to hospital for T.B. Test.
- The treatment of T.B. is a costly affair. Therefore, every effort should be made to save from the disease of T.B.
- By birth low weight and malnourished children should also be given B.C.G. vaccination to protect them from T.B.
- To prevent T.B. disease in infant and children, the children should be breastfed properly for proper nutrition.
- After six months children should be served nutritious supplementary diet in the form of cow milk, pulse water and vegetable water.
- The infants should be breastfed even during illness.
- The weight of child should be taken to see the proper growth of child.
- The treatment of adult T.B. patients should be started immediately so that they could not infect other persons.
- The T.B. patients should keep small towels to cover their mouth and nose to prevent the spread of T.B. germs.
- T.B. patient should not spit at open space.
- The patient should spit in a pot which should be buried or burnt.
- The family members of T.B. patient should visit hospital for T.B. examination to remove doubt.
- The brain T.B. is a killer type of T.B. Majority of children met death.
- The surviving children become mentally disabled.
- Lungs T.B. is also very dangerous disease. The children do not cough but they suffer from high fever. They become idle.
- The T.B. also affects our backbone and as a result hynch sign appears in back.

- The T.B. also affects swellings. They increase in size and turn into wounds.
- It is better to take preventive steps than going for treatment of the disease.
- The treatment of T.B. goes for months. Its treatment should go as per advice of the doctor.
- The disease of T.B. may cause disability in children.
- Multidrug therapy is given to a T.B. patient.
- As soon as treatment starts, the germs of cough and spit get destroyed. Now, there is no fear of contagious disease.
- Full doze treatment should be taken by T.B. patient and finally get proper check-up.

Leprosy

It is a communicable skin disease caused by a bacteria. Any person can become victim of leprosy whether rich-poor, child-adult, male-female and literate-illiterate. It can be cured by proper treatment. Its treatment should be started immediately. On starting treatment, this disease does not spread from one person to another person. Only 15-20 per cent leprosy patients are infectitious. Nearly, there are 40 lakh leprosy patients in India. The number of leprosy patient, below the age of 15 years, is 8 lakh. This disease has been reported from all states of our country. But the states of Andhra Pradesh, West Bengal, Odisha and Tamil Nadu have more number of leprosy patients. If the disease is diagnosed and treatment is started timely physical deformity due to disease can be prevented. Our Government has started scheme to identify and treat this disease, but some more arrangements needs to be done. This disease causes deformities to nose, lips and fingers of hands and feet. Some persons become disable. They need occupational training. The leprosy patients and their family have to face stigma and discrimination. Therefore, the Government should take step to prevent discrimination against leprosy patients and their families. It is fitness of the thing to present here the facts related to how leprosy is caused and how it can be prevented and cured.

Some Chief Scientific Informations about Leprosy

Some main scientific informations related to leprosy are as follows:

- The leprosy is caused by a bacteria.
- It is a communicable disease.

- If treatment is started, then it does not spread in other person.
- The disease of leprosy can be cured completely.
- The quick treatment of disease prevents physical deformities in the body of patient.
- Families of leprosy patients should not be isolated from the community. They should be allowed to live in the community.
- Leprosy patients needs rehabilitation by the cooperation of family and community.
- Leprosy affected disabled persons should be given occupational training.
- Sufficient attempts should be made to prevent and treat leprosy patient.

Some Other Scientific Information Related to Leprosy

Some other scientific information about leprosy are as follows:

- There is very bad concept that leprosy is caused by the curse of Gods and Goddesses.
- It is also a wrong conception that this disease is result of bad deeds in this life or previous life.
- As a number of diseases are caused by germs and bacteria, in the same leprosy is also caused by germs or bacteria.
- This disease is not hereditary.
- The children of leprosy patients are quite normal and healthy.
- Leprosy patients can arrange marriage and lead happy married life.
- The disease of leprosy can occur to any person at any time.
- This disease affects children in the age of 8-15 years very much.
- This disease is spread not by all leprosy patients. But only 15-20 per cent leprosy patients are infectitious.
- If a person lives with an infectitious leprosy patient for a long time, then this disease can spread in the person in contact.
- The germs or bacteria of leprosy spread by coughing, spiting, and sneezing.
- The patient of leprosy should have small towel at mouth and nose at the time of coughing, sneezing and spiting.

Symptoms of Leprosy

The signs of leprosy disease are as follows:

- White or red spot on skin.
- Plane spot and dry or smooth skin.
- The spot bereft of touch feeling.
- The spot which does not pain on touch.
- The part of body which does not indicate hot or cold.
- It is not necessary that all spots appearing at skin are sign of Leprosy. Therefore, doctor should be consulted immediately for diagnosis and treatment.
- There is no vaccination of leprosy prevention. Therefore, other means should be adopted for prevention and cure.
- The Leprosy Disease is fully curable.
- It is a bad notion that leprosy disease is non-curable and patient should be isolated from family and community.

Measures to Cure Leprosy

The following means should be adopted to cure leprosy:

- Now, effective medicines are available which cure leprosy completely.
- The treatment of disease should be started immediately after diagnosis.
- The treatment should be continued as per the suggestion of the doctor concerned.
- The beginning of treatment at the earlier prevents physical deformity.
- Quick start of medicine prevents the spread of disease in other persons.
- The patient meeting regular treatment is not infectious for others.
- Leprosy disease affects our bodily system as a result the fingers of hands and feet of some persons get bent and feel pain in movement.
- Leprosy disease creates deformity in nose, lip, forehead, and ear.
- The leprosy patients who do not under go treatment in the beginning may have chance of more physical deformities.
- To prevent physical deformity due to leprosy, treatment must be started soon after identification. Delay in treatment is sure to cause deformity.
- The early stage deformities may be controlled by oil massage and exercise.
- Some deformities are cured by operation.

- The best way to become free from deformity is immediate treatment, continuity and full course.
- Leprosy germs do not cause wounds. It affects our nervous system. As a result leprosy patients do not feel cold, hot and pain.
- Sometimes, wounds appear in patient's body due to insertion of glass, iron, wood, pin etc.

Cooperation of Family and Society

It has been observed that leprosy patients are isolated from the family, community and society because of social stigma attached to the diseases. Rather leprosy patients need full cooperation of family, community and society. The rehabilitation of leprosy patients is possible by the cooperation of family, community and the Government. The following efforts should be made in this regard:

- The family members and community can be convinced that all leprosy patients are not infectitious.
- The infectitious or uninfectitious nature of leprosy can be found out by examination or test under supervision of a doctor.
- The infectitious leprosy patients should be isolated from family and community. The treatment should be started at right time till right period properly.
- Leprosy patients, whose treatment start at right time and continues as per advice of doctor, can live in family.
- Such patients can continue their occupation.
- The family and community should accept leprosy patients.
- Family and community should contribute positively in rehabilitation of leprosy patients.
- The children of leprosy patient should be sent to school.
- The teachers should convince other children and their guardians that leper's children do not spread leprosy.
- The leprosy patients should be given equal opportunity in education, occupation and marriage.

Leprosy Prevention and Treatment Arrangement

For leprosy control and treatment, our Government has established institutions and organizations. They are as follows:

- There are network of units both in rural areas and urban areas to prevent and treat leprosy.

- These units treat leprosy patient free of cost.
- Multi Drug Therapy (MDT) has been introduced in leprosy affected areas.
- Members of family and community should know about the places where leprosy control and treatment units have been established.
- Members of family and community should also know about the long time period of treatment.
- School teachers, health workers and community members should play positive role in identification, treatment and rehabilitation of leprosy patients.

8

Folk Classification and Primary Treatment of Diseases

It is a common feature of folk communication that they categorize or classify all things of their world where they live. These traditions are continuing generation after generation as folk knowledge. Folk communities take cognigance of these classifications as they have folk thought or meaning. They reveal cultural significance of the community. Like other things and events, they classify their health events like disease and treatment. The folk classification of diseases and their treatment reveals the knowledge, thought and meaning hidden behind classification. Thus, from the point of view of cognizance and meaning, the classification of diseases occupies significant place.

Folk communities classify diseases in following ways:

- Age-based disease
- Sex-based disease
- Common diseases
- Untouchability based disease
- Divinal curse based disease
- Seasonal disease
- Accident prone disease
- Disease based on life-style.

Now let us discuss about these folk classification of disease one by one.

Age-based Disease

The members of folk community classify their diseases on the basis of age group. For example disease of infant, child, and aged.

Sex-based Diseases

Folk communities classify diseases according to sex groups such as disease of male and female and transgender.

Common Disease

The disease which affects all sex and age groups.

Season-based Disease

Folk communities classify diseases according to season. For example, disease of summer, rainy and winter seasons. People fall ill when one season ends and other season starts its beginning.

Infection-based Diseases

Folk communities classify diseases on the basis of infections. The patients suffering from leprosy, T.B., cough, cold, allergy, diarrhoea are treated as suffering from contagious and infectitious diseases. Such patients are treated as keeping in isolation and social-distancing.

Divinal Curse Based Disease

The people of folk communities classify diseases on the basis of divinal curse. For example, deaf, dumb, pox, cholera, leprosy, and barrenness.

Accident-based Disease

The members of folk communities classify diseases on the basis of accident. For example different kinds of fractures.

Diseases Caused by Lifestyle Change

Some diseases are caused by change in lifestyle. For example: sugar, B.P. hypertension, heart disease.

Folk Primary Treatment of Diseases

Folk people have their own concept of primary treatment. They take help of

Jhar-phuk, worship, sacrifice, folk medicine, herbal *Jari-buti* and even some allopathic medicines available in village shop for primary treatment of disease. When diseases are not controlled by primary treatment, they visit hospital and doctors. Description about *Jhar-phuk* method, worship method and scientific method has been presented in chapters 5th, 6th and 7th. Therefore, here we are going to discuss only domestic primary treatment methods of diseases. Now let us discuss diseases and their primary treatment methods followed by folk communities. For the purpose of study, it can be discussed under the following headings:

- Child diseases and primary treatment
- Aged disease and primary treatment
- Male diseases and primary treatment
- Female diseases and primary treatment
- Common diseases and primary treatment
- Seasonal diseases and primary treatment
- Body parts diseases and primary treatment
- Cursed diseases and primary treatment
- Accident and quarrel-based diseases and primary treatment
- Skin diseases and primary treatment
- Hairfall diseases and primary treatment
- Face diseases and primary treatment
- Lifestyle related disease and primary treatment.

Child Disease and Primary Treatment

There are some diseases which affect children more than other age groups. They are termed as pediatric child disease. The child diseases and their primary treatment in folk communities are being presented as follows:

Cough

Infants and children suffer from cough frequently. They need more care by family and community. To avoid the disease of cough in children, lactating mothers have to observe a number of taboos related to food. They have to take such food materials which could not exceed or cause the disease of cough. The garlic is cooked in mustard oil for some time on slow heat. This cooked oil is applied over the body of children four-five times in a day. The children are covered with a sheet. They are allowed to wear full dress. Lactating mothers keep infants on breast feeding. But after six months, children are given extra food like cow milk, goat milk, pulse water, starch and vegetable water. The *ghee* is also applied on body of children suffering from cough. Mother is allowed to take turmeric powder mixed milk at bed time. The cough is cured naturally in a week. But when it continues, the help of doctor is seek.

Cold

The cold affects children very much. They fall ill and suffer from cold and fever. The folk people treat cold primarily with hot natured diet given to lactating mother. The lactating mother is asked to eat egg, meat, onion, ginger and garlic so that the cold of children could be recovered after breast feeding. Post-breast feeding stage children are served extra food mixed with few drops of *ghee* or mustard oil. Garlic cooked in mustard oil is applied over the body of child. The *ghee* of sheep is applied over lungs, throat and forehead. The juice of leaves of Seez plant (a kind of thorny plant) is given to the children suffering from cold. The juice is taken out by heating the leaves on stove. The juice of ginger, garlic and onion is taken out, heated gently and served to the children with spoon. Mustard oil is applied on the body of children time to time.

Kukur Khansi (Dog Cough)

When the face of child becomes red by coughing and cough does not come out, it is known as that the child is suffering from *kukur khansi.* This disease is confirmed further by continuation of same type of coughing for two weeks. Now, the child is brought before a doctor for treatment. But before bringing child to a doctor, the primary treatment of disease is made in the same way as in case of cough and cold. The child is served loaf sugar cooked in *ghee.* The leaves of Tulsi is boiled in water and served to the child five-six times in a day. The old *ghee* of cow is applied over the lungs and heart of child. Turmeric powder mixed in milk is served to the child. When all such efforts fail and coughing continues, the child is brought to hospital.

Pneumonia

It is regarded as very dangerous disease of infants and children. In this disease, the throat and lungs are filled with phlegm or cough and the child feels suffocated in breathing. When pneumonia is confirmed, the child is brought before doctor immediately. But before bringing the child to a doctor, some primary treatment is given. This includes application of old *ghee* of cow on lungs and heart, serving few drops of cow's *ghee,* juice of

Seez plant leaf and Tulsi leaves boiled in water. The body of child is covered with full dresses and a sheet. The fire is kept burning round the clock. But when primary treatment does not bring effective result, the child is brought to hospital immediately.

Gala Ghontu (Tetanus)

The disease of *Gala Ghontu* is known as Tetanus in English. In local language, it is known as *Gala Ghontu* because this disease kills the children by exerting more and more pressure on throat. It is also known locally as *Dhanush Tankar,* because the body assumes the shape of a bow in this disease. This disease occurs when naval of child is cut with rusty knife or a child meets injury with old iron implements. The body of child is soaked with slightly hot Mahua oil. The fire is kept burning. But when primary treatment does not prove effective, the child is brought to a doctor immediately.

Sukha Rog (Weight loss)

Weight loss is a serious disease of a child. It may occur due to malnutrition. But it may also occur due to liver and stomach disease. The weight loss due to malnutrition can be cured by providing sufficient nutritious diet. But when weight loss is caused by liver or stomach diseases, it requires special care. Juvenile jaundice may be a cause of weight loss in children. The ultimate treatment of this disease is by a doctor. But before reaching to a doctor some primary treatment is given in house. This includes no application of oil on body. Powder is applied and the child is kept in sun for some time. Mother's milk is never stopped. The children above six months are served honey drops five-six times in day.

Hichaki

Hichaki is a disease of children in which a child breathes with a sound like *Hacha-Hacha.* That is why it is known as *Hichaki.* Infants are served mother's milk time to time as primary treatment to prevent *Hichaki.* But a child above six months is served liquid food time to time to prevent *Hichaki.* Honey drops are also served to the child.

Gas Formation

Some children show complaint of gas formation. It is believed that mother has not observed taboos related to food. Her milk may cause gas in child stomach. The lactating mother is asked to take *Ajawine* water, *gur* and black salt. If the child is above six month, the child is also served water of *Ajawine*. *Jafar* is also served. Dabour Janma Ghuti is given to the child as primary treatment.

Kai-Dasta (Diarrhoea)

The disease of *kai-dast* (vomiting and loose motion) is taken very seriously by parents of infants and children. It is considered as a fatal disease. The child is brought before a doctor urgently. But before bringing to a doctor some first aid like treatment is given to the child. Now-a-days ORS is available in every village shop. Parents do not want to take any chance of wait and watch. They give ORS solution to children immediately. ORS solution has been included in primary treatment of diarrhoea. If ORS is not available, sugar-salt solution is given to the children as first aid.

Not Suckling

This is also taken as a child disease. In this disease, the child does not show interest in breast feeding. This behaviour indicates that there is something wrong with the child. This indicates symptoms of cough, cold, allergy, gas, stomach pain or fever. The mother tries to know the reason and starts primary treatment accordingly. *Jhar-phuk* treatment is done. *Totaka* of burning red chilly is done. If child does not start suckling, he/she is brought in hospital.

Fear

Sometimes, the child gets frightened by hearing fearful sounds. He/she starts weeping. He/she neither shows interest in suckling nor playing. He/she goes on weeping continuously for hours. The mother attempts to drive out fear from the child. The child is taken in lap and every attempt is made to divert the fear. Sounds of toys are created, songs are sung, and the body of child is touched here and there with hands. If child does not stop weeping, he/she is brought to a doctor

Disease and Primary Treatment of Aged

The diseases of aged and their primary treatments are as follows:

Falling Teeth

Falling Teeth is taken as a disease of ageing because it creates trouble in chewing every kind of food. Only soft foods are taken. Hard food is avoided. To prevent falling teeth, the primary treatment followed is keeping teeth quite clean with green *Nim* stick and mustard oil with salt.

Not Hearing

Not Hearing is also a geriatric disease. As a primary treatment of this, garlic cooked in mustard oil is put in ears regularly as drops. This practice clears the ears and the aged feel relax in hearing.

Blindness

Dim vision properly is also a disease related to old age. For curing this disease, the eyes are washed regularly with cold water. The milk of cow and goat is dropped in eyes regularly. This primary treatment practice helps the aged in improving visibility.

Bodyache

Regular bodyache is also a problem of old age. As a primary treatment to cure body pain, the body is massaged with mustard oil heated with garlic. The practice is repeated daily.

Indigestion

Indigestion is also a disease related to old age. In old age, the digestion power decreases. The problem of indigestion increases. As a primary treatment, the aged person is not served spicy and oily foods. Lemon juice and pickle of lemon and Amla are served. *Kala namak* and jaggery are given.

Male Diseases and their Primary Treatment

Some of the diseases of males and their primary treatments are as follows:

Night Fall or Dream Fall

This is a kind of disease in which the semen ejaculates during night sleep.

When this happens repeatedly, it is known as a disease. The male finds himself copulating with a female and ultimately his semen fall as drops. The cloth of male get wet. This disease makes a male anxious. He does not find himself fit physically or mentally. He talks to his friends. Friends suggest him to control some food. When family members come to know this, some treatments are given. Hot food and sour foods are avoided. Spicy and only hot food materials are also not served. Milk is served daily after night meal. He is not asked to sleep alone. Honey and *peepal* powder are given. *Trifla churna* is also given to patient daily in the morning.

Impotency

This is a male disease. In this disease the erectile power of male is decreased due to which he is not in a position to do sex with his wife. This disease occurs due to hand practice or malnutrition. This disease puts a dark sport on the power of a male. The male suffering from sugar, B.P. and heart disease also develops impotency. Persons suffering from mental diseases also suffer from impotency. Primary treatment of this disease is balanced diet. The patient is served meat, chicken, fish, egg, fruits, dry fruits, onion, garlic and green vegetable. Thus, by giving nutritious and balanced diet, the disease of impotency is removed by primary treatment. But when primary treatment becomes ineffective, the patient is brought in a hospital for treatment under a doctor.

Male Sex Disease

Sometimes, male suffers from sex disease like swelling in sex organ, wound in sex organ and dirty smell from sex organ. These are such diseases about which a male does not like to disclose in the beginning. But when he becomes disable, he has to disclose it to his family member. Now the primary treatment is started. The primary treatment includes washing sex organs with *Nim* leaves boiled in water after each urination. Toddy of *Nim* is given to share. Oil of *Nim* and oil of *Karanj* are applied over the organ. If the disease is not cured by these primary treatment, the patient contacts doctor for the treatment.

Female Disease and Primary Treatment

For the purpose of study, we can present female disease and their treatment in the following ways:

Barrenness

This is regarded as a very serious disease for a woman. Such woman cannot produce children and become mother. That is why she is termed as *Banjh* (barren). A woman suffers from this disease due to malnutrition, irregular menstrual cycle, mental diseases and ovary related diseases. Sometimes barrenness occurs due to impotency of husband or his sperm formation related disease. As a primary treatment, women suffering from barrenness are adviced to take nutritious balanced diet. She is given regular intake of milk, fruits, green vegetables, honey and peepal powder and *trifala churna* and toddy of *khajur*. Such women are adviced to offer worship to deities. When primary treatment fails, such women go to hospital for treatment.

Ovary Related Disease

In case of some women, their ovary gets diseased. The mouth of ovary gets swollen, regular flow of foul liquid takes place and sometimes irregular bleeding takes place. When the ovary become diseased, such women are adviced primary treatment like washing with *Nim* leaves boiled water regulary four-five times or after each urination. *Nim* oil and *Karanj* oil is adviced to put inside organs. The water of *Chiraita* plant is asked to drink in the morning before breakfast. But when primary treatment does not solve the problem, the patient is brought to hospital for treatment.

Hysteria

This is regarded as a female disease which occurs in adolescent girls. In this disease a girl looses its mental balance and behaves sometimes as a mad or mental case. The gir suffering from this disease goes on repeating the same words or sentence without any break. She does not listen to any one. Community members think that she has become a mental case. As a primary treatment *Jhar-pukh* method is used. But the best remedy of this disease is her marriage. After marriage, this disease is recovered.

Breast Related Disease

Lactating women have to suffer breast related diseases. Sometimes wound appears in breast. This disease is known locally as *Thanail*. In folk and peasant society, this disease is controlled by *Jhar-phuk* method. The breast is treated with a wooden comb. But when primary treatment is not effective, the patient is brought to a hospital for treatment.

Not Flow of Milk

This is a disease of lactating mother. Such mother does not breast feed her baby. As a part of primary treatment such woman is adviced to allow child to suckle again and again. Mother is asked to take milk and water of pulse. Mother is given *Halua* of turmeric and loaf sugar cooked in pure *ghee.* But when all such primary treatments become ineffective, the woman is brought in hospital for treatment.

Not conceiving

Not conceiving is also a female disease. In this disease, a woman does not conceive. In the beginning it is not taken as a serious disease. But as time passes, this disease disturbs woman and the family members. As a part of primary treatment, *Jhar-phuk* method and *Puja-path* are used, besides giving nutritious balanced diet regularly. But when these primary treatments fail, woman is brought to a doctor for treatment.

Abortion

Abortion is also taken as a woman disease. Sometimes, the pregnancy turns into abortion or miscarriage. It is taken as a serious disease. As a primary treatment, the *Jhar-phuk* method and *Puja-path* are used. The family members take every care of her. She is not asked to fetch water, bring water, lift heavy weights, to much walking, climbing up and down and not going alone anywhere. But when all these primary treatments become unsuccessful, the woman is brought to hospital for treatment under a doctor.

Delivery Related Disease

Woman has to suffer from delivery related disease, too. This includes delivery pain, trouble in delivery. As a primary treatment, an experienced woman of the community remains twenty four hours with her to assist in delivery. *Mahua* made wine is applied over stomach to facilitate normal delivery. But when complexity arises due to turn of baby in stomach or narrow delivery path, she is brought to hospital for treatment under supervision of a doctor.

Common Disease and Primary Treatment

There are some diseases which occur to all ages—child, young, adult and aged and all sex groups—male, female and transgender. That is why they are known as common diseases. They are treated primarily in the following ways:

Allergy (Sardi)

According to folk concept, this disease occurs when there is change of season—cold to hot or hot to cold. It also occurs due to some food materials, dust and smoke. It is taken as a contagious disease because it spreads from one individual to another. In the disease of cold, nose and throat start burning. The fall of water starts from the nose. Although people get physically disturbed in the disease of allergy, but it is not taken as a serious disease. They believe that it will be recovered naturally in few days by avoiding some food and using some special food.

As a primary treatment of *sardi,* people do the following practice:

- Intake of Tulsi leaves tea.
- Intake of ginger, onion and garlic cooked in pure *ghee.*
- To take loaf sugar cooked in pure *ghee* at night.
- To take *ghee* in hot water.
- Intake of *Golmircha* powder and *Talmisri* cooked in pure *ghee.*
- To take *ghee* and *Litti* as a special night meal.
- To take meat or chicken cooked in onion and garlic.
- To take egg.
- To take turmeric powder with hot milk.
- To take juice of hot Seez (Thorny) plant.
- To observe fast at night.

These days, anti-allergic tablets are also available in village shop. People have included them in primary treatment.

Coughing (Khansi)

According to folk concepts, sardi and *khansi* both occur together. It is believed that *sardi* affected person will suffer from *khansi.* If *sardi* is not followed by *khansi,* it will bring adverse effect upon chest and heart of concerned individual. In *khansi,* the throat starts irritating. The folk people take following steps as primary treatment of *khansi:*

- To take tea of Tulsi seeds and leaves.
- To take onion, ginger and garlic cooked in pure *ghee.*
- To take *Talmisri* and a black chilly cooked in pure *ghee.*

- To take old *ghee* and old loaf sugar at night.
- To drink hot milk with turmeric powder.
- To eat meat and chicken.
- To eat egg.
- To take *Chayavanprash* with milk.

Of late, cough syrup is also included in primary treatment.

Bukhar (Fever)

Fever is a common disease which affects people belonging to all age groups and sex groups. The allergy and *khansi* also cause fever. In fever, the temperature of body goes up. The patient looses appetite and energy. When body temperature exceeds 100°, it is taken as serious. The folk people take following steps as primary treatment:

- Measuring body temperature regularly.
- To take hot milk, hot water, hot curry or soup.
- Covering body on feeling cold.
- Putting less clothes on body when temperature rises above 100°.
- Washing face and body with towel soaked in cold water.
- To put band of clothes on forehead, navels and feet soaked in water or milk.
- Cold oil is applied in summer fever and hot oil is applied in winter fever.
- Towel is rubbed in feet.
- *Chiraita* water is served to the patient.
- Honey and *peepal* powder is served to the patient.

Now-a-days paracetamol tablet is included in primary treatment of fever, because it is available in village shops.

Miyadi Bukhar (Complex Fever or Typhoid)

It is a complex form of fever. The fever goes after a fixed period say a week, two weeks, three weeks, four weeks, five weeks and so on. In the morning, there is no fever. But after breakfast temperature starts rising. From evening, the temperature starts decreasing. The trends of rising and decreasing fever continues for a fixed period or *miyad.* That is why it is termed as *miyadi* fever. The folk people follow following practices as primary treatment:

- To take temperature in morning, noon and night.
- To give *chiraita* water in the morning.
- To give milk soup and curry.
- To give honey and *peepal* powder.
- To keep clothes of patient clean.
- To wash body of patient regularly with wet clothes.
- To serve meals as per desire of the patient.
- To give Paracetamol tablets available in village soap.

Malarial Fever

Malarial fever is locally termed as *Tharthari.* It is because when malarial fever rises, it brings severe cold. The patient starts shaking hands and body. The patient cries sound like *Hum-Hum.* The fever rises up to 100°-103°. The fever gets down by sweating. The main sign of this disease is rise in temperature by feeling cold and down in fever by sweating. The folk people do following practices as primary treatment to cure the disease:

- Keeping body of patient hot by covering with clothes and sheet.
- Keeping fire burning nearby the patient.
- Serving water of *chiraita* plant in empty stomach.
- Serving *Golmircha* powder and honey.
- Giving *Nim* leaves to chew.
- Serving tea, soup, milk and curry to the patient.
- Serving onion, garlic and ginger fry to eat.
- Serving omlet and curry of meat and chicken.
- Giving tablet of *kunain* available in village shop or village quack.

Loose Motion

This is a very common disease which occurs in all age groups and sex groups. In this disease loose motion starts. This occurs due to extreme cold, extreme summer, rainy season and indigestion. The primary treatments given by the people are as follow:

- Lemon pickle and old loaf sugar are served to the patient.
- *Ajawain, kalanamak* and loaf sugar are given.
- Syrup of sugar, salt and lemon juice is given.
- Syrup of burnt *zira* and churned curd is given.
- *Hing* is given to the patient.
- Syrup of mango in salt or sugar is given.

- Tablets or syrup Pudinhara is given.
- ORS is given.
- Pickle of Amla is given with gur.
- *Trifala churna* is given.
- When loose motion is not controlled by above primary treatment, the patient is brought to hospitals for treatment under a doctor.

Vomiting

Vomiting is a common disease. It may occur due to cold attack, hot attack, over intake of food and digestion problem. In order to control vomiting, the following practices are done as primary treatment:

- To observe fast.
- To take lemon tea.
- Lemon, sugar and salt syrup is given.
- Lemon, *kalanamak* and *ajawain* are given.
- Loaf sugar, *golmircha* powder and *kalanamak* are given.
- Liquid food such as milk, pulse, curd, churned curd are given.
- *Trifala churna* is served.

Lahar (Sunstroke)

It is also a common disease which occurs due to attack of excessive heat of sun. The patient starts loose motion, vomiting and high fever. To cure sun stroke, following practices are done as primary treatment:

- The patient is asked to have a white onion in pocket.
- Green mango syrup is applied over the body.
- *Andi* oil or *Amla* oil is put on forehead and even in entire body.
- Green mango syrup with salt and sugar is served.
- *Bel* syrup is also served.
- Pudinhara tablet or syrup is served.
- Juice of sugarcane is given.
- Green fruit is given.
- Cloth band wet in goat milk or cow milk is put on forehead, navel and feet.
- Towel is rubbed in feet.
- Face is washed with towel wet in cold water.
- Honey is served.
- Lemon juice syrup is given.

- Loaf sugar and *kalanamk* are given.
- *Bel* syrup is also served.
- *Sattu* syrup is served.
- *Trifala churna* is served with hot water.

Tight and Irregular Motion (Constipation)

This is also a common disease which occurs in all age and sex groups. In this disease, a person feels trouble in defecation. The night soil becomes hard and does not come out. Patient feels motion but motion is not released. The patient feels pain at the time of easing. The folk community members attempt to cure this disease by following primary treatment:

- The patient is served hot milk half an hour after night meal.
- In the morning *Trifala Churna* is given with hot water.
- More and more liquid food is served.
- Spicy and oily food is avoided.
- A glass of water is taken in the morning after leaving bed.
- Rice and curd is given to eat.
- Old loaf sugar is given at night.
- Sugarcane juice is served in the morning.
- Soap is applied at the exit point of night soil.

Gas Formation

This is a common disease which occurs in all age and sex groups. Folk community and peasant community members practice following primary treatments to control gas formation:

- Taking very simple diet.
- Avoiding spicy and oily foods.
- Avoiding readymade foods.
- Eating *khira, kakari,* apple and guava regularly.
- Eating light food.
- Avoiding eating too much in one time.
- Eating something several times.
- Avoiding pickles of different types.
- Eating *sattu* solution.
- Avoiding Tea and Coffee.
- Taking *Ajawain, Hing* and *Kalanamak.*

Indigestion

This is also a common disease which occurs to all age and sex groups. In this disease, the food taken is not digested. As a result patient feels uneasy. He/she feels vomiting tendency or pain in stomach. He/she looses appetite. The folk and peasant people attempt to cure this disease by following primary treatment:

- To observe fast till a stomach is not empty.
- To take light liquid food such as curd, churned curd, pulse water.
- To take loaf sugar, *ajawin* and *kalanamak.*
- To take sugarcane juice.
- To take lemon juice and *kalanamak.*
- To eat *khichari.*
- To eat *Amla* and lemon pickles.
- To take *hing* and loaf sugar.
- To take *trifala churna.*

Hichaki

It is a common disease in which air of digestive canal comes out irregularly making sounds like *Hicha-Hicha.* That is why it is termed as *Hichaki.* The folk and peasant community members attempts to cure it by following primary treatment:

- To take water up to full stomach.
- To take *kalanamak* and loaf sugar in mouth.
- To take churned curd.
- To close both noses and mouth for some time.
- To say that patient has stolen salt.

Bodyache

This is a common disease which occurs to all age and sex group people. Folk and community members cure this disease by following primary treatment:

- The massage of body is done by mustard oil.
- The garlic is cooked in mustard oil and applied over the entire body.
- Ginger, turmeric and loaf sugar cooked in *ghee* is taken twice in a day.

- *Mahua*-liquor is applied over the body.
- *Mahua*-liquor is also taken.

Cold-stroke

This is also a very common disease which occur to all age and sex groups. As sun-stroke occurs in summer in the same way cold-stroke occurs in winter. To cure cold-stroke, folk and peasant community practice the following primary treatments:

- The body of patient is made hot.
- Fire is kept burning.
- *Mahua* oil is applied over the body.
- Hot food materials are served.
- Hot milk is given.
- Hot lemon tea or liquor tea is given.
- Loaf sugar, turmeric and ginger cooked in *ghee* is taken.
- Meat or chicken curry is given.
- Eggs are given.
- *Mahua*-liquor is served as medicine.

Seasonal Diseases and Primary Treatment

There are a number of diseases which occur in different seasons. They are known as seasonal diseases. They are as follows:

- Sun-stroke
- Cold-stroke
- Allergy
- Cough
- Loose motion
- Vomiting
- *Chechak* (Pox).

Apart from *chechak*, the primary treatments of all above diseases have already been described. Hence, they are not repeated. The primary treatment of *chechak* has been provided in cursed disease.

Body Parts Disease and Primary Treatment

Our body is made up of different parts and in each body parts disease occur.

Hence, primary treatments of diseases according to body parts are being given here. They are as follows:

Head Disease and Primary Treatment

Headache

Headache is a common disease which puts an individual restless. There may be different causes of headache such as sun-stroke, cold-stroke B.P. and hypertension. Trouble in menstrual cycle creates headache in women. An individual cannot feel calm while suffering from headache. The folk and peasant community members attempt to cure headache by following primary practices:

- Putting Amla, pumpkin and *Andi* oil on forehead.
- Putting *Til* oil on head.
- Massaging the head and forehead.
- Putting mustard oil on head during winter.
- Massaging forehead with *Mahua* oil.
- Putting head before burning fire.
- Putting a cloth band on forehead.

Half Headache

Sometimes headache occurs in half part of head. Hence, it is known as half headache. As a primary treatments of this disease all above mentioned practices are followed. Besides, *Jhar-phuk* method is also followed:

Kiramwah

This is a kind of headache which appears before sunrise and disappears after sunrise. For the primary treatment of this disease all above mentioned practices are followed. The help of *Jhar-phuk* method is also taken.

Eye Diseases and Primary Treatment

A number of diseases occur in eyes such as becoming red, swelling and burning. The members of folk and peasant community treat eye diseases with following primary treatments:

- Cleaning eyes with hot or cold water.
- Putting milk of mother, cow or she goat in eyes.
- Soaking eyes with towel wet in hot water.
- Soaking eyes with hot rice kept in a cloth as ball.
- Putting *Gulabjal* (rose water) in eyes.

Nose Disease and Primary Treatment

Some diseases occur in our nose. They are *nakara,* swollen nose, closing nose and coming sound from it. The folk and peasant people attempt to cure their nose disease by following primary practices:

- Cleaning nose properly in the morning.
- Putting mustard oil drop in nose in morning and evening.
- Not cutting hair of nose.
- Not putting finger in nose.
- Inhaling garlic smell.

Eye Diseases and Primary Treatment

Some diseases occur in our ears such as ear pain, closing ear, sounding and not listening. Folk and peasant people follow following primary treatment behaviours to cure their ear diseases:

- Putting garlic cooked mustard oil.
- Putting gentle hot onion juice in ear.
- Putting hot leaves of moraba plant on ear.
- Putting mild hot leaves of *Akawan, mahua* and *dhatura* on ears.
- Regular putting of mustard oil in ears.

Tooth Diseases and Primary Treatment

Some diseases occur in our teeth. Such as toothache, swelling in gum, germ attack in teeth and others. The folk people treat their teeth disease by following primary practices:

- Massaging teeth gum with salt and mustard oil.
- Using fresh *Nim, Karanj, Ber* stick for cleaning gum and teeth.
- Washing teeth with hot water.
- Putting *lavang* powder at the place of toothache.
- Putting *Fitkiri* powder at the place of toothache.
- *Jhar-phuk* treatment of toothache.

Mouth Diseases and Primary Treatment

The folk and peasant community members treat their mouth diseases like mouth wounds by following primary practices:

- Using old *ghee* of cow or sheep over tongue and inner parts of mouth.
- Putting mustard oil on navel.
- Taking gentle hot food.
- Taking gentle hot milk.
- Taking help of *Jhar-phuk* method.

Throatache and Primary Treatment

There are some diseases which occur in our throat. They are throat swelling, throat burning, throat pain and coughing throat. The folk and peasant people treat their throat diseases with following primary practices:

- Washing throat with salty hot water four five times daily.
- Taking hot water.
- Soaking throat with clothes.
- Hot *Mahua* seed is put on throat.
- Tieing throat with towel at night.
- Taking help of *Jhar-phuk* method.
- Taking Chayavanprash with milk.

Neck and Shoulder Diseases and Primary Treatment

The people suffer from neck pain and shoulder pain during change of season. It is a very common disease during change of season. The folk and peasant people take help of following primary practices for treating neck and shoulder disease:

- Not using pillow.
- Garlic cooked mustard oil is massaged four-five times.
- *Mahua* oil is heated and applied over the affected area.
- The affected part is soaked with a cloth having *mahua* flower, *choker, Ajawain* and salt.
- The liquor of *mahua* is applied over swollen part.
- The *mahua* liquor is taken as medicine.
- *Mahua* leaves, *Moram* leaves and *Dhatura* leaves are heated and tied in neck and shoulder with the help of cloth.

Back and Waist Diseases and Primary Treatment

The folk and peasant people suffer from back and waist pain frequently. They use their own primary treatment methods. They are as follow:

- Massage of back and waist by massage doer.
- Regular massage with garlic cooked in mustard oil by self.
- Regular massage by *mahua* oil.
- Soaking with cloth having *mahua* flower, choker, *ajawain* and salt at night.
- Covering waist and back with hot leaves of *Moram, Mahua* and *Dhathura* and finally tied with cloth for whole night.
- Applying *mahua* liquor
- Taking *mahua* liquor as medicine.

Thigh, Knee and Foot Disease and Primary Treatment

Folk and peasant people suffering from thigh, knee and feet disease use following primary practices for curing diseases:

- Massage with a massage doer.
- Self massage with garlic cooked in mustard oil.
- Massage with *mahua* oil.
- Soaking with *mahua* flower, *choker, ajawain* and salt tied in a cloth.
- Putting hot *mahua* leaves, moram leaves, *dhathura* leaves on affected area at night and with a cloth.
- Taking *mahua* liquor as medicine.
- Applying *mahua* liquor at affected area.

Stomach Disease and Primary Treatment

Folk and peasant people suffering from stomach diseases follow following practices as primary treatment:

- Taking liquid food.
- Taking mild hot milk.
- Taking sugarcane juice.
- Taking pumpkin and papaya juice.
- Taking lemon juice and *kalanamak.*
- Taking loaf sugar, *Ajawain* and *kalanamak.*

- Taking *Bel* syrup.
- Taking *Trifala churna.*
- Taking *Hing* and *Ajawain.*
- Observing fast, if necessary.

Cursed Disease and Primary Treatment

There are some diseases whom members of folk and peasant society categorize as cursed disease. They are Cholera, Pox, Jaundice and Leprosy. They treat these cursed diseases with primary practices. They use these treatments as primary treatment.

Cholera

This disease spreads in rainy season. It is believed that when mother Goddess Bhagwati becomes displeased, this disease spreads. It is a contagious disease. The folk and peasant people treat this disease with following primary practices:

- Patient and all members are adviced to take boiled water.
- To wash clothes and bed sheet of patients with surf and hot water.
- To use phenyl in rooms, courtyards, bath rooms and latrine.
- Serving hot liquid food to patient.
- Giving tablets of loaf sugar, *Ajawain* and *kalanamak.*
- To approach patient covering hands, nose and mouth.
- Attendant is advised to take care of not only cleanliness of patient, but his/her own health as well.
- Serving *mahua* liquor.
- Serving hot Chiraita water.
- Serving *Nim* boiled water.
- To make promise to mother Bhagwati for a special worship.
- To report the health worker.

Pox and Primary Treatment

Pox is disease which occurs at the time of change of seasons. It is believed that this disease is also caused by the curse of mother Goddess Bhagwati. When she becomes displeased, she sends this disease to community. This is contagious disease and spreads from individual to individual. It is of two types—*Bari Mata* (big mother) and *Choti Mata* (small mother). In case of *Barimata,* the wounds are bigger, but in case of *Choti Mata* the wounds is smaller. The *Bari Mata* is more dangerous than *Choti Mata.* The folk people observe following primary treatment to cure this disease:

- The patient is kept in a separate room.
- A promise is made to offer a special worship in the temple of Devi Mai.
- The caretaker of patient keeps hands and face covered with clothes. He/she keeps special care of hygiene.
- Phenyl is spread on floors of each rooms and courtyards.
- The clothes and bedsheet of patient is washed in surf and hot water.
- *Nim* leaves are spread on the bed of patient.
- The body of patient is washed with *Nim* leaves boiled water.
- The patient is served simple food without spices and oil.
- Now-a-days dettol is used for washing body and clothes of patient.
- After cure, a special worship is offered.

Leprosy and Primary Treatment

Leprosy is also taken as a disease caused by Sun-God. It is a contagious disease and a great social stigma is attached to it. The members of folk and peasant community practice following methods as primary treatment:

- Leprosy patient is kept in a separate room.
- The patient is served simple food.
- *Nim* toddy is served.
- *Nim* oil and *karanj* oil are applied on affected areas.
- Patients are asked to observe sun worship daily.
- Patients are advised to take blessing of mother Goddess Bhagwati.
- Patients are served food in separate utensils.
- Utensils are washed with burning ash.
- The care taker member has to take care of his/her own health.
- The patients are brought to leprosy cure centre as early as possible.

Jaundice and Primary Treatment

Jaundice is regarded as a disease cursed by the Sun-God. The body of patients become yellow. The bed and clothes also become yellow. The folk and peasant community members observe following practices as part of primary treatment:

- Serving *Mar-bhat,* salt and lemon juice.
- Serving non-spicy and non-oily vegetables.

- Serving boiled green leafy vegetables.
- Not serving pulse.
- Serving churned curd.
- Serving sugarcane juice.
- Serving orange and apple fruits.
- Giving cucumber and water melon.
- Giving sugar syrup.
- Giving milk without fat.
- Avoid meat, chicken, eggs and fishes.

Accident and Quarrel based Disease and Primary Treatment

In accidents and quarrels, our body parts gets broken, fractured, burnt and cut. The accident affected person is known as accident victim and need treatment like patient. In case of accident some primary treatment is necessary. Primary treatments related to accident based disease are as follows:

Fracture and Primary Treatment

When bones of hands, legs, neck, shoulder met an accidental fracture, they are cured by folk and peasant community members by observing following primary treatment:

- The broken body parts are kept straight and tied with sticks to keep them fixed.
- Turmeric powder and lime are heated and applied over the effected part.
- *Chotsazi* is crushed to make paste and applied over the body parts.
- Leaves, bark and roots of *Harjora* plant are crushed to make a paste for applying over the fractured parts.
- The patient is brought to hospital for secondary treatment.

Burn and Primary Treatment

The cases of burning occur at the time of cooking, falling hot milk, falling hot oil, fall of hot foods, falling hot tea and others. The incidence of burning requires primary treatment. The members of folk communities treat the case of burning primarily with following practices:

- Not pouring water on burn scar.

- Putting potato paste on burnt part.
- Soaking with clothes mildly.
- Carrying victim to hospital.

Cut and Primary Treatment

Our body parts get cut while cutting vegetables, touching blades and knives, dashing against stones, falling on stones and in quarrelling. The incidence of cutting requires primary treatment. The folk and peasant people follow following practices as a part of primary treatment:

- The wound is covered with a clean cloth.
- Before covering with cloth, urine is put.
- The juice of *Genda* flower leaves is applied.
- *Nim* leaves paste is applied.
- The wound is kept away from salt, ash and cowdung.
- Injection of Tetanus is taken.
- The bandage is changed everyday.
- The patient is brought to hospital for secondary treatment.

Skin Disease and Primary Treatment

There are some diseases which affect our skin. The members of folk and peasant communities attempt to treat their skin diseases with primary practices. They are as follows:

Jurpiti and Primary Treatment

Jurpiti is a skin disease which appears during change of season. In this disease, red spots appear on the body here and there. The folk and peasant people treat this disease with following primary practices:

- Vermillion is mixed in mustard oil, and applied over the skin.
- After application of vermillion paste, the body is covered with a blanket.
- Fire is burnt for sweating.
- After appearing sweating, the disease is cured.

Kal-kal or Khujali (Irritation)

This is a disease in which irritation appears in skin. This disease attack in fingers, thighs, upper hands joint with shoulder. When this disease occurs, heavy irritation starts. Patient start rubbing the body parts. In rubbing body parts, the patient feels pleasure. But after rubbing he/she feels burning sensation. The members of folk and peasant community employ following practices as primary treatment:

- Wet milky soil is applied over the affected body parts.
- The body is allowed to become dry in sun.
- Bathing properly after an hour.
- Applying *Nim* oil and *Karanj* oil.
- Taking *Nim* toddy.
- Taking water of *Chiraita* plant in the morning while empty stomach.
- If not cured, bringing patient to a doctor.

Dinay (Eczima)

The disease of Dinay is very serious skin disease which appears at any parts of body as ring worm or eczema. Water starts flowing from the wounds after irritation. The folk and peasant community members attempt to cure this disease with following primary practices:

- Cleaning the eczema or ring worm with milky soil.
- Now-a-days, Nim soap and Dettol soap is used.
- After washing, *kapur* mixed in coconut oil is applied.
- *Chiraita* water is served in empty stomach.
- *Nim* toddy is served before breakfast.
- *Nim* leaves paste is applied over the diseased parts.
- The clothes and bed sheet of patient is washed in surf.
- The patient is not asked to touch soda and surf.

Hair Disease and Primary Treatment

Untimely fall of hairs is taken as a serious hair related disease. The folk people and peasants practice following primary treatments to cure the fall of hairs. They are as follow:

- Less and less use of soap and shampoo in hairs.
- Washing hairs with milky soil.
- Not washing hairs with hot water.
- Daily use of coconut oil in hairs.
- Daily use of mustard oil.
- Washing hairs with dry Amla powder.

- Washing hairs with pulse flour (*Besan).*
- *Mehandi* powder is applied.

Face Disease and Primary Treatment

The skin of face becomes shaded, line appears and skin becomes dry. They are treated as face disease. They make a person old in look. The folk and peasant people cure this disease with following primary practices:

- Daily wash of face with *Besan* (Pulse flour).
- Application of milk on face.
- Application of butter on face.
- Application of curd fat (*Chhali).*
- Application of Turmeric and pulse ointment (*ubatan).*

Lifestyle Change Disease and Treatment

Now-a-days, some diseases have also appeared in folk and peasant communities due to change in lifestyle. Folk and peasant attempt to treat these disease with primary practices. They are as follows:

Sugar Disease (Diabetes) and Primary Treatment

Now-a-days, the disease of sugar has also appeared in folk and peasant societies. It is because the members of those communities have also brought changes in their lifestyle. They attempt to treat this disease with own primary treatment. They are as follows:

- Not eating sweet food items.
- Not eating too much in one time.
- Eating green karaila and *karaila* powder.
- Eating *methi* powder.
- Eating bread four-five times in a day in little quantity.
- Eating a pulse of *masur* and *mung.*
- Eating green and leafy vegetables.
- Not eating potato.
- Eating *Jamun* seed powder and mango seed powder.
- Eating vinegar of *Jamun.*
- Chewing new leaves of *Nim,* guava and bel plants.
- Walking regularly in the morning.

Blood Pressure and Primary Treatment

Blood pressure has also become a dangerous disease of folk and peasant communities. The folk and peasant community members attempt to cure this disease with following primary practices:

- Taking only boiled foods.
- Not taking oily and spicy foods.
- Less and less use of salt.
- Taking seasonal fruits.
- Use of *karela* vegetables.
- Use of pumpkins
- Use of *khira, kakari* and watermelon.
- Taking vegetable of *sahejan* or *munaga.*
- Taking leaves of *sahejan* or *munaga.*
- Taking patient to hospital for secondary treatment.

Heart Disease and Primary Treatment

Now-a-days, heart disease has also appeared in folk and peasant communities. Folk and peasant community members attempt to cure the disease with following primary practices:

- Less and less use of salt in vegetables.
- Less and less use of oil, *ghee* and fats.
- Use of mustard oil or Pisi oil in very little amount.
- Using *Arjun chhal* bark water regularly in morning during empty stomach.
- Taking juice of onion, ginger, lemon and apple together after cooking for sometime.
- Taking patient to hospital for treatment.

9
Impediments to Health

As has been dealt earlier that the greatest wealth on this earth is *Nirogikaya* (Disease free body). In other words we can say that health is the greatest wealth. It is above money, gold, silver and diamond. That is why we want to remain healthy and we practice different healthy behaviours. For example food behaviour, sleep behaviour, work behaviour, rest behaviour, *yoga* and *pranayama* behaviour, folk medical behaviour, modern medical behaviour, walking and exercise behaviour. By adopting such behaviours we want to remain healthy and make our life long. To live healthy is our human right. No Government or individuals can deny our this right. In democratic country like India, it has become responsibility of the Government to keep people healthy. But it is not possible without our positive cooperation. Today, there are Governmental, non-Governmental, international organizations and media which are working for the health of poor, deprived, exploited and neglected lot of the community. They are women, children, aged, S.Cs, S.Ts and OBCs. A number of health improvement related programmes have been formulated and implemented from the very first five years plan. A number of new health promotion programmes have also been introduced time to time. But on the basis of study of health indicators, we are lagging far behind. This reveals clearly that health has to face some impediments. Factors responsible for impediments to health are as follows:

- Individual factor
- Social factor
- Geographical factor
- Natural factor
- Educational factor
- Physical factor
- Cultural factor
- Economic factor
- Political factor

- Nutritional factor
- Psychological factor
- Industrial factor
- Migration factor
- Communicational factor
- Habit factor
- Corruption factor
- Genetic factor
- Sexual factor
- Religious factor
- Magical factor
- Developmental factor

Now, let us discuss about these factors related to impediments to health one by one.

Individual Factor

Individual factor creates impediment to health. Although health is related to community and society. But the ultimate victim or loser of health is individual. There are some individuals who do not obey social and community value related to health. They are indulged in smoking, drinking, tobacco chewing and even in prostitution. Their such anti-social and deviant behaviours destroy their physical and mental health. They become pathological cases for the society. Thus, individual factor creates impediments to health.

Social Factor

Social factors also come in the way of maintaining health. In our society there are resourceful and resourceless or people—haves and have nots. The resourceful persons visit super speciality hospital for treatment of diseases. They are in position to make heavy expenditure on treatment. On the other hand, there are some people who are at the bottom of social stratum. They are resourceless. They are exploited, oppressed and deprived section of society. They struggle hard to maintain their existence. They do not know what is balanced died and what is proper nutrition. They eat whatever they get. They do not think of balanced diet and nutrition. Again in our society girls are discriminated in nutrition. They are deprived of proper nutrition. Thus, social factors come in the way of health.

Geographical Factor

Areas such as hill, plateau, forest, plain, coastal, desert and island come in health maintenance. Each geographical area has its own environment. In different environment different diseases appear and affect the health of people. Different geographical areas create trouble in proper delivery of health services. As a result, people are not in a position to avail health services provided by the Government. Thus, geographical factor creates impediments to health.

Natural Factors

Natural factor like flood, earthquakes, starvation and epidemic come in the way of health. During flood and earthquakes health service delivery system is badly affected. Transport system, communication system, water supply system and other systems are disturbed and people are not in a position to get food, water, clothes, shelter, medicine and others. Flood and earthquakes also invite a number of new diseases. Since delivery system is disturbed, people do not get food, water and medicine to fight against the diseases. Thus, natural factor creates impediments to health.

Educational Factors

In our country, a good number of people are still illiterate. Because of this they are not in a position to avail a number of health delivery facilities. They do not show their participation in health delivery system. They do not get benefit of Anganwadi Kendra, health sub-centres, health centres and hospitals. They do not show interest in vaccination, safe maternity, safe delivery, safe reproductive health behaviour and safe children health. They still spend time in *Jhar-phuk* and Pujapath for curing diseases. Thus, illiteracy comes in the way of health.

Physical Factors

In our country, there are a good number of people who are deaf, dumb, blind, lame, handless, mentally retarded and physically challenged. They are, now, known as *Divyang*. They are dependant on society for their health and existence. Our Government has established institutions to take care of them, to educate them and to keep them physically fit. But they are not in a position to avail.

Cultural Factors

Cultural factors also come in the way of health. In our culture, women cook food, serve to all members and themselves share in the last. Sometimes no food is left for them. They do not go to cook again. Rather they go to sleep with taking water. This cultural factor makes woman malnutrient. In this way, cultural factors create impediment to health.

Economic Factors

It is true that health is the greatest wealth. But it is also true that wealth is essential to remain healthy. There are people in our society who lead life below poverty line. Crores of people remain hungry and go to sleep without food. Such people are bound to become victim of malnutrition. They suffer from a number of diseases. They are not in a position to avail proper treatment. They do not live in clean environment. They do not have clean drinking water sources, airy house, latrine and drains in house. They lack kitchen and wash room. They live in such a pitiable condition that they cannot maintain good health due to poor economic condition. Thus, economic factor creates impediment to health.

Political Factors

Political factor also comes in the way of health. Now-a-days, health has been integrated to human right. To remain healthy and to maintain health is our human right. No individual and Government can deny it. In our country, it is duty of the Government to keep people healthy and take special care of non-priviledged sections. For this purpose our Government has established many layered health institutions where free treatment and medicines are provided. But proper health delivery does not reach to all people. B.P.L. cards are given to those who are below poverty line. In the selection of health beneficiary, partiality is maintained. Real beneficiaries are not selected. Besides this many health services, delivery schemes of Central Government are not implemented in some states for political rivalry. This is unfortunate. Thus, lack of political will appears before us. In this way political factor creates impediment to health.

Nutritional Factors

Our health is directly related to nutrition. What is our concept of nutrition. How we provide nutrition to our body, how many times we provide nutrition and what we include under nutrition determine our health. But nutrition has relation with income. Families with low income do not place emphasis on balanced nutrition. They provide, somehow, nutrition to their bodies, but they do not provide balanced nutrition. In such cases, they are bound to become malnourished.

Now-a-days, people are using refined in place of *ghee*, mustard oil and Tisti oil. People are using varieties of ready made species. Refined and spices are spoiling our health.

Also, people are dependant on ready made fast foods, restaurant foods and restaurants. These practices are also affecting health adversely. People are becoming victims of diabetes, B.P., heart diseases and intestine diseases.

Psychological Factors

Today we are living in an age of marketism, consumerism, and meterialism. Our needs are created by the market. Varieties of consumer goods are available in the markets. They are reaching people through advertisement. Through advertisement false propaganda is created about the best quality of goods. But in practice they are of low quality. In the age of marketisation, we do not have satisfaction. We are buying consumer goods on loan. More and more burden of loan has made us mentally disturbed. In place of peace, fraternity and cooperation, people are becoming jealous and competitive. To see neighbour richer, happier and peaceful, people are becoming anxious and mental patient. A number of members are taking help of corruption, bribery, crime and social pathology to become rich and richer. But in fact, they are turning into psychological cases and mental patient.

Thus, psychological factors come in the health. We are loosing our mental health, we are disintegrating our personality, family, community and society.

Administrative Factors

Administrative factor is also coming in the way of public health. The success of the Government depends upon administrative system. The responsibility of formulating policies and programmes, implementing them, monitoring them, evaluating them and following up them depends upon administrator. The health administrators have to play significant role in delivery of health services to the people. But, people are not getting health benefits of a number of health promotion programmes launched by the Government. Thus, administrative factor comes in the way of public health.

Industrial Factor

Now-a-days, we have a number of big industrial complexes. Majority of industrial complexes are in towns, cities, or metropolises. They are located on the bank of rivers, tanks and seas. Industries produces not only goods to be sold in markets. But they also produces waste materials in the form of solid, liquid and gas. Solid and liquid industrial wastes are flowing in rivers. They are polluting soil and water. Industries emit smoke. Smoke is polluting our air. Industries are also emiting sound as a result of which sound pollution appears. Due to industrial complexes, we are bound to live in a polluted environment which is affecting our health negatively. We are becoming victims of blind, dumb, deaf, throat cancer, lung cancer, intestine cancer and others. Thus, industrial complex create hindrance in health.

Migrational Factor

Today we are migrating from rural to urban areas in search of jobs, works, business and trade to towns, cities and metropolises. We are migrating to foreign countries too. The only goal behind migration is to earn more and more money. For this, we are leaving our family, community and society. We are going to live in towns, cities and metropolises. We do not get proper space to live, we live in slum. We do not have food security. We eat in hotels and depends upon readymade food. We do not have safe drinking water. We have to work more and more hours. We become victim of drinking and prostitution. We neither save money nor our health. We return home becoming victim of AIDS, T.B., malnutrition and a number of diseases. Thus, migration creates impediments to health.

Communicational Factors

Communicational factor is also creating hindrance in health. Our Government has launched a number of health promotion schemes. But a good number of them could not attain success due to lack of communication. The success of a programme depends upon the manner in which beneficiaries are communicated and convinced. We have Governmental, non-Governmental, international and media as agents of health development. But in spite of these agencies, health promotion programmes are not attaining success because traditional agencies are being ignored. In vaccination, family welfare, maternity benefit, AIDS, leprosy, safe maternity, we are not getting success up to expectation. It is due to not proper communication. Thus, communication creates impediment to health.

Habit Related Factors

Personal habits also come in the way of our health. It is said that habit is the second nature. Once it makes victim, the victim continues for ever. Wine, liquor, tobacco, biri, cigarettes, opium, marijuana, *zarda* and drug are our habits. We consume them, because we do not have control on ourselves. We start taking them under control as habit. Intake of intoxicants and others make us ill physically, mentally and economically. We become patient of T.B., Asthama, Heart, B.P., Cancer and others. Thus, personal habits also creates a lot of impediments to health.

Corruption Factor

Corruption also comes in the way of health. In our countries some parameters or standards have been decided for food materials. The traders are supposed to follow them. But due to prevalence of corruption the standards related to food are not maintained. We have to eat adulterated foods and food materials. We do not get pure food materials. Intake of impure food materials has made us ill physically and mentally. Thus, corrupt practices create hindrance in maintenance of health.

Genetic Factors

There are some disease which are transferred from parents to children. They are known as genetic diseases. Due to genetic factor children are short statured, physically handicapped, non-motile, blind, deaf, dumb and cross-gender. Thus, genetic factors affect our health in many ways.

Sexual Factors

Homosexuality and prostitution creates a number of sexually transmitted disease such as HIV/AIDS. Unsafe sex relations make us victim of sexually transmitted diseases. Much sexuality also destroys our health. Controlled sex life keeps us fit physically and mentally. In this way, sexual factor also affects our health negatively.

Religious Factors

Religious factors also create hindrance in maintenance of our health. In our society epidemic, barrenness, impotency, and non-curable diseases are taken as curse of deities. T.B., Polio, Leprosy, Cancer, and pox are taken as curse of Gods and Goddesses. Such patients have to observe a number of taboos. They have to offer worship. Social stigmata is also attached to these diseases. Such belief create delay in modern treatment of disease. As a result, many of them loose their health and meet untimely death. Thus, religious factor comes in the maintenance and treatment of health.

Superstitions

These factors also come in the way of health maintainance. In our society a number of diseases are blieved as a result of witchcraft or black magic. People correlate all events of serious and non-curable diseases as a result of witchcraft and black magic. People spend valuable time in *Jhar-phuk* and quarrel with neighbours, community members, relatives and villagers. For barrenness, widowhood, infant or child mortality, mother mortality, adult mortality, leprosy, T.B., cancer and others, witchcraft or black magic is taken as responsible. In doubt of magical attack, people spent time in visiting to *Ojha, Guni, Shaman, Pandit, Padari* or *Maulavi* and magical performances under their supervision. When patient is not given proper treatment, he/she is bound to loose health for ever. Thus, magical factor creates impediments to health.

Developmental Factors

Developmental factors also put hindrance in health maintenance. Now-a-days, we are using more and more chemical fertilizer, patent seeds, and insecticides to get more and more produce from the field. But we are bound to eat polluted grains and vegetables. Such polluted food intake is affecting our health adversely.

Also, we are testing nuclear bombs. They are also affecting our health.

Today, we are living in an artificial environment. We live in air-conditioned room and houses. We work in A.C. office. We travel in A.C. car, bus and train. Artificial environmental conditions are affecting our health condition. We are becoming victims of new and new diseases.

From the above account, it is quite clear that our health is affected negatively by a number of factors. They act as impediments to health.

10
Health Agents

Ever since his emergence on this earth, man has been engaged in experiencing, understanding, knowing and diffusing knowledge of health, disease and treatment. The agents, whom man has entrusted to explore and diffuse information of health, disease and treatment in society, are known as health agents. They are also termed as health communicators. The main functions of health agent have been to make people aware of health, to inform about diseases affecting health, to tell people about the treatment of different diseases, to say about the signs and symptoms of some disease, to treat the diseases, to inform people about treatment centres and hospital to tell about medical stores and to communicate people about ways by which healthy life can be led. As they have been busy in communicating health, diseases and their treatments, it is but natural that they are designated as health communicator or health agents.

For the purpose of study, we may divide health agents into following types on the basis of their role in different periods of time:

- Traditional Health Agents
- Modern Health Agents
- International Health Agents.

Now, let us discuss about the these agencies of health one by one.

Traditional Health Agent

In our communities, there are some persons or institutions which have been assigned duties of health, disease and treatment since time immemorial. They are as follows:

- Family
- Neighbourhood
- Medicine man

- Kusarain, Dagarin or Chamain
- Massage doer
- Snakebite *Jhar-phuk* doer
- Scorpion-bite *Jhar-phuk* doer
- Jackal-bite *Jhar-phuk* doer
- Mongoose-bite *Jhar-phuk* doer
- Dog-bite *Jhar-phuk* doer
- Toothache *Jhar-phuk* doer
- Headache *Jhar-phuk* doer
- Body pain *Jhar-phuk* doer
- Jaundice *Jhar-phuk* doer
- Pahan or Baiga
- Priest
- Sage
- Faqir
- Bhagat
- Bhagatin
- Ojha-Guni
- Vaidya
- Maulavi
- Father
- Ayurvedic Centre
- Homoeopathy Centre
- Yoga Centre
- Naturopathy Centre
- Siddha Centre
- Jyotishacharya.

Now, let us discuss about these traditional agents of health one by one.

Family

Family is primary school and mother is regarded as first teacher. As a first teachers she teaches about good health habits to children, besides their proper breast feeding and nutrition. She is not only first teacher, but also first doctor who takes care of health of not only children but husband and other aged members of the family. She cooks nutritious and healthy food and nourishes all family members. She knows names of a number of common diseases and their primary treatment by folk medicines and herbal medicines. When the disease is not controlled by primary treatment, the family head brings member to hospital for treatment. Thus, family acts as a traditional agent of health.

Neighbourhood

Neighbourhood also acts as traditional agent of health. When a member of the neighbourhood falls ill seriously, all members of the neighbourhood and community become serious and anxious. They tell about varieties of folk and herbal medicines and medicine man to approach for the treatment of the person concerned. They bring and provide herbal medicine for the patient. They also accompany patient family to visit the house of medicine man. When the first treatment is not effective, they help concerned family in carrying to hospital for better treatment. The neighbourhood also teach small children about good health habits. They try to control the bad habits of children. Thus, neighbourhood works as traditional health agent of the community.

Medicine Man

The folk and peasant societies have medicine man. The medicine man's post is hereditary and continues from father to the eldest son. The medicine man has knowledge of diseases and their treatment by folk or herbal medicine. Members of folk and peasant communities suffering from disease approach the medicine man for treatment and medicine. The medicine man provides already prepared medicine or asked the patient to provide medicine after preparation. He gives some medicines in liquid form or as syrup and some as tablets. The patients are cured by his treatment. Thus, medicine man plays the role of traditional agent of health.

Kusarain, Dagarian or Chamain

Kusarain, Dagarin or Chamain is regarded as traditional delivery expert in folk and peasant communities. This post is also hereditary and goes to first *Putoh* (daughter-in-law) from *Sas* (mother-in-law). As they are delivery expert, their services are hired in folk and peasant communities. In folk and peasant-communities delivery of child generally takes place in house. Therefore, Kusarain, Dagarian or Chamain plays significant role. From delivery to *Chhathi* ceremony, they keep watch on health of mother and infant. They are paid good prize for their services in cash, kind and food materials.

Massage Doer

In folk and peasant communities, some men and women are expert in massage doing. They do body massage with mustard oil or special oil prepared for the purpose to aged men and women. Male massage doer does massage to a male only and female massage doer does the massage of female only. They are paid in cash and kind. Thus, they act as traditional agent of health.

Bone setter (Haad Vaidya)

In folk and peasant communities, some persons are expert in setting broken, fractured or dislocated bones. That is why they are known as bone setters. They do setting of bone by traditional method without operation and X-ray. They fix the bone and tie with sticks for support. The patient is adviced for rest. Some ointment prepared from herbs are given for applying on the broken part. *Harjorawa* plant bark is crushed, heated and applied. Turmeric and lime paste heated and applied over the portion affected. Bone setters are paid in cash and kind. They take up cases of hurt, swollen, simple fracture. But for compound fracture, they advice the patient to go to hospital. They also do bone setting of cattle. They act as traditional agent of health.

Snake Bite Jhar-phuk Doer

In folk and peasant communities some persons are expert in curing snake bite by *Jhar-phuk* method. As they take help of *Jhar-phuk*, they are also known as *Jhar-phuk* doer. Either patient is carried to their house or they come to attend patient in house. They utter mantra and try to bring down the poison at the place of bite. Then poison is taken out by *Jari-buti* applying over the bite. If necessary, they make a cut at the point of bite to get the poison flow outside with poisoned blood. In this way, they act as traditional agent of health.

Scorpion Bite Jhar-phuk Doer

There are some persons expert in curing scorpion bite by *Jhar-phuk* method. They know the mantra by which the poison of scorpion bite is got down at the point of bite. Then they take out poison from the bite place out by applying *Jari-buti.* The *Jari-buti* absorbs the poison.

Jackal Bite Jhar-phuk Doer

In folk and peasant communities, the incidence of jackal bite is common. The poison of jackal bite is cured by *Jhar-phuk* doer who are known as expert in depoisoning the Jackal bite. They recite some mantra and do *Jhar-phuk.* After reciting mantra, they put *Jari-buti* on bite place which cures the patient. They work as traditional agent of health.

Mongoose Bite Jhar-phuk Doer

In folk and peasant communities, there are some persons who cure mongoose bite by *Jhar-phuk* method. They are expert in curing mongoose bite through *Jhar-phuk* method. The take help of mantra and herbal *Jari-buti* in curing the mongoose bite. They are traditional agent of health.

Dog Bite Jhar-phuk Doer

Dog bite is very common feature in folk and peasant communities. There are some experts who cure the dog bite by *Jhar-phuk* method. In this method, they take help of reciting mantras and *Jari-buti* medicine. They are known as traditional agent of health.

Toothache Jhar-phuk Doer

Toothache is very common tooth disease. In folk and peasant communities, this disease is cured by *Jhar-phuk* method. The *Jhar-phuk* doer takes helps of some mantras and herbal medicine in curing the toothache. Thus, he/she is known as traditional agent of health.

Headache Jhar-phuk Doer

In folk and peasant communities, there are some persons expert in curing headache by *Jhar-phuk* method. They take help of *Jhar-phuk* method and herbal medicine in curing headache. He/she is known as traditional agent of health.

Bodyache Jhar-phuk Doer

In folk and peasant communities we have some experts who cure body ache by *Jhar-phuk* method. In this method they recite mantras first and then do massage with *Jari-buti* medicine.

Jaundice Jhar-phuk Doer

In our folk and peasant communities, there are some persons expert in curing Jaundice by *Jhar-phuk*. In this method, they take help of reciting mantras and giving *Jari-buti* medicine to the patient. The patient feels relief by *Jhar-phuk* method. They also act as traditional health agent.

Pahan or Baiga

In tribal communities, priests are known as *Pahan* or *Baiga*. A Pahan/Baiga is also expert of disease and treatment by *Jhar-phuk* method and *Jari-buti* medicine. In this way, *Pahan* acts as traditional health agent.

Priest

In peasant communities, some persons act as village priest and temple priest. They have knowledge about disease and treatment through *Jhar-phuk* method and *Jari-buti*. They act as traditional health agents.

Sage

In folk and peasant communities, some sages take shelter by erecting a hut under a lonely place. They also have knowledge of disease and treatment through *Jhar-phuk* method. They also act as traditional health agent.

Faqir

In folk and peasant communities, some persons as *Faqir* wander from village to village for begging. They also cure disease by *Jhar-phuk* method. They act as traditional health agent.

Bhagat

In folk and peasant communities, some male members are expert of driving *Bhut-Preta* and witchcraft. They are known as *Bhagat.* They cure disease caused by *Bhuta-Preta* and witchcraft. They act as traditional health agent.

Bhagatin

In folk and peasant communities, there are some female members who are expert in driving out *Bhut-Preta* and witchcraft. They are known as *Bhagatin.* They act as traditional health agent.

Ojha-Guni

In folk and peasant communities, there are some persons well expert in curing diseases caused by *Bhuta-Preta,* witchcraft, evil-eyed mouthed and evil-voiced. They are known as *Ojha Guni.* They are traditional health agent.

Maulavi

In Muslim communities, persons who cure diseases by *Jhar-phuk* method are known as *Maulavi.* They are also traditional health agent.

Father

In Christian communities, father of church acts as traditional health agent. He cures diseases by prayers and *Jhar-phuk*.

Vaidya

In folk and peasant communities, there are some persons who act as Vaidya. The *Vaidya* has knowledge of Ayurvedic and *Jari-buti* medicine. He cures diseases by his Ayurvedic and *Jari-buti* medicine. His occupation is known as *Vaidyagiri.* He acts as traditional agent of health.

Homoeopathy Centre

In folk and peasant communities, some persons have established Homoeopathy centre for the cure of different diseases. They act as traditional health agent.

Ayurvedic Centre

In folk and peasant communities, some persons have established Ayurvedic centres for treatment of diseases. They cure diseases by Ayurvedic medicine and work as traditional health agent.

Naturopathy Centre

Some persons of folk and peasant communities have established Naturopathy centre. They cure diseases by Naturopathy and work as traditional health agent.

Yoga Centre

Some persons of folk and peasant communities, run yoga centre and cure diseases through yogic practices. They act as traditional health agent.

Jyotishacharya

In peasant communities there are Jyotishacharya who belong to priestly community. They attempt to cure the diseases of a person by observing his/her horoscope, palm and face. They provide gems to wear in ring and suggest special worship to Lord Shiva, Vishnu, Hanumana, mother Goddess and Rahu-Ketu. They also act as traditional agent of health.

Modern Health Agent

Now-a-days, we are living in era of modern science and technology. We have developed latest technology and super-speciality hospitals with expert doctors for treatment of different diseases. There are following modern health agents:

- Anganwadi Kendra
- School
- Health Sub-centre
- Primary Health Centre
- Extra Primary and Subsidiary Health Centre
- Referral Hospital
- Sadar Hospital
- Government Medical College and Hospitals
- Private Medical College and Hospital
- Private Nursing Home
- Super Speciality Hospital
- Acupressure Centre
- Electropathy Centre
- Pathological Laboratories
- Ultrasound Centre
- C.T. Scan Centre
- Medical Shops and Stores
- Nurses
- X-Ray Technician
- Veterinary Doctor
- Ministry of Health
- Medical Companies
- Medical Representatives
- Private Clinic
- Ministry of AYUSH
- Ayurvedic College and Hospital
- Homoeopathy College and Hospital
- Yoga College and Institute
- Naturopathy College
- Siddha College
- Unani College.

Now, let us discuss about these modern health agents one by one.

Anganwadi Kendra

This is a modern health agent which communicates people about health of pregnant woman, infant and lactating women. It invites pregnant women for health check up, injection, balanced diet, safe delivery and vaccination of children. Thus, Anganwadi Kendra is encouraging pregnant and lactating women and their children to maintain reproductive, lactating, safe delivery and infant health through modern medical treatment. Anganwadi Kendra has played significant role in improving reproductive health, lactating health and infant and children health. They have reduced mother and child mortality rate. Anganwadi Sewika, Sahayika and supervisor work for this purpose.

School

School is a modern agent of health. It teaches about good habit and good health. It teaches about cleanliness personal hygiene and sanitation to the children who attend school. The school inculcates the value of good health character for a good citizen of country. It also teaches students about modern first aid technique to fight cold, cough and fever. It controls the bad health habits.

Health Sub-centre

Our Government has established health sub-centre combining two or more Panchayats for modern treatment of diseases. In health sub-centres nurses, compounder and health worker live to serve the people during illness. Doctor also pays a visit time to time. Health sub-centres make survey of illness and health conditions of the people. Family welfare camp and vaccination camp is organized time to time. The health sub-centres indicate the value of modern health, disease and treatment. It has made people aware of modern methods of treatment and disease control by modern medicines. Thus, health sub-centres act as modern health agent.

Primary Health Centre

In each block headquarters, there is a primary health centre. Mostly it has four medical officers, nurses, trained *Dai,* and health visitor. All doctors and staff of primary health centre act as modern health agent and provide modern treatment to the people. It is also known, now, as community health centre.

Extra-Primary and Subsidiary Health Centre

In addition to primary health centre, our Government has established extra primary and subsidiary health centre on a population of 20,000 to 30,000. It has two medical officers, nurses, *Dai,* and health workers. All doctors and staff work as a modern health agent. They help people in getting treatment through modern method and medicine.

Referral Hospital

In each referral hospital, there are four posts of expert doctor in medicine, gynae, pediatric and surgery. There are nurses, *dai,* compounder, health workers and other staff. They all work as a modern agent of health. They help people in treatment of diseases through modern technique and medicines.

Sadar Hospital

In each district, there is a Sadar Hospital. There is a chief medical officer, other expert doctors, nurses, *dai* and other workers. All together function as modern health agent. They expend help to the people in treatment of diseases through modern technique and medicines.

Government Medical College and Hospital

Our Government has established a number of medical colleges and hospitals in each state to provide modern treatment through modern expert doctors and medicines. They also impart medical education to students. Thus, Government medical colleges and hospitals work as modern agent of health.

Private Medical College and Hospital

In our country, there are a number of private medical colleges and hospitals engaged in imparting medical education to students and provide modern treatment to the people through expert doctors, technicians and medicines. They also act as modern health agent.

Private Nursing Home

There are a number of private nursing homes where private doctors and technicians do treatment of patient through modern techniques and medicines. They act as modern health agent.

Super Speciality Hospital

In our country, a number of super speciality hospitals have been established where treatment is done by multi-specialist doctors, technicians and other staff. They act as modern agent of health.

Acupressure Centre

Now-a-days, a number of acupressure centres have been established where modern treatment is provided with acupressure techniques. These centres also act as modern health agent.

Electropathy Centre

To assist doctors in modern treatment of diseases, a number of pathological laboratories have been established where blood, urine, stool, sugar, cholesterol, and other tests are done through modern techniques. They act as modern health agent.

Ultrasound Centre

To assist specialist modern doctors, a number of ultrasound centres have been established where disease affected parts of liver and stomach are photographed by latest modern techniques and medicine. They act as modern health agent.

Medical Shops and Stores

There are a number of medical shops, pharmacies, and stores where modern medicines are sold and bought on the prescription of a doctor. They act as modern health agent.

Nurses

There are a number of nurses in each hospital to assist and take care of patients. They are associated with modern hospitals on monthly salary. They act as connecting link between doctor and patient. They are modern health agent.

X-Ray Technician

In hospitals or outside hospitals, there are a number of X-Ray technicians where X-Ray is done by modern technology and medicine. They act as modern health agent.

Veterinary Doctor

There are a number of veterinary doctors posted in block by the Government to provide modern treatment to domestic animals. There are some private veterinary doctors also. They work as modern health agent.

Veterinary Colleges

Our Government has established a number of veterinary colleges to impart education to veterinary students. They act as modern health agent.

Ministry of Health

Ministry of health is most powerful modern health agent. It controls all medical institutions and provide budgetary provision to each medical institution.

Medical Companies

There are a number of medical companies involved in production of medicines. They produce modern medicines and, thus, act as modern health agent.

Medical Representative

Each medical companies employ a number of medical representatives to promote and increase sale of company products. They visit doctor to doctor and provide samples for prescription to the patient. Thus, they act as modern health agent.

Private Clinic

There are a number of private clinics in our country which are providing modern treatment to the patient with modern medicine and technology.

Ministry of AYUSH

Our Government has established Ministry of AYUSH to impart education, training and treatment in Ayurveda, Yoga, Unani, Siddha and Homoeopathy through modern knowledge and technology. Attempts have been made to modernize traditional medical systems. They are, now, working as modern agent of health.

Ayurvedic Colleges and Hospitals

Our Government has established Ayurvedic colleges and hospitals to impart education in Ayurveda and to provide treatment to the people through modern Ayurvedic medicines. They act as modern health agent.

Yoga Colleges and Hospitals

Our Government has established colleges and hospitals to impart education in Yoga and to provide yogic treatment for physical and mental health of people. They act as modern health agent.

Naturopathy College

Our Government has established naturopathy colleges in different parts of the country to impart education, training and treatment in naturopathy through modern technology.

Siddha Colleges

In South Indian States, our Government has established Siddha colleges to impart Siddha medical education, training and treatment through modern knowledge and technology.

International Health Agent

Now-a-days, health is not limited to family, community, and nation, rather it has assumed an international dimensions. All countries of the globe are facing the problem of Cancer, AIDS, Ibola, Coronavirus and others. All countries of the world are facing problems of air, water, soil and sound pollution related diseases. All countries of the world have to face the problem of earthquakes, floods, Tsumani and others. Such natural disasters bring a number of diseases. In order to fight health problems at global level, there are certain global health agents. They extend help in maintenance of health during a natural calamities and others. They are as follows:

- UNICEF
- World Health Organisation
- Red-Cross
- CARE.

Now let us discuss about these world health agents one by one.

UNICEF

This is an international health agent which is extending help in maintenance of children health at global level. It is controlled by an international council. It provides funds for children health and education in developing countries to run children health and education programmes through N.G.Os. It extends cooperation in supply of health kits, advice, training research and evaluation of the programmes undertaken. Under Integrated Child Development Scheme, it provides weighing machine, films, projcctors, typewriter, duplicators, K.B. scale and toys to Anganwadi Kendras. Health card is provided to each beneficiary.

World Health Organisation (WHO)

It is an international health agent. It is controlled by Economic and Social Council of United Nations. It plays significant role in health of international community. In our country, it is playing significant role in control of Diarrhoea, pox, malaria, AIDS, Cancer and Kalajar. It has provided jeep, trailor, spraying machine, poster, banner to run the programme with its aids. It provides significant health services during storm, quakes, flood, starvation, tsunami and other natural calamities and disasters.

Red Cross Society

It is an international health agent. It has office in all developing countries. In India, it is known as Red Cross Society of India. In our country, each state has its office. Its main objective is to create health awareness in poor women to develop healthy habits in them and to make them able to look after their health by themselves. It has own vehicle, doctor, nurse, and other staff. They arrange camp for women by moving village to village. They distribute medicine free of cost. The institution organize operation camp in village and meet all expenditure. It distributes food, clothes and blankets among the patients. Thus, it is extending full cooperation in women health empowerment. It also performs significant role during flood, earthquakes, Tsunami, epidemic and other natural disaster.

CARE

This is an International health agent. It has its office in capitals of all countries. It is named after the country, for example CARE India. In state, it is known after state. For example CARE Jharkhand, CARE Bihar and others. It makes valuable contributions towards child development and maternity health. It extends help in running ICDS properly. It is private, volunteering, profitless, secular International Health Agent. It tries to protect the health of poor, exploited, oppressed, deprived and natural disaster victims. It provides them a life to lead respectfully. It lays emphasis upon children health, maternity health, reproductive health, community health and health statistics. CARE is known as Cooperative for Assistance and Relief Everywhere. It was established in 1948. It is functioning in India since 1986.

11
Jungle and Jari-buti (Herbal) Medicine

There has been a very close relationship between man and forests since time immemorial. When man emerged on this earth from his animal ancestry, he was not a producer. He was simply a consumer of forest produce and other naturally available things. As a consumer of natural things he lived for millions of years. He become producer of grains during Neolithic period nearly 8000-6000 B.C. In this way nature nurtured man. It is quite natural that man developed intimacy with flora and fauna available in Jungle. Both became inter-dependent, interrelated and maintained their co-existence for millions of years. This relation is still maintained by tribals and others who live in forests. Their main means of stay is forest.

Man earned knowledge not only for food gathering, hunting, shifting cultivation and fuel wood, but he also earned knowledge about the medicinal values of flora and fauna available in forest. He recognized his diseases and used parts of flora and fauna as medicine to cure disease. Even today, forest dwellers use root, bark, leaves, flowers, fruits, seeds and stems of forest-plants as medicine or *Jari-buti* found in forest. He collects root, shoot, stem, bark, leaves, flowers, fruits and seeds. He prepares ointment to be applied, syrup and tablets to be taken. The medicine man diagnoses the diseases and provide *Jari-buti* medicine to patients. Patients are cured. Some *Jari-booti* are eaten raw, while some are eaten as cooked. Some are prepared as syrup, tablets and ointment. For treatment of diseases mixture of medicine is also prepared. Generally, herbal medicines are taken with hot water, empty stomach, once, twice or thrice in a day. Similarly, ointment is applied once, twice or thrice time in a day. Some are taken with loaf sugar, *kalanamak* or milk. Some *Jari-buti* medicines are prepared in house because parents have common knowledge of medicinal plants and their use in diseases.

The medicinal properties of forest flora were recognized and used not only by tribals, but also by Aryan Hindus, who laid the foundation of Ayurveda. Our Hindu *Rishi-Munis* and *Acharyas* had identified medicinal properties of forest plants and trees. They prepared medicines for different diseases from their roots, bark, leaves, flower, fruits and seeds. They established Ayurveda system of medicine which is continuing even today. But our folk and peasant people are still using different parts of flora and fauna as raw, cooked and boiled in different diseases. Their such knowledge tradition is continuing since time immemorial. Their knowledge may be based on scientific, partly scientific and non-scientific tradition. So, there is urgent need to explore the real medicinal value of those flora which have been identified as medicinal plants and are continuing generation after generation.

Now, attempts are being made to present here names of plants and trees whose root, shoot, stem, bark, flower, fruits and seeds are used as medicine. Since past our forests have been blessed with plenty of plants and trees of medicinal value through out the length and breadth of our country. The communities living in and around forest have identified them and preserved them since past. Sometimes, the whole plant is used as medicine, sometimes their root, stem, bark, leaves, flowers, fruits or seeds are used in different diseasse. Some examples in this regard are as follows:

- *Bark:* Arjuna, Ashoka, and Kachanar.
- *Flower:* Urahul, Gulal and Har Singar.
- *Fruit:* Bel, Amla, Amaltas, Kela, Mango, Apple and Jamun.
- *Leaf:* Tulsi, Nim, Ghrita Kumari, Brahmi and Karipatta.
- *Root:* Sarpagandha, Mulethi, and Chikauri.
- *Seed:* Mango, Imali, Jamun, Isabgol and Karanj.
- *Shoot:* Turmeric, Ginger, Onion and Amarlata.
- *Whole plant:* Chiraita, Brahmani.
- *Wood:* Chandan, Khair, Pine.

Now, a brief description of some medicinal plants is being given below. The plants may be common or may differ from forests to forests, i.e. different ecology.

Aam (*Mongifera indica*): The fruits and seeds of mango have medicinal value. The syrup of green mango is useful in sunstroke. The seeds of mango is useful in sugar and diarrhoea. The ash of leaves powder cures teeth smell and diseases.

Aasan (*Termenelia tomentosa*): The paste of fresh and soft leaves is useful in vomiting and loose motion. The ash of its bark is mixed in *Til* oil and applied over wounds to get relief. The juice of leaves cures ear pain.

Adula (*Adeto dawasik*): Its root and leaves are used as medicine. It is very much useful to cure bronchitis, asthma, cough and cold. Its leaves and roots are dried in shadow. They are crushed to make powder and are made small tablets by mixing in *Golmircha.* The tablets, thus, made cure cough, cold and asthama.

Ajawain: It is a perennial plant. Its leaves, flowers and fruits are used as medicine. It is especially useful in thread worm and round worm. It cures fevers, enhances digestive power and removes gas.

Akawan (*Calotropis gigantia*): Its roots are used to cure the disease of fileria or Hathi Pawn. Paste of leaves cures muscular and joint pain. Flower powder cures Asthama, cough, cold, indigestion and irregular menstruation. Its milk is used to cure dog bite. Its leaves are also useful in joint pain.

Amarbel (*Carcutariflexa*): Paste prepared from it is useful in hurt and swelling. Its decoction is useful in toothache and hairfall.

Amarlata (*Cassica fistula*): Its root, leaves and fruits are used as medicine. Its fruits and leaves cure loose motion or dysentery. Its roots are boiled in milk and given to T.B. patient to cure T.B. The paste of root cures wounds. The root is boiled in water and taken to cure composite fever. The leaf paste is applied on burnt part to get relief.

Amla (*Ambalica afisinalis*): It is a medicinal plant whose bark, leaves, fruits and roots are used as medicine. It is an important constituent of *Trifla Churna* which is used to cure stomach. Its fruits are beneficial in liver, stomach and pile diseases. Its use promotes hemoglobin. Its fruits cure leucoria.

Anantamul (*Hemidemnus indicus*): Its root has medicinal value. Roots are dried in shadow and crushed to make powder. The powder, thus, made is used to cure of fever, sugar, indigestion, joint pain and skin disease and leucorrhoea. Its root is also used for *Jhar-phuk* treatment of Jaundice disease.

Arandi (*Recinus conmunis*): Its oil has medicinal value. It is useful in sunstroke. Its oil is also used for controlling pregnancy. Its leaves are taken with curd to cure Jaundice.

Arjuna (*Terminelia arjuna*): This is a big evergreen tree. It is also known as Kumkum or Nadi Sarja. It is found on the bank of river, drain and tank. Its bark is beneficial for heart patient. Its bark is boiled in water and the filtered water is used as medicine with spoon in empty stomach.

Ashoka (*Saraca indica*): It is a medicinal plant whose bark, flowers sand fruits are used as medicine. Its bark is boiled in water and taken as medicine to cure irregular menstruation. Its flowers are useful in blood dysentery. The seeds are useful in diabetes.

Ashwagandha (*Vidania semnifira*): Its roots and fruits are used as medicine. Its roots are used to cure T.B., weakness and joint pains.

Babul (*Acasia archica*): Its fruits remove weakness. Its bark removes swelling. Its fruits cure impotency.

Bahera (*Terminesia Belerica*): Its powder cures indigestion, increases appetite. It is important constituent of *Trifala, Chayavanprash,* and *Madhavani.* It cures mental disease and leprosy.

Bar (*Gigicus Mauritina*): Its fruits powder cures leucoria and removes impotency. Its root boiled in water is used for curing dog bite.

Bargad (*Ilastica*): Its bark powder cures urine diseases. Its fruits cures indigestion.

Bel (*Agle marmelus*): Its fruit is useful in stomach and heart disease. Its leaves are used for controlling sugar. Its syrup is used in sunstroke. Its root is used for *Jhar-phuk* treatment.

Beljan (*Codia Mix*): Its bark powder cures gastric and irregular mens.

Bengsag, Brahmanic (*Centila Asiasica*): It is useful in stomach disorder, sugar, jaundice and gastrics. The entire plant has medicinal value. Its leafy vegetable cures a number of diseases.

Bhelwa (*Simicarapus Anacardium*): It is useful in joint pain and cancer menstrual cycle.

Bhograj (*Pusidenum Dhana*): The juice is beneficial for obtaining potency.

Bhumi Jam (*Premnakarvesia*): Its root powder is useful in removing gastrics.

Chir (*Pinus raux berghi*): Tarpin oil is extracted from it, which is very much useful in curing joint pain. It cures old cough.

Chirchiri (*Acarenthus aspera*): Its root has medicinal value. It is used for curing scorpion bite and snake bite. It is also used in *Jhar-phuk* treatment of diseases.

Dhatura (*Dhatura festuosa*): Its leaves are used for curing the diseases of joint pain. Its leaves juice kills germs of stomach.

Dhawai (*Urfordia faticosa*): Its flower is useful in T.B. and indigestion.

Eucalyptus (*Eucalyptus Globuls*): Its leaves juice cures stomach pain. Its bark juice cures cough, cold and allergy. Its oil cures headache.

Future (*Crotonaraxberghi*): Its milk cures eye diseases.

Gajar (*Daucus carota*): It is useful in skin diseases and heart diseases. Its juice is useful for child health.

Gamhar (*Gamelia arboria*): It is useful in snake bite, scorpion bite, killing stomach worm. It is useful in restoring urine flow.

Gandha Purna (*Gaul theria fregretima*): Its oil is very much useful for curing liver diseases and stomach worms.

Ganja (*Camewis cetiva*): It is used as intoxicant which increases hunger, brings sound sleep and clears the stomach.

Ganna (*Secerum aficinerum*): Its juice clears stomach and cures the diseases of Jaundice. Loaf sugar is useful in many kinds of stomach, cough and pain related diseases.

Gawar Patha (*Alobera*): It is useful for curing rough skin and liver diseases.

Gendafool (*Tegetus erecta*): Its leave paste is useful in curing wounds and burn.

Ghorwach (*Acorus clamus*): It is useful in gastrics, increases hunger, kills stomach worms, controls asthama and regulates menstrual cycle. It is also useful in disease of Mirgi.

Ghrita Kumari (*Aloy barbedensis*): The juice of its leave kills stomach worms and is useful in burn. It provides nutrition to hairs. Its juice prevents conception. Its leaves are taken as appetizer.

Giloy (*Tibosmora cardilia*): It cures bile related diseases and women related diseases. Its root is used for causing vomiting.

Gular (*Ficus Glomirata*): It is useful for regulating menstrual cycle, stomach related diseases and controlling vomiting during pregnancy. Its ripe fruits act as blood purifier.

Gunj Per (*Abrus prictorius*): It is used for bringing a senseless person in to sense.

Haldi (*Kurkuma domestica*): It cures cough, cold, fever and swelling. It is used as beautifying element.

Har Singar (*Nictenthus arabar tris-tris*): It is used for curing fever, sugar and joint pains.

Harjor (*Sijan pilos pariesus*): It is helpful in fractures.

Harre (*Terminalia chhebula*): It is useful in cough, cold and indigestion. It is an important constituent of Trifala churna.

Illaichi: Its seeds are full of medicinal value. It cures indigestion and enhances hunger.

Imali (*Tamarindus indica*): The fruit, seed and leaf have medicinal value. The bark ash removes eczema. Syrup of fruits cures sunstroke fever and irregular menstrual cycle. Its leaves acts as digestive. Its seeds cure leucoria and scorpion bite. Its fruit cures intoxication of *Bhang*.

Isharmul or Ishwari (*Aristolochia indica*): Its root cures tooth ache. Powder of roots and stems is used as digestive. It cures irregular menstrual cycle, too. It controls fever and diabetes. It creates vomiting and abortion on taking too much.

Kachanar (*Bauhenia bharigata*): Its buds powder is helpful in indigestion and piles. Its roots, bark and flowers are useful in skin diseases.

Kadam (*Anthrocifesis Kadamlao*): Its bark powder cures fever. Its flower and fruits provides nutrients.

Kamraj (*Seeda aqueta*): The paste of its root is useful in ear and joint pain.

Kanel (*Themesia perubhiyana*): Its leaves are useful in skin diseases.

Karam (*Edina cordifolia*): Its bark paste is useful for skin diseases. Its juice prevents conception. Its leaves are useful for curing wounds.

Karanj (*Pogamia pinata*): Its thin green stick removes teeth diseases. Its oil cures skin diseases. Its bark powder is useful in pile. Its oil controls pregnancy.

Karela (*Memoradica chireciar*): Its fruits are useful in controlling sugar and blood pressure.

Kaucha (*Mukuna putita*): Its seeds are useful in curing wounds. Its roots are used for treating malaria fever.

Kauchala (*Striknus bomica*): Its seeds are used in *Jhar-phuk* treatment.

Kela (*Musparadici aka*): It is useful in controlling loose motion, and digestion. Green banana is useful in controlling sugar diseases.

Khaini (*Nicotiana tewecuru*): It is useful in curing joint pain, ear pain and skin diseases. Its stalk cures toothache.

Khair or Kattha (*Acasia ketechu*): Its root paste is beneficial in curing joint pain. It also removes fever and controls blood pressure.

Khapara Sag (*Anthema portula castum*): It is useful in sugar, indigestion, clearing stomach, liver and kidney diseases. It cures uterus related diseases and *kala jawar.*

Khira (*Cucumis cetimus*): It is useful in diabetics, indigestion, sunstroke, cholera and stone diseases.

Kohara (*Kukurbita moscata*): Its leaves, flower, fruits and seeds have medicinal value for curing gastric and joint pain.

Kulinjan (*Alwinia galauga*): It provides nutrition to head hairs and cures headache.

Kunain (*Sicona oficinelis*): Its bark-powder is used as medicine. It cures malaria disease. It is also useful in pneumonia, amoebic dysentery, and eye diseases.

Kusum (*Sechali chera Oleosa*): Its bark powder cures loose motion. Its oil removes skin diseases and provides nutrients to head hairs.

Kutum (*Coccinia cordifolia*): Its fruits are useful in stomach pain, indigestion and gastric.

Kutumar (*Solenum indicum*): This is useful in asthama, stomach, cough, urine, and gastric diseases.

Lahsun (*Aliyun Setimum*): It cures ear ache, opens heart blockage, removes joint pain and cures stomach related diseases.

Lajvanti or Chui-Mui: This is useful in snake bite, scorpion bite and ear pain.

Lal Dudhi (*Uberbiahita*): The entire parts of plants are used as medicine. This plant is useful in curing heart, liver, T.B., Asthama, cough and cold. Its root controls vomiting.

Mahakal: Its root is poisonous and used for curing pain.

Mahua (*Madhuca Beauty*): Mahua leaves, flowers, fruits and seeds have medicinal value. Its leaves flowers and seed oil is used for removing joint pain and swelling. Its liquor is used as medicine to recover pregnancy health. Its oil is useful in cough and cold.

Maida (*Litsia Polyantha*): Its bark paste is applied over fracture and swelling.

Makchunda (*Chuclipta Alba*): Its flower juice removes hotness of stomach.

Mardaraj: Its bark removes impotency.

Mayor Chundia (*Elephatap Siescever*): Its root is used for terminating pregnancy.

Mehandi (*Lavsonia Inermis*): Its leaves cures urine disease. It cures dandruff.

Muli (*Refnus Cetivus*): It removes gastric.

Munaga (*Morinza Olifera*): Its root, leaves, flower, fruits and seeds are used as medicine in sugar, heart and blood pressure disease. Its fruits prevent pox disease.

Nagfeni (*Opuntia pilocled*): Its paste is useful in skin disease. Its juice removes ear pain.

Nim (*Ajediracta indica*): Its leaves, bark, oil and toddy are used as medicine for curing skin diseases, sugar, and preventing conception. Its leaves are used during pox disease on bed and washing body.

Nimbu (*Citrus aurentifolia*): It is used as appetizer, it enhances hunger and removes indigestion. It opens heart blockages and reduces fats in body. It cures dandruff.

Palak (*Spinesia oleresia*): Its leafy vegetable cures stomach diseases and eye diseases.

Pathar Chatta (*Bryophylum pinetus*): The juice of leaves cures stone diseases.

Pechaki (*Colokesia esculanta*): It removes swelling and joints fractured bones, when its paste is used.

Phutakal (*Ficus inbectoria*): Its leaves are useful in stomach diseases.

Pipal (*Pipal langun*): It cures fever, increases appetite, and removes piles.

Piper (*Ficusrelegiosa*): Its fruits and leaves cure stomach diseases. Its powder cures piles.

Pitaunji (*Putan Jeva sexberghi*): It cures skin allergy.

Plas (*Beauliamonosperma*): Its bark juice is useful in stomach diseases and broken bones.

Prishna Parni (*Ureria pituk*): It cures fractures and gastrics.

Pyaj (*Aliyum sepa*): Its juice cures cough and cold. Its paste cures swelling.

Rengani (*Armimon Maxina*): It cures hydrocele growth. Its seeds cure tooth ache.

Sadabahar (*Minca rezia*): Its leaves and flowers cure diabetics and fever.

Sanjiwan Buti (*Lycopodium*): It cures the disease of not seeing at night (*Ratondhi*). It brings senseless in to sense. It cures diabetics and joint pains.

Sarpagandha (*Raulfia sarpentina*): Its seeds is used in scorpion bite, snake bite, and stomach ache. Its root cures malaria. Its powder is used as energy giver and improves impotency.

Saunth (*Zinziber okisinela*): It is a medicine of cough and cold.

Semal (*Bombex ceita*): It cures barrenness and blood urea.

Sharifa (*Anonasquamosa*): Its leaves and seeds are used for killing dandruff.

Shisham (*Dalberzia sised*): It removes stomach diseases and improves potency.

Sindawar (*Mitex nigando*): It cures all kinds of fever. It is helpful in skin diseases.

Sukdarshan (*Crinum deficsum*): Its seed powder cures impotency.

Surya Mukhi (*Helienbus etem*): Its oil controls cholestrol.

Urad (*Feciolas ganga*): Its decoction is useful in the disease of *Lakawa*.

Urahul (*Hebiscus rosinensis*): It is a medicinal plant. The juice of its buds cures impotency when taken regularly in empty stomach. Its bark cures urine diseases. Its flower powder cures irregular menstrual cycle. The root is useful in cough and cold.

Fauna and Folk Medicine

The members of folk and peasant communities use horns, feathers, meat, teeth, nail and fat of birds and animals as medicine. They are as follows:

Bhauri Kira: It is a black colour creature which swims on water. It cures epilepsy when taken with loaf sugar.

Kenchua: It also cures epilepsy when eaten with loaf sugar.

Kabutar: Its meat cures stomach stone.

Kutta: Its meat cures the disease of T.B.

Bageri: Its meat removes the disease of impotency.

Haril: Its meat cures Asthama.
Vanmurgi: Its meat cures cough and cold.
Chamgadar (Bat): Its meat cures Ratondhi and Asthama.
Snake oil: It cures leprosy.
Shahil: Its meat cures epilepsy.
Siyar blood: It cures skin disease.
Dear horn: It is useful in curing piles.
Elephant Teeth: It is useful in curing piles.
Tiger teeth: It is used in *Jhar-phuk* treatment.
Elephant Nail: It is useful in *Jhar-phuk* treatment.
Sahil feather: It is used for *Jhar-phuk* treatment.
Peacock feather: It is useful in *Jhar-phuk* treatment.

12
Health Demography

In India, a national health policy was formulated in 2002. In that policy formulation, emphasis was made on an approach of public health system and equality in advantages of different classes. It was found that the benefit of public health was not equal in different classes. Its excess was good in the rich but the poor and vulnerable groups were not equally benefited. The poor were deprived of health benefit. In National Health Policy 2002, emphasis was placed on uprooting the inequality of health benefit between rich and poor. Attempt was made to bring all citizens of our nation in mainstream of health development. Some key health indicators are being presented in the table given below.

Key Health Indicators

Table 12.1: Status of Key Health Indicators in India

Sl. No.	Health Indicators	Scheduled Castes	Schedu- led Tribes	OBCs	Other	Total
1.	Infant mortality rate	83	84.2	76.0	61.8	67.0
2.	Neonatal mortality rate	53.2	53.3	50.8	40.7	43.4
3.	Child mortality (1yr—5yr)	39.5	46.3	29.3	22.2	29.3
4.	Below 5 yrs child mortality	119.3	126.3	103.1	82.6	94.9
5.	Percentage of 4yr Institutional Delivery	26.8	17.1	36.1	40.1	33.6
6.	Percentage of Women with Anaemia	56.0	64.9	50.7	47.6	51.8
7.	Percentage of undernourished children	42.2	26.4	43.0	46.8	42.0
8.	Childhood Vaccination (Full Immunization)	40.2	26.4	43.0	46.8	42.0
9.	NHC Test (predelivery)	61.1	56.5	64.6	71.3	65.4

Source: National Health Survey, 1998-1999.

The above table reveals clearly that in all key health indicators, Scheduled Castes, Scheduled tribes and OBCs are lagging far behind. This also indicates that the benefit of public health system has not been achieved equally by all communities. Therefore, there is urgent need to bring all communities in mainstream of nation so that all may attain equal health benefits.

Total Fertility Rate

Total fertility rate is being presented in the Table given below:

Table 12.2: Distribution of total fertility rate in India by castes

Sl. No.	Castes	Total Fertility Rate
1.	Scheduied Castes	3.15
2.	Scheduled Tribes	3.06
3.	Other Backward Castes	2.83
4.	Other Castes	2.66
	Total	2.92

Source: National Family Health Survey, 1998-99.

The above table shows that the total fertility rate in India is 2.92, but total fertility rates in S.Cs, S.Ts, OBCs and other castes are 3.15, 3.06, 2.83 and 2.66 respectively. At national level total fertility rate in S.Cs and S.Ts are more than OBCs and other castes.

Use of Family Welfare Programme

Family planning method is one of the family welfare programmes. It helps in birth control and spacing between two children. The problem of unwanted pregnancy can be solved by using family planning method. It also helps in maintaining a suitable gap between two births. This method is very much useful for family welfare.

Table 12.3: Use of family planning method in India by married couples.

(In percentage)

Sl. No.	Family planning method	Scheduled Castes	Scheduled Tribes	OBCs	Other castes	Total
1.	Male sterilization	1.9	3.1	1.6	1.9	1.9
2.	Female sterilization	34.4	28.8	37.2	31.1	34.2
3.	IUD	0.7	0.9	1.5	2.4	1.6
4.	Other method	44.6	39.1	46.8	53.5	48.2

Source: National Family Health Survey, 1998-99.

The above table indicates clearly about inequality in adopting family planning methods in caste and sex groups. Male sterilization was lower in Scheduled Castes than Scheduled Tribes. Female sterilization was more in Scheduled Castes than Scheduled Tribes. The use of IUD was more prevalent among other castes than SCs, STs and OBCs. The use of other methods was also more in other caste categories.

Need of Family Planning

The use of family planning method is required to control family size and to maintain desired difference between births of two children. The unmet need for family planning is given in the table below.

Table 12.4: Unmet Need Limiting in India

Sl. No.	Castes	Percentage
1.	Scheduled Castes	8.2
2.	Scheduled Tribes	7.0
3.	Other Backward Castes	7.1
4.	Others Castes	7.5
	Total	7.5

Source: National Family Health Survey, 1998-99.

Observation on above table reveals that the per centage of Unmet need limiting was high in Scheduled Castes (8.2%). It was 7.0 per cent in Scheduled Tribes, 7.1 per cent in other backward castes and 7.5 per cent in other castes.

Unmet Need Spacing

The unmet need spacing in India is given in the table below.

Table 12.5: Unmet Need Spacing in India

Sl. No.	Castes	Percentage
1.	Scheduled Castes	8.6
2.	Scheduled Tribes	8.8
3.	Other Backward Castes	8.6
4.	Others Castes	7.7
	Total	8.3

The above table shows that the per centage of unmet need spacing was high in Scheduled Tribes (8.8 %). Its per centage was 8.6 each in Scheduled Castes and other backward castes and low in other castes (7.7 %).

Total Unmet Need in India

The per centage of total unmet need in different caste categories has been given in the table below.

Table 12.6: Total Unmet Need in India

Sl. No.	Castes	Total unmet Need in India (Percentage)
1.	Scheduled Castes	16.8
2.	Scheduled Tribes	15.9
3.	Other Backward Castes	15.7
4.	Others Castes	15.2
	Total	15.9

Source: National Health Survey, 1998-99.

The above table reveals that there is difference in different castes so far as total unmet need is concerned.

Its per centage in SCs, STs, OBCs and OCs was 16.8, 15.9, 15.7 and 15.2 respectively.

Meeting of Married Women to Family Planning Agent

The meeting of married woman to a family planning agent has been presented in the following table.

Table 12.7: The meeting of married women to a family planning agent at least once in India

Sl. No	Castes	Percentage
1.	Scheduled Castes	13.4
2.	Scheduled Tribes	17.9
3.	Other Backward Castes	13.6
4.	Others Castes	11.3
	Total	14.05

Sources: National Family Health Survey, 1998-99.

The per centage of married women who had met with a family planning agent at least once in her married life was also different in different caste categories. It was 13.4 per cent in S.Cs, 17.9 per cent in S.Ts, 13.6 per cent in OBCs and 11.3 per cent in OCs.

Nutritional Deficiency

The national family health survey indicates towards nutritional deficiency. Due to nutritional deficiency, people become victims of malnutrition and anaemia.

Malnutrition Nutritional Defficiency in Women

The nutritional deficiency in women has been shown in Table 12.8.

Table 12.8: Nutritional Deficiency in Women in India

Sl. No.	Castes	Percentage
1.	Scheduled Castes	42.1
2.	Scheduled Tribes	46.3
3.	Other Backward Castes	35.8
4.	Others Castes	35.8
	Total	30.5

Source: National Family Health Survey, 1998-99.

The above table reveals clearly the nutritional deficiency is prevalent in women belonging to different caste categories. Its per centage for SCs was 42.1, for STs 46.3, for OBCs 35.8 and for OCs 30.5. It also appears that nutritional deficiency in women in India was a fact beyond caste categories, though their per centage was different.

Anaemia in Women

Anaemia in women belonging to different caste categories is also a crucial issue, but its per centage differs from one caste category to another. The per centage of anaemic women in different caste categories have been presented in Table 12.9.

The table reveals that the per centage of anaemic woman in more in Scheduled Castes and Scheduled Tribes than other Backward Castes and other castes. In Scheduled Castes the per centage of women suffering from anemia was 56.0. Among Schedule Tribes the per centage of anemic women was 64.9 while among other Backward Castes, the percentage of anaemic women was 50.7 and in other castes this percentage was 47.6.

Table 12.9: Percentage of Anemia Women in Different Castes in India

Sl. No.	Castes	Percentage of Anemia
1.	Scheduled Castes	56.0
2.	Scheduled Tribes	64.9
3.	Other Backward Castes	50.7
4.	Others Castes	47.6
	Total	54.8

Source: National Family Health Survey, 1998-99.

Childhood Vaccination

Our Government has launched programme for childhood vaccination to save children from life threatening diseases. If a child is given full dozes of vaccination, his/her life becomes secure from number of childhood diseases. The per centage of full childhood vaccination in different caste categories is given below.

Table 12.10: Percentage of Full Childhood Vaccination in India in Different Castes

Sl. No.	Castes	Percentage of Full Childhood Vaccination
1.	Scheduled Castes	40.2
2.	Scheduled Tribes	26.4
3.	Other Backward Castes	43.0
4.	Others Castes	46.8
	Total	39.1

Source: National Family Health Survey, 1998-99.

The above table indicates that per centage of full childhood vaccination is not same in different caste categories. In SCs, the per centage of full childhood vaccination was 40.2, but in S.Ts this per centage was only 26.4. In other backward castes and other castes this per centage was 46.8 and 39.1 respectively.

B.C.G. Vaccination

Table 12.11 reveals that the awareness towards B.C.G. vaccination is found in all caste categories. But its per centage in different caste categories is not same. In Scheduled Castes the per centage of children given B.C.G. vaccination was 69.9. In Scheduled Tribes this per centage was 60.0. But in other Backward Castes, this per centage was 71.6 and in other castes it was 76.1 per cent.

Table 12.11: Percentage of B.C.G. Vaccination in Different Castes

Sl. No.	Castes	Percentage of B.C.G.
1.	Scheduled Castes	69.9
2.	Scheduled Tribes	60.0
3.	Other Backward Castes	71.6
4.	Others Castes	76.1
	Total	69.4

Source: National Family Health Survey, 1998-99.

DPT III Vaccination

The per centage of D.P.T. III vaccination in different caste categories in India has been given in table below.

Table 12.12: DPT III Vaccination in India

Sl. No.	Castes	Percentage of Children
1.	Scheduled Castes	52.7
2.	Scheduled Tribes	37.5
3.	Other Backward Castes	56.7
4.	Others Castes	60.4
	Total	57.8

Source: National Family Health Survey, 1998-99.

The above table shows that total per centage of DPT III vaccination in children in India was 57.8. This per centage in different caste categories was different. In SCs the per centage of children given DPT III vaccination was 52.7 followed by 37.5 in STs, 56.7 in OBCs and 60.4 in OCs.

Polio III Vaccination

The per centage distribution of polio vaccination in different caste categories has been shown in the table below.

Table 12.13: Percentage of Polio III Vaccination in India

Sl. No.	Castes	Percentage
1.	Scheduled Castes	61.3
2.	Scheduled Tribes	49.0
3.	Other Backward Castes	65.6
4.	Others Castes	65.6
	Total	60.4

Source: National Family Health Survey, 1989-99.

Table 12.13 reveals that the total per centage of children given Polio III vaccination in India was 60.4. This per centage in SCs, STs, OBCs and OCs was 61.3, 49.0, 65.6 and 65.6 respectively.

Vaccination of Measles

Under full vaccination programme, vaccination of measles has also been included. This has brought influence on families of different caste categories. The per centage of vaccination of measles in different caste categories has been shown in the table below.

Table 12.14: Percentage of Measles Vaccination in India

Sl. No.	Castes	Percentage
1.	Scheduled Castes	47.6
2.	Scheduled Tribes	34.3
3.	Other Backward Castes	50.7
4.	Others Castes	57.1
	Total	47.4

Source: National Family Health Survey, 1998-99.

The above table reveals that the total per centage of measels vaccination in India was 47.4. But it was 47.6 in SCs, 34.3 in STs, 50.7 in OBCs and 57.1 in OCs.

Childhood Malnutrition

When children do not get proper and balanced diet, they become malnutrient. In our country, children belonging to all caste categories are victims of malnutrition. But per centage of malnutrient children differs from one caste category to another caste category. The per centage of malnutrient children in different caste categories is given in the table below.

Table 12.15: Percentage of Malnutrient children in different caste

Sl. No.	Castes (Weight for Age)	Percentage
1.	Scheduled Castes	53.5
2.	Scheduled Tribes	55.9
3.	Other Backward Castes	47.3
4.	Others Castes	41.1
	Total	49.45

Source: National Family Health Survey 1998-99.

Table 12.15 reveals that in our country the per centage of children suffering from malnutrition is 49.45. But this per centage differs in different caste categories. The per centage of malnutrient children in S.Cs, S.Ts, OBCs and OCs is 53.5, 55.9, 47.3 and 41.1 respectively.

Status of Anaemia in Children

In our country, children belonging to each caste category are victim of anaemia. But per centage in different caste categories is different. The per centage of children suffering from anaemia in different caste categories has been given in the table below.

Table 12.16: Percentage of Anaemic Children in Different Caste Categories

Sl. No.	Castes	Percentage
1.	Scheduled Castes	78.3
2.	Scheduled Tribes	79.8
3.	Other Backward Castes	72.0
4.	Others Castes	72.7
	Total	75.7

Source: National Family Health Survey, 1998-99.

Table 12.16 shows that in our country 75.7 per cent children are suffering from anaemia. This per centage is different among different caste categories. The per centage of children victims of anaemia in different caste categories is given in the table above. Anaemia victim per centage of children in SCs, STs, OBCs and OCs is 78.3, 71.8, 72.0 and 72.7 respectively.

Drinking Water

To remain healthy, clean drinking water is a must. It is because dirty water causes a number of disease in our body. But unfortunately, in our country all people do not have access to safe drinking water sources. The per centage of families using different sources of drinking water in India is presented in the Table 12.17.

Table 12.17 reveals clearly that people in our country are dependant on different sources of drinking water. 36.6 per cent families were dependant on tape, 35.7 per cent on hand pump, 5.6 per cent on tubewell, 18.2 per cent on well, 1.0 per cent on tank or lake, 1.0 per cent on river-canal, 0.7 per cent on stream and 1.2 per cent on other sources.

Table 12.17: Percentage of Families using Different Sources of Drinking Water in India

Sl. No.	Sources of Drinking Water	Percentage of Families
1.	Tap	36.7
2.	Handpump	35.7
3.	Tubewell	5.6
4.	Well	18.2
5	Tank or Lake	1.0
6.	River-Canal	1.0
7.	Stream	0.7
8.	Others	1.2

Source: Census Reports 2001.

Castes of Families by Sources of Drinking Water

Attempt has been made to know the sources of drinking water in different caste categories. The per centage distribution of castes of families by sources of drinking water has been presented in the following table.

Table 12.18: Percentage Distribution of Families of Different Caste categories using Different Sources of Drinking Water

Sl. No.	Water Sources of Drinking	Percentage of Families of Caste Categories		
		SCs	STs	General
1.	Tabe	32.2	20.0	40.1
2.	Hand Pump	43.6	35.8	33.6
3.	Tubewell	5.3	5.9	5.6
4.	Well	15.5	28.4	17.5
5.	Tank-Lake	0.9	1.4	1.0
6.	River-Canal	0.8	3.2	0.8
7.	Stream	0.4	3.9	0.4
8.	Others	1.2	1.5	1.1

Source: Census of India 2001.

The above table reveals clearly that all caste categories of families are dependant on different drinking water sources. The per centage of families dependant on tap water in SCs, STs and OBCs was 32.2, 20.0 and 40.1 respectively. 43.6 per cent SCs families were using hand pump, 35.8 per cent STs families were using hand pump and 33.6 per cent General Caste families were using hand pump as a source of drinking water. The per centage of SCs, STs and GCs categories families using tube well was 5.3, 5.9 and 5.6 respectively. In SCs 15.5 per cent families were using well, in STs 28.4 per cent families were using well and GCs 17.5 per cent families were using well. The per centage of tank-lake user as source of water in SCs was 0.9, in STs was 1.4 and for GCs 1.0. The river-canal user per centage for SCs, STs and GCs was 0.8, 3.2 and 0.8 respectively. The per centage of stream users in SCs, STs, OBCs was 0.4, 3.9 and 0.4 respectively. The per centage of other sources users among SCs, STs and GCs was 1.2, 1.5 and 1.1 respectively.

Location of Drinking Water Sources

Attempt was made to know the location of drinking water sources in different caste categories. The distribution of families of different caste categories according to location of water sources is presented in the table below.

Table 12.19: Location of Water Sources in Different Caste Categories in India

Sl. No.	Location of Water Sources	Percentage of Caste Categories		
		General Castes	Scheduled Castes	Scheduled Tribes
1.	Inside house	45.2	27.0	39.0
2.	Nearby house	40.0	53.5	44.3
3.	Distant from house	14.4	19.5	16.7

Source: Census Report 2001.

The above table reveals that the location of water sources is inside house, nearby house and distant from house in all above three caste categories, but per centage in different caste category was different. In general castes the per centage of families having water sources inside house, nearby house and distant from house was 45.2, 40.0 and 14.4 respectively. In Scheduled Tribe categories, the per centage of families having water sources inside house, nearby house and distant from house was 39.0, 44.3 and 16.7 respectively. In SCs the per centage of families having water sources inside house, nearby house and distant from house was 27.0, 53.5 and 19.5 respectively.

Location of Water Sources in Rural India

Attempt was made to know the location of water sources in different caste categories in rural India, which is being presented in the Table 12.10.

The Table 12.10 reveals that rural families belonging to different caste categories had water source located in house, nearby house and distant from house, but their per centage was different. In General Caste 69.4 per cent families had water sources inside house, 22.6 per cent had water sources nearby house and 8.0 per cent had water sources away from house. In case

Table 12.20: Location of water sources in Rural India by caste categories

Sl. No.	Location of Water Sources	Caste Categories			
		General Castes	Scheduled Castes	Scheduled Tribe	Total
1.	Inside house	34.1	20.9	10.6	28.7
2.	Nearby house	48.5	58.2	59.6	51.8
3.	Distant from house	17.4	20.9	29.8	19.5
	Total	100.0	100.0	100.0	100.0

Source: Census Report 2001.

of Scheduled Castes 48.5 per cent families had water sources inside house, 36.8 per cent had water sources nearby house and 14.7 per cent had water sources away from house. In Scheduled Tribes, 46.9 per cent families had water sources inside house, 35.7 per cent had water sources nearby house and 17.4 per cent had water sources away from house.

Availability of Toilet

Sanitation is closely related to health. To remain healthy and to keep environment healthy, there is urgent need of toilet in house. But it is unfortunate that proper attention towards toilet in houses was not paid. Toilet facility was available only to rich families. An attempt was made to know the availability of toilet facility in families of caste categories, which has been presented in the table below.

Table 12.22: Availability of Toilet in families Belonging to Different Caste Categories

Sl. No.	Caste Category	Percentage
1.	General Castes	42.3
2.	Scheduled Castes	23.7
3.	Scheduled Tribes	17.0
	Total	27.7

Sources: Census of India, 2001.

The above table indicates per centage difference in availabilities of toilet in families of different caste categories. At the time of survey, 42.3 per cent families of General castes had toilet facilities in their houses. 23.7 per cent families of Scheduled Castes had toilet facility in their houses. In Scheduled Tribes 17.0 per cent families had toilet facility in their houses.

Availability of Drainage System

An attempt was made to know the drainage system in families belonging to different caste categories, which has been presented in the table below.

Table 12.23: Drainage system in Different Caste Categories in India

Sl. No.	Caste Categories	Drainage System (Percentage)
1.	General Castes	50.6
2.	Scheduled Castes	42.9
3.	Scheduled Tribes	21.8
	Total	38.43

Source: Census Report, 2001.

The above table shows that all families belonging to different caste categories do not have drainage system in their house for the flow of dirty water. The table indicates that the per centage of GCs, SCs and STs families having drainage system was also different. In GCs 50.6 per cent families had drainage system in their house. In SCs, 42.9 per cent families had drainage system in their houses. In STs, 21.8 per cent had drainage system in their house.

House and House Structure

Our health is influenced by our house and its structure. Clean environment of house affects the health of family inmates. The house structure of different caste categories in India has been presented in the table below.

Table 12.24: Pucca House structure in Different Caste Categories in India

Sl. No.	Caste Categories	Percentage of Pucca House
1.	General Castes	57.7
2.	Scheduled Castes	42.8
3.	Scheduled Tribes	24.4
	Total	41.63

Source: Census Report, 2001.

The above table indicates that in our country all families do not have pucca houses. 41.63 per cent families in India owned pucca houses. The per centage of families having pucca houses in different caste categories was different. In General castes, 57.7 per cent families had pucca houses, while

42.8 per cent SC families owned pucca houses, but only 24.4 per cent Scheduled Tribe families had pucca houses.

Availability of Electricity in Houses

Availability of electricity in houses also affects our health. We need light during night to cook food, to share food and to visit toilet. In darkness, we can fall down and get our bones fractured. Availability of electricity in houses of different caste categories have been given in table below.

Table 20.25: Availability of Electricity in Houses among Different Caste categories

Sl. No.	Caste Categories	Percentage of Houses Having Electricity Facility
1.	Common Castes	61.4
2.	Scheduled Castes	44.3
3.	Scheduled Tribes	36.5
	Total	47.4

Source: Census Report, 2001.

The above table indicates clearly that all families in our country do not avail electricity facility. Only 47.4 per cent families had electricity facility in their houses. But this per centage was different for different caste categories. While 61.4 per cent General caste families had electricity facility in their houses. 44.3 per cent Scheduled Castes families had electricity facility in houses. But this figure for Scheduled Tribe families was only 36.5 per cent.

13
Health Promotion Programme

Our country India is a democratic country. To maintain the health of citizens of our country is responsibility of the Government. To remain healthy is our human right. Ever since Independence, our Government is launching health promotion programmes to bring all people in the mainstream of nation. Some basic health programmes introduced during very First Five Year Plan are still continuing. Some new health promotion programmes have also been launched time to time in different plan periods. The most recently launched health promotion programme is Ayushman Bharat—Pradhanmantri Jan Arogya Yojana, which have been launched on 15th September, 2018 by our Hon'ble Prime Minister Sri Narendra Modi. Our Government is trying its best for bringing qualitative and quantitative changes in health promotion programmes and their beneficiaries of rural and urban areas. As a result of all such efforts, positive results have started coming up.

It will be fitness of the thing to present here description of some public health promotion programmes. In order to deliver public health services in rural and urban areas, our Government has established Anganwadi Kendra, health sub-centre, health centre, community health centre, referral hospital, Sadar hospital and Government medical college and hospitals. A number of private nursing homes and medical colleges have also come up under the control of the Government. Government met all kinds of expenditure on Government medical institutions. It provides lands and security to private medical institutions. The Government also takes help of N.G.Os in health promotion scheme. Now, a description of some national level health promotion programmes is being presented here.

Minimum Needs Programme

Through this special health promotion programme, attempt has been made to provide better health services and facilities in rural areas. Under this programme, Referral hospitals, Primary health centres, Extra primary supplementary health centres and health sub-centres were established. In each Referral hospital, four posts of doctors have been created. These four posts are of pediatrics, gynaecology, surgery and medicine. At each Block four posts of medical officers have been created under Primary health centre, at each extra primary supplementary health centre, two posts of medical officers have been created. At each health sub-centre, posts of compounder, nurse and health worker have been created.

Under this programme, 21513 health sub-centres (15% of total, 3610 Primary health centres (15.75% of total) and 604 community health centres (19.45% of total) have been established in tribal areas. Since tribal population is found in hilly, plateau, forest, coastal, desert and island areas, therefore, some relaxation in population norm was followed in the establishment of health sub-centres, primary health centres, community health centres and multipurpose workers.

Information about population norms for establishment of basic health institutions in rural tribel areas is given in the table below.

Table 13.1: Health Infrastructure Norms in Rural and Tribal Areas

Sl. No.	Infrastructure Facility	Population Norms	
		Rural Area	Tribal Area
1.	Health Sub-centre	5,000	3,000
2.	Primary Health Centre	30,000	20,000
3.	Community Health Centre	1,20,000	80,000
4.	Multi-purpose worker	5,000	3,000

Source: Report 2005 : Task Group on Development of Scheduled Castes and Scheduled Tribes, Planning Commission, Govt. of India.

National Malaria Control Programme

Malaria has been a complex public health problem in India. Before 1948, 7 to 8 crore of people used to die each year in our country. To eradicate this complex public health problem, malaria eradication programme was launched. Under this programme, spray of DDT was made. The spray of DDT had brought positive and encouraging result. Under this programme, malaria victims were identified and blood samples were collected for investigation.

Malaria eradication revised programme was launched by our Government since 1.4.1977 and is continuing even today. Under this programme, spray of DDT and identification of patients suffering from malaria was done. This programme was implemented by dividing it into four areas. These areas were other areas sub-plan, Tribal Area sub-plan, Urban Area programme, and Tribal Urban Area Programme.

Under this programme, there is a post of Chief Malaria Officer at state level, a post of Divisional Malaria Officer at division level and a post of District Malaria Officer and Assistant Malaria Officer at District level. At block level, all workers work under local doctor incharge of malaria control.

95 per cent population of our country resides in such areas where there are chances of spread of malaria. Out of total malaria infected area, 11 per cent is contributed by North-East states. This area contributes only 4 per cent in our national population. Our Central Government is meeting all expenditure on malaria eradication in North-East States since 8th December, 1994.

From September 1997, An Enhanced Malaria Control Programme has been launched for tribal areas of eight states. It is known as EMCP in short. It was implemented in the states of Andhra Pradesh, Chhattisgarh, Jharkhand, Gujarat, Madhya Pradesh, Maharashtra, Odisha and Rajasthan. Selection of districts was made on the basis of incidence of more than 30 per cent occurrence of P. Phalciperum, 25 per cent tribal population in primary health centres and incidence of death due to malaria.

The main objectives behind implementation of this programme was to provide preference to tribal areas in malaria control, to implement long term cost effective strategy, to bring improvement in quality of service delivery, to build efficiency and start new approach.

This programme was implemented in 1045 Tribal Development Blocks of 100 Districts in 8 States. A detailed account of this has been given in the table below.

Table 13.2: Enhanced Malaria Control Programme by States and Districts

Sl. No.	Name of State	No. of District	No. of Primary Health Centres
1.	Andhra Pradesh	10	79
2.	Jharkhand	10	109
3.	Gujarat	09	239
4.	Madhya Pradesh	17	155
5.	Chhattisgarh	09	94
6.	Maharashtra	14	182
7.	Odisha	21	153
8.	Rajasthan	10	34
	Total	100	1045

Source: Same as Table 13.1.

In 1997, 2.66 million cases of malaria were identified in laboratory, in which 1.04 million cases were of P. Phalciperum. In 2008, 33 per cent decrease in malarial cases was observed. The number of P. Phalciperum was reduced to 0.80 million showing 18 per cent decrease in 2003. During this period total decrease of 38 per cent was observed. In 1997, there were 1.19 million cases of malaria which was reduced to 0.74 million in 2003.

National T.B. Control Programme

This is a programme of Central Government in which cent-per-cent expenditure is met by our Central Government. According to an estimate nearly 0.18 per cent people are victims of T.B. in our country. In order to control this serious disease, National T.B. Control Programme is running in our country since 1962. But this programme could not have achieved desired result. Therefore, a Revised T.B. Control Programme was launched which is known as DOTs. DOTs have been implemented in different phases under recommended strategy of World Bank. Its purpose was to raise the treatment rate of new cough positive cases up to 85 per cent and to identify 70 per cent new cases. For Scheduled Tribes the population norm was reduced from 5 lakh to 2.5 lakh. For micro centres, population norm was reduced from 1 lakh to 50,000. Emphasis was made on establishment of more and more Dots. Special attention was made on meeting of medicine expenditure and journey expenditure of patients and family members. In tribal area, this programme was implemented under Tribal Sub-plan. In our country, extension area of DOTs is increasing fastly. Leaving one district in Nagaland and two districts in Tripura entire North-eastern States including Sikkim have been included under it. To make access of this programme to all classes, all Government medical colleges, private medical colleges, general hospitals and N.G.Os have been integrated.

National Leprosy Eradication Programme

Leprosy is a big health problem. Social stigma is attached with this disease. Lepers are looked down in society and community. They are isolated from family, community and society. They are given separate room, and separate utensils for food. They are prohibited to walk in the morning so that nobody could see their face. They were not invited and allowed to participate in social and religious functions. They were forced to leave community, to make suicide or to lead a life of beggar. Those who wanted to live used to survive as beggars near temple of Gods and Goddesses.

After implementation of Leprosy Eradication Programme, a change in attitude towards leprosy and lepers has taken place. They are not isolated, rather they are being rehabilitated. Our Central Government met cent-per-cent expenditure on this programme.

An encouraging scheme for the eradication of leprosy has been launched by our Central Government. This is known as Multidrug Therapy. Under Multidrug Therapy (MDT), doses of B. Jefaupicine, Laprin and Depson are given. This disease is cured by Multi Drug Therapy in six months to two years. This programme has been implemented in all districts of all states. The entire population of our country has been covered under this programme. At state level, there is state leprosy eradication officer and at district level, there is district leprosy eradication officer.

The following units are functioning under leprosy eradication programme:

- Leprosy Control Unit
- Revised Leprosy Control Centre
- Survey, Education and Treatment Centre
- Temporary room of 20 beds
- Leprosy Rehabilitation Room
- Epitomiological Survey Team
- Leprosy Training Centre
- Sample Survey-cum-Evaluation Unit
- Supplementary Centre.

In order to create awareness towards leprosy and lepers and to find out hidden cases, four revised leprosy eradication campaigns were launched in all areas. Through these campaigns hidden cases were identified and awareness towards leprosy eradication was created. As a result, patients and family members had started visiting the investigation and treatment centres. Now, there was no hesitation in getting investigated.

The 5th Revised Leprosy Eradication Campaign was launched in 8 states. They are Bihar, Jharkhand, Chhatisgarh, Uttar Pradesh, Pashchim Bengal, Odisha, Andhra Pradesh and Mahrashtra.

For distantly located and inaccessible areas, a special action programme SAPEL was launched. In the period between 2001 and 2004, a total 1440 SAPEL programmes were decentralized.

Our Central Government has also taken help of N.G.Os in eradication of leprosy in different parts of the country. N.G.Os were funded by the Government. Attempt was made to remove all misconceptions related to leprosy and its treatment and lepers could be rehabilitated.

National Blindness Control Programme

Our Government is running blindness control programme since 1981-82. At state level eye bank has been established. Operation of cataract is done and transplantation of eye is done. All medical colleges and hospitals have been attached to this programme.

National Fileria Control Programme

This programme is being launched by 50 per cent assistance from Central Government and 50 per cent assistance by State Government. In order to control fileria, fileria control centre and fileria clinic have been established by the Government. All medical colleges and hospitals have been attached to this programme.

National Iodine Deficiency Control Programme

Through this national level programme, attempt has been made to control diseases which occur due to iodine deficiency. This programme has two main objectives:

- To supply iodized salt in place of common salt in all states.
- To make a survey of diseases caused by iodine deficiency.
- This is a centrally sponsored progamme.

National AIDS Control Programme

This national level programme is being launched by our Central Government since 1992-93. For this purpose AIDS clinics have been established. Each centre is given Rs. 5,000 and each cell is given Rs. one lakh.

YAWS Eradication Programme

It is a centrally sponsored scheme. It was established in 1996-97 by National Infectitious Diseases Institution. This disease creates disability in body and we become disabled. It is an infectious disease. It is cured by a doze of penicillin injection. This scheme has been launched in eight states. They are Andhra Pradesh, Assam, Chhattisgarh, Gujarat, Jharkhand, Madhya Pradesh, Maharashtra, Odisha, Tamil Nadu and Uttar Pradesh.

Efficiency Building Project

Under the joint aegis of World Health Organisation and Indian Medical Research Council, Efficiency Building Project was launched for tribals since April 1999. This project lays emphasis upon care taking of tribal health. Its main purpose is to collect baseline data and complexity related to tribal health. In this programme health workers are taken from the community. They are trained to look after health of tribal communities. The health workers assist in small diseases and delivery. They are given kits and cycles.

National Family Welfare Programme

Our country is the biggest demographic republic of the world. Our country has 2.4 per cent land area of the world. We contribute 16 per cent in world population. To control population, our Government has launched National Family Welfare Programme. This is a centrally sponsored scheme. The Central Government bears all kinds of expenses on this programme. This is a self-volunteered programme. Its main purpose is to create a special environment for the welfare of family. Its purpose is to control family size so that parents and children could lead a healthy life. This programme was known as Family Planning Programme. But from Ist April, 1996 this is known as Family Welfare Programme. In this programme target free approach has been adopted. Again in 1997-98, community need evaluation approach was adopted in place of target less approach. Under this approach community leaders such as village head, village priest, Women Health Association, Primary school teachers were integrated with family welfare programme to look after community health. Attempt has been made to provide family welfare facility to all families. For this purpose, health sub-centres, primary health centres, community health centres, referral hospital, Sadar hospital, government medical college and hospitals and private medical college and hospitals have been attached with this programme. Some NGOs have also been attached to that programme. The help of media, seminar, conferences, video show, cinema, slides and other audio-visual media are taken to make this programme successful.

Kalajar Control Programme

This national programme was launched in financial year 1991-92. This is a centrally sponsored scheme. Kalajar Control Centres have been established where test of bone-marrow is done to identify the case of Kalajar patient.

Integrated Child Development Scheme (ICDS)

This is a centrally sponsored scheme in which cent-per-cent expenses are met by Central Government. It was realized that children are backbone of a nation. They are future hope of a country. That is why special attention should be paid on children right from conception to the age of 6 years. Parents play significant role in physical, mental and psychological development of children. The pregnant and lactating women should be provided health and nutritional education essentially. Keeping in view the protection of health of pregnant and lactating women and children up to 6 years of age, Integrated Child Development Scheme was launched. This programme is run through Anganwadi Kendra, where pregnant women, lactating women and children in the age group of 0-6 years are given nutritional diet to save them from malnutrition. This programme has following objectives:

- To provide nutrition to children in the age group of 0-6 years and to improve their health status.
- To lay the foundation of proper psychological, social and physical development.
- To reduce infant and the child mortality rate.
- To reduce malnutrition.
- To reduce the number of drop-out children from school.
- To encourage child development through coordination between different ministries and departments.
- To impart training to mothers for proper nutrition and healthcare of children and themselves.

The unit of this programme is Block. According to the norms of this programme in urban and rural areas one Anganwadi Kendra has been established at every one thousand population. But in tribal areas this norm has been reduced to 700 population. Women and children receive all kinds of benefit from Anganwadi Kendra. At each Anganwadi Kendra 100 beneficiaries have been included in which number of children and women should be 88 and 12 respectively.

Under this scheme children and women of below poverty line are beneficiary and receive six types of infrastructural services. They are as follows:

- Supplementary Food
- Immunization
- Health test

- Directive services
- Nutrition and Health Education
- Pre-school informal education.

In each integrated child development scheme, there is a post of project officer. Each Anganwadi Kendra has an Anganwadi Sevika and Anganwadi Sahayika. At every 20 Anganwadi Kendra, there is a woman supervisor. At each 5 Anganwadi Kendras in general area and 100 Anganwadi Kendra in tribal area there is an Assistant Child Development Project Officer. All administrative expenses are met by Central Government, but expenditure on supplementary food is met by the State Government.

Supplementary Food

Children below six years of age and pregnant and lactating mothers of BPL families get supplementary food in Anganwadi Kendras. It is given for 300 days in a year. Local food is served as supplementary food. Identification of malnutrition is done on the basis of age for weight or on the basis of measurement of upper arm circumference. Kits have been given at each Anganwadi Kendra. Tape has red or yellow colour symbols. Tape helps in knowing the level of malnutrition. In case of serious malnutrition, double supplementary food is provided.

Immunization

At each Anganwadi Kendra, attempt has been made to provide full immunization of children. The children are given all vaccinations till 5 years of age free of cost. The vaccination saves children from Diphtheria, B.C.G., Black cough and tetanus, Polio and T.B. After health test, protein and iron tablets are given to pregnant women. There is a provision of four time tests during pregnancy period. Whenever there is a problem, pregnant women is sent to hospital.

Health Checkup

Under this programme, regular predelivery tests are done. Urine, blood, blood pressure and weight are tested regularly. During pregnancy period tetanus injections are given. After tests, besides supplementary food, protein and iron tablets are given to pregnant women. A pregnant woman is subjected to tests four times. If there is any trouble in tests, the woman is referred to hospital immediately.

Lactating mothers and children are also subjected to regular medical check-up. In the beginning tests are done at house. But after six to eight weeks, mother goes to Anganwadi Kendra along with child for check-up.

Health and Nutrition Education

Lactating women and pregnant women are imparted health and nutritional education to look after their health and health of children. They are also educated to take care of children and to maintain a gap of at least two years between birth of two children. They are given education of family planning.

Rural Drinking Water Programme

As water is essential for our health and life, our Central Government and State Governments have placed special emphasis on supply of pure drinking water in rural areas. Under this programme, 40 litres of fresh and pure drinking water is made available for each male and female. For 250 people a hand pump has been provided. Drinking water source should not be far away from 1.6 km in plain area and not more that 100 metre high in plateau area. UNICEF also makes contribution in providing fresh drinking water in rural areas. At present, the Government has launched 'Har Ghar Nal Jal Yojna.'

Urban Drinking Water Project

This is a centrally sponsored scheme in which special attention is paid on providing fresh drinking water to urban people. Scheduled Castes, Scheduled Tribes and slum areas are also included in this scheme. In this project fresh drinking water is supplied on the basis of per individual. 70 per cent population having water pipe connection in houses is supplied drinking water 70 per Pcd. 30 per cent population having water pipe connection in houses is supplied drinking water 40 per Pcd. In this project 1051 towns were included whose population was less than 50,000. In this scheme, towns of IV, V and VI categories were included. The contribution of Centre and State for this scheme is 50 : 50.

Rural Sanitation Programme

To maintain cleanliness in rural areas, our Government has launched following schemes:

- Construction of sanitation toilets for BPL families.
- In tribal tolas, construction of a sanitary toilet for 10 houses.
- To convert mobile toilets into sanitary toilets.

- Construction of separate toilet for women.
- Construction of street and drainage in villages.
- Construction of Pucca soak pits and garbage.
- Cementation of street.
- Urban Sanitation Programme.

To maintain cleanliness in urban area is responsibility of municipality or municipal corporation. Roads, streets, drainage and toilets are constructed by the Nagar Nigam/Nagar Palika. Water connections are provided to town dwellers. 'The PHED of the State Government makes valuable contribution in maintaining cleanliness in towns. Low cost sanitation programme has been launched by the Government.

Pradhan Mantri Bharat Swachh Abhiyan

This programme has been launched in our country from 2014 by Central Government. Under this programme, toilet facilities have been provided in all Government educational institutions of rural and urban areas. In rural and urban areas each BPL family has been given a sum of Rs. 12,000 for construction of sanitary toilet. This programme has provided sanitary facilities in poor houses and Government institution. This programme is intended to stop open defecation and has brought revolutionary change in lifestyle of rural and urban poor.

Swachchhata Hi Sewa Karya Karma

This programme has been launched by our Central Government on 15th September, 2018 to keep environment of house neat and clean because cleanliness is the best service for leading a healthy lifestyle.

Ayushman Bharat Yojana

This is a centrally sponsored scheme launched by our Government for the treatment of BPL family members. This scheme is also known as Pradhanmantri Jana Arogya Yojana. This programme has been launched on 2nd October, 2018. Under this programme, a member of BPL family can avail medical treatment up to a cost of Rs. 5 lakh in any medical institution in India who have been included in this programme. Medical treatment cost is met by the Government. This programme is regarded as very promising and valuable programme for the rural and urban families having red and yellow card or BPL Card.

14
Folk Biology

Folk biology is practice of biology by folk communities. Since this biology is practiced by the people living as folk, or peasant communities, it is also known as Ethnobiology. The folk and peasant communities are practicing domestication of plants and animals since Neolithic period. They have accumulated scientific knowledge of rearing and caring of plants and animals. These scientific knowledge are continuing from generation to generation and have led the foundation of agricultural civilization. The folk and peasant people are the best biologist for the plants and animals they domesticate. In course of rearing and caring of plants and animals, they have acquired knowledge to classify them in folk categories, to identify their diseases, to treat their diseases and for artificial fertilization. Thus, folk biologists are real practitioners of biology for their own economy and society.

There was a time in the history of mankind, when man was not producer. Rather he was simply a consumer of natural goods. His all basic needs were fulfilled by nature. He used to do hunting and gathering in the forests. He used to live in caves. He used to drink water from streams or river. He used to wear leaves and bark. Man led this type of life for millions of years. But during Neolithic period (6000 B.C.-8000 B.C.) man learnt to domesticate plants and animals. In Chalcolithic age (3000 B.C.-5000 B.C.) he began to settle in river valleys and started domestication of plants and animals on large scale by making canal from the river. In this period specialisation of labour took place. Copper smiths and potters emerged as specialists. In Bronze age (3000 BC) urban revolution took place. Now potters, carpenters, coppersmiths, bronzesmith and priest emerged as specialists. The concepts of urbanization and urban administration developed. But in villages domestication of plants and animals continued. They produced grains, cereals, vegetables, milk, meat, wool, clothes cotton etc. They exchange their produce with potters, carpenters, bronze smiths and copper smiths. Thus, by reaching in the age of urban civilization, people knew to produce more and more grains and cattle to meet their various kinds of needs. Thus, a complex structure of specialists in relation to folk and peasant communities emerged.

From Neolithic period till now the folk biology witnessed a number of positive changes so far as folk production, disease, treatment, fertilization and biotechnology related to domestication of plants and animals are concerned. Folk communities have given birth to folk biology on the basis of their experience and practice with plants and animals domesticated. They have preserved their folk technology of producing more and more yield of grains, meat, milk, wool and calves through traditions which have been handed down from generation to generation.

On the basis of their experience and practice, folk people knew that plants and animals also need water, air and food for healthy growth. They also have respiratory, digestive and excretory system. Lack of proper care and nutrition also make them ill. Germs and bacteria also make them infectious. If proper care and nutrition is not provided, they attain death like man. Therefore, plants and animals also need healthy life to lead. Ill health of plants and animals also make us ill. Thus, concept of ill health, disease and treatment for plants and animals came in to existence among folk and peasant people. Their experience with breeding of plants and animals led them develop folk biotechnology for producing hybrid species of plants and animals. The hybrid varieties were yielding more milk and meat.

Our knowledge about medical anthropology will not be complete without dealing with folk biology. Folk people use animals for riding, getting furs, for begging, for playing, getting fuel. Folk people rear animals for getting skin and getting money by selling them in market. Folk people rear birds for eggs, meat, money, play and time passing friend.

Folk people domesticate ox, cow, buffalo, camel, goat, sheep, pig, monkey, ass, donkey and horse. They rear pigeon, cock, hen, *titer, batter,* duck, parrot and other birds. Great kings used to domesticate lion, tiger, deer, elephant for status and prestige.

In domesticating birds and animals, emphasis is placed on proper care, nutrition and fertilization to continue the progeny of animals and birds domesticated. Cow, buffaloes, camel and goat are domesticated to get milk. Cow, she buffalo, and she camel give calves. He calves are sterilized to till lands and draw carts. Some of them are left unsterilized for fertilization. The calves of she goat are sold to get money. Their meat is also eaten. Dogs are domesticated to keep watch of house during night. He goats (rams) are also sacrificed in the name of Gods and Goddesses. Sheep are tamed to get milk and calves. Their meat is also eaten. Their furs are collected to prepare blanket. Bear and monkey are domesticated to earn money by showing their dances in folk fairs. Goat fight and sheep fight are also organized in folk fairs. Ass, donkey and short horses are domesticated to carry goods and passengers.

Like cattle, birds like hen, cock, pigeon and titer are domesticated to get their eggs and meat for eating. They are also domesticated for sacrifice at the time of worship. Parrot and maina are tamed for entertainment and time pass.

Thus, from above account it is quite clear that folk communities and peasant communities are closely related to domestication of animals and birds to supplement their economy and meet a number of social and religious needs.

Branches of Folk Biology

There are two main branches of Folk Biology. They are as follows:

- Folk Zoology
- Folk Botany

Now, let us discuss about these branches one by one.

Folk Zoology

Folk Zoology deals with zoological knowledge of folk people such as fertilization, hybridization, rearing, caring, feeding, identifying diseases and treating them for cattle domestication. It also deals with folk classification of cattle, their trade and market.

Theme of Folk Zoology

The following constitute the theme of folk zoology:

- Domestication of cattle and birds
- Classification of cattle and birds
- Fertilization of cattle and birds
- Hybridization of cattle and birds
- Caring of pregnant cattle and birds
- Rearing and caring of calves and children of birds
- Feeding of cattle and birds
- Milking milch cattle
- Identification of disease of cattle

- Folk treatment of cattle diseases
- Sale and purchase of cattle
- Preparation of manure from dung
- Preparation of fuel from dung
- Communication with cattle
- Worship of cattle
- Sterilization of cattle
- Construction of cattle shed
- Death ritual of cattle.

Now let us discuss about these aspects of folk biology one by one.

Domestication of Cattle and Birds

Members of folk communities domesticate cattle and birds for purpose like getting milk, getting meat, tilling land, drawing cart, carrying goods.

Classification of Cattle

Folk people classify their animals on following basis:

On the Basis of Age

The folk people classify animals according to age such as bachcha, jawan and burha. Bachcha is for children, Jawan is for adult and Burha is for old.

For example bachcha hiran, jawan hiran and burhka hiran. The categories bachcha, jawan and burha is applied for age of all kind of animals.

On the Basis of Colour

The folk people classify animals on the basis of colour too. For example black cow, white cow, red cow, brown cow and spotted cow. Similarly black ox, white ox, red ox, brown ox and spotted ox. Black buffalo, grey buffalo and spotted buffalo. Red horse, white horse, black horse. Thus, folk people classify cattle on the basis of colour of the animals.

On the Basis of Stature

The folk people use length of cattle as a category for classification. For example *Barka bail* (tall ox), *Manjhila bail* (middle ox) and *chhotaka* or *Natawa bail* (small ox). In this way they classify ox, horses, buffalo and other animals.

On the Basis of Horn

The members of folk community take structure of horn as a criteria for classifying animals. For example horned cow, non-horned cow, moving horn cow, fixed horn cow, down horn cow, straight horn cow, zigzag horn cow. These categories are applied for buffalo and ox too.

On the Basis of milk giving

Cow and buffaloes are categorized on the basis of milk giving. For example milch cattle and non-milch cattle. Similarly *Dhudharu Gay* (milk giving cow) and *Natha* (non-milk giving) cow.

On the Basis of Reproduction

Cows, buffaloes, camel are categorized on the basis of reproduction of calves. Each year giving calf is termed as *Dhanpurahi* and after two years giving calf is termed as *Baken.*

On the Basis of Sex

The members of folk communities classify animals on the basis of sex. For example:

- *Gay–Bail* (cow-bull)
- *Bhains–Bhainsa* (She buffalo-he buffalo)
- *Bakari–Bakara* (She goat-he goat)
- *Bheri–Bhera* (She-sheep-he sheep)
- *Suari–Suar* (She pig-he pig)
- *Hathini–Hathi* (She elephant-he elephant)
- *Baghin–Bagh* (Tigress-Tigar)
- *Sihani–Singh* (Lioness-Lion)
- *Kuti–Kuta* (Bitch-Dog)
- *Gadahi–Gadaha* (She ass-he ass)
- *Khacharin–Khachar* (She donkey-he donky)
- *Hirani–Hiran* (She deer-he deer)
- *Utani–Uta* (She camel-he camel)
- *Bilai–Bilar* (She cat-he cat)
- *Siyarin–Siar* (She Jackal-he Jackal)
- *Khargoshin–Khargosh* (She hare-he hare)
- *Chuhia–Chuha* (She mouse-he mouse)

- *Bandaria-Bandar* (she monkey-he monkey)
- *Bhaluain–Bhalu* (She bear-he bear)
- *Kachhui–Kacchua* (She turtle-he turtle)
- *Ghariyalin–Ghariyal* (she crocodile-he crocodile).

On the Basis of Species

Folk people classify animals on the basis of species. For example—*Gay, Bhais, Bakara, Sher, Hiran, Bandar, Bhalu* and others. Each type of animal classify a species. They mate with opposite sex member of the same species.

On the Basis of Domestication

The folk people classify animals as wild and domestic on the basis of domestication.

On the Basis of Fertility

Cows, she buffalo and she camels, mares are classified on the basis of fertility. Non-fertile ones are termed as *Bhahila* and fertile ones are known as *Sahila.*

On the Basis of Area

Folk people classify animals on the basis of area such as *Dehati* (local or rural) and *Videshi* (foreign). For example: *Dehati Gai* and *Videshi Gai.*

On the Basis of Place of Purchase

Folk people classify their animals on the basis of place of purchase or market. For example *Chhatarwali Gay, Dadari Wali Gay, Barahpur Wali Gay* and others. The name of place is added for classifying other animals too.

On the Basis of Food

Folk people classify animals on the basis of food eaten by them. For example non-vegetarian and vegetarian. Tiger, Lion, Jackal, Hyena are meat eater animals (carnivorous). But cow, buffalo, camel, ox, sheep, goat, elephant are grass eater animals (herbivorous).

On the Basis of Nature

Folk people classify animals on the basis of nature such as aggressive and submissive.

Lion, tiger, leopard and wolf are aggressive animals. But cow, buffalo, goat, sheep are submissive animals.

On the Basis of Disability

Folk people classify their animals on the basis of disability, too. For example blind cow, one eyed cow, lame cow, deaf cow. In the same way other animals are also categorized on the basis of physical disability.

Classification of Birds

Folk people classify birds on the basis of following categories:

On the Basis of Species

The folk people classify birds on the basis of species. For example crow, peacock, patridge, heran, haril, parrot, panduk, maina, gauraiya, koel, nilkantha, bageri and others. Each bird lives in its own species and reproduce own kinds.

On the basis of Sex

Folk people classify birds on the basis of sex. For example:

- *Toti–Tota* (she parrot-he parrot)
- *Kaui–Kaua* (she crow-he crow)
- *Suggi–Sugga* (she parrot-he parrot)
- *Koeli–Koel* (she cuckoo-he cuckoo)
- *Maini–Maina* (she starlin-he starlin)
- *Titari–Titar* (she patridge-he patridge)
- *Baguli–Bagula* (she heren-he heren)
- *Panduki–Panduk* (she dove-he dove)
- *Harili–Haril* (she wood pigeon-he wood pigeon)
- *Ulluin–Ullu* (she owl-he owl)
- *Badurin–Badur* (she bat-he bat)
- *Gaurayi–Gauriya* (she sparrow-he sparrow)
- *Hansin–Hans* (she swan-he swan)

- *Baterin–Bater* (she quail-he quail)
- *Morani–Mor* (Peahen-peacock)
- *Kabutari–Kabutar* (she pigeon-he pigeon)
- *Bataki–Batak* (Duck-Drake)
- *Bajani–Baj* (she felcon-he falcon)
- *Garurin–Garur* (she adjutant-he adjutant)
- *Giddhani–Giddha* (she vulture-he vulture)
- *Chilani–Chil* (she kite-he kite)
- *Nagin–Nag* (she cobra-he cobra)
- *Sarasi–Saras* (she crane-he crane).

On the Basis of Colour

Members of folk community classify a bird on the basis of colour. For example white pigeon, red pigeon, black pigeon, gray pigeon and spotted pigeon. In the same way they classify other birds.

On the Basis of Age

The members of folk community classify a bird on the basis of age. For example child pigeon, adult pigeon and old pigeon. In the same way, they classify other birds on the basis of age.

On the Basis of Size

Members of folk communities classify birds on the basis of size, too. For example small birds, big birds, very big birds and small kite, big kite and very big kite.

On the Basis of Length of Leg

Folk communities classify birds on the basis of length of legs. For example short legged and long legged.

For example sparrow and crane.

On the Basis of Food

Folk communities classify birds on the basis of food they eat. For example meat eater and fruit eater. Kite, vulture, eagle are meat eater. Parrot are fruit eaters.

On the basis of domestication

Members of folk communities classify birds on the basis of domestication. They call parrot, pigeon, maina, titar, duck as domesticated birds and kite, vulture, eagle as wild birds.

Fertilization of Cattle and Birds

Members of folk communities know very well about the breading season of each animals. They know very well the mating season of cow, buffalo, goat, camel and pig whom they domesticate. They know the signs of heat period of cow, buffalo, goat and camel. For this purpose they have bull, he buffalo, he-goat and he-camel. They remain wandering in the folk areas. On hearing heat symbols males are attracted towards females. Copulation takes place in field. The expert of folk community extends help in copulation. Copulation continues for several times. After copulation, it is believed that fertilization has taken place. When heat period is not repeated after 21 days to 30 days, it is believed that cow, she-buffalo, she-camel or she-goat has canceived. Members of folk community remain conscious during heat period. They bring their cow, she buffalo or she camel to male counter-parts for mating. Goats and sheep flock consist of male and female members. Therefore, mating can take place anytime. Males feel the smell of heat period of females. They are attracted towards females and copulation occurs while grazing grasses.

In birds, males and females are reared together. They always remain together. Fertilization takes place at the time of picking up grains, insects and other food materials. Pigeon, duck, sparrow, parrot, patridge, quail all live in pair. That is why no conscious attempt is made by the people for their copulation and fertilization.

Hybridization of Cattle and Birds

Members of folk communities know to develop hybrid variety of animals and birds by selecting males of desired variety. For example crossing of a small cow with a big bull. As a result, cross fertilization takes place and improved variety of offsprings are delivered. They are long, healthy and give more milk. For the purpose of hybridization, they do counselling of gene. For genetic counselling, they select male of improved variety for copulation during heat period. Hybridization is very common practice in folk community for domestication of animals. For this purpose, they cover a distance of 10 to 15 km in search of an improved variety of male partners of cattle.

Artificial Insemination

Now-a-days, knowledge of veterinary science has reached even in folk communities. Now, they do not wander from place to place in search of a suitable male partner of concerned cattle for fertilization of their cows, she-buffaloes, she-goats and she-camel. Rather they visit the veterinary doctor for artificial fertilization. The veterinary doctors have semen bank. They inject semens in reproductive organ of female cattle through a needle. Thus, artificial fertilization takes place.

In case of birds, they do genetic caoncelling by selecting a male partner of desired colour and variety for fertilization. Now-a-days, artificial fertilizer of eggs also take place in hens and ducks.

Care of Pregnant Cattle and Birds

The owner of cattle takes proper care of pregnant cattle and birds. They know about the pregnancy period of cow, goat, pig, she buffalo, she-camel and other whom they domesticate. The pregnancy period of cow, she-buffalo, she-camel, she-ass, she-donkey, mare remains generally of ten months. In the early months they are allowed to graze in open fields with other animals. The herd boy remains in the flock to avoid quarrel between expectant animals and other. It is because quarrel may lead to termination of pregnancy. In last two months, special care is taken in food, nutrition and other. The expectant cow, she-buffalo, she-camel, she-goat or she-pig is not allowed to go in grazing ground. She is kept in cattle shed. Food and water are given timely. To avoid black magic and evil eye, a black cloth is kept at entrance gate. A black thread is tied in neck of pregnant animal. The cow shed is kept clean. A promise is made to shed God to offer a special worship after successful delivery. The owner keeps watch during night time too. He keeps his bed near the cow in shed till delivery does not occur. If there is any complication, he visits to the animal delivery expert and seeks his help in delivery. When the calf is turned, then complication occurs. The expert brings the calf in right direction and pulls out with hands.

As soon as delivery occurs, fire is burnt. Mild hot water or fresh water is given to mother. The navel cord is cut with a clean blade or bamboo knife. Mango leaves and bamboo leaves are served to mother to clear the waste from the stomach. As soon as reproductive waste comes out, it is thrown quickly outside the house. The mother is not allowed to eat the waste because eating reduces the milk of mother.

In case of pregnant birds like duck, hen, cock, the couple birds take every care of eggs delivered. The owner provides protection from dog and cats who destroy their eggs. The male and female bird looks after eggs one by one in day time. In night, they take care together. They take care till kids hatch out from the eggs. Hatching out takes place within a month.

Care of Calves and Kids of Birds

Within an hour of delivery, the calf is allowed to suckle the mother. The calf does not show interest in the beginning. But regularle attempts by master develops suckling interest in calf. For a month, the child is allowed three time suckling. But after a month, two time suckling is allowed. For a month, the calf is kept on milk. After a month, water is given. After two months grasses are served in the mouth of calf. The calf learns eating grasses quickly.

The colostrums is regarded very pious and nutritious. It gives full nutrition to the calf. Colostrums is cooked in loaf sugar and served to Gods, Goddesses and ancestors. It is shared by family and community member as Prasad.

To avoid black magic and evil eye, a black thread is tied on feet and neck of child. Black spot is made on forehead. Special worship is done in the name of Gods, Goddesses and ancestors for successful delivery.

Father and mother birds take care of their kids twenty four hours. When furs appear on body, kids are brought out for picking up food. The owner provides protection to kids from dog and cat. At night, they are covered with a big net basket for protection. During day, they are served rice grains to eat.

When calves of animals become young, they are allowed to go in field for grazing grasses.

Feeding of Animals and Birds

Members of folk community know that animals and birds domesticated required feeding. In folk communities, animals are feed twice in a day besides grazing. In the morning and evening they are served straw, hey, grains, waste of oilseeds, dry *mahua* flower and husk of pulse as feed. Straw, hey, grasses and leaves are also served as feed. At both ends they are served water. People preserve straw, hey, *mahua* flower, pulse husk, broken rice of grains, waste of oilseeds to be served as feed, besides grazing in field. They also cut grasses and break leaves to serve them as feed. Calves are served three-four times feed, but young, adult and old are served feed twice in a day.

On festive occasions, animals are also served *khir-puri* as *Prasad* of worship. Special feed is given to milk giving cows and buffalo to fetch more and more milk. Oxen are given special feed during agricultural season because they have to plough the agriculture fields.

Cart drawing animals are served special feed. Oxen carrying back, loads are also served special kind of feed. All cattle are served special food as medicine.

Feeding of birds, and their kids are done time to time, besides allowing them to pick up foodgrains, insects and other from the field, street, drains, courtyards and other places. They are served rice grains, pulse grains, wheat grains, maize, millet, marua, makeya, jinora as feed.

Milking Milch Cattle

As referred to earlier, folk people domesticate cow, she-buffalo, she-camel, she-goat and she-sheep to get milk. Hence milking is required expertise. Some members of family are expert in milking milch cattle. For the purpose of milking they tie the legs with a rope so that animal could not attack with leg on person who milks the cow or other animals. Milking is done twice in a day—morning time and evening time. If calf is alive, the calf is allowed first to suckle milk. After sometime, the calf is detached from suckling but calf is kept nearby the cow. The cow starts tongue combing the calf and the milking is started. Some milk is left for suckling the calf. When the milking is over, the calf is allowed to suckle again. But milking a cow or buffalo whose calf is not alive is very difficult. In this case the cow or she buffalo is served special food for milking.

Disease of Cattle and Folk Treatment

The health of animals is influenced by change in season. They also get infected inside body. Their eyes and ears also become infected. Dirty water intake bring a number of disease inside their body. They also meet accident and get legs and thorns broken. They also face infection in mouth and stomach. They also suffer from constipation and loose motion. In this way, disease and accident are also truth for animals domesticated. Some animal diseases and their treatment are as follows:

Summer Fever

Animals also get attacked by sunstroke. Sunstroke brings fever inside their body. Animals suffering from fever do not share food, do not urinate and their ear becomes cold. Seeing animals neither eating nor urinating, the owner understands that something wrong has happened with the cattle. He/she touches the ears and body to confirm the fever. Hot body and cold ears confirm all about the suffering form the fever. On confirmation folk treatment is done. *Til* oil is put on the forehead, head and horn. Green mango syrup is applied over the body and served to the animal with the help of a bamboo instrument called *Chonga* (cylindrical bamboo instrument). The leaves of bamboo and mango are served to eat. Churned curd, salt and loaf sugar are given. Juice of sugarcane and lemon are served to the animal. With these folk treatments attempt is made to remove the fever. If fever is not down, *Chiraita* water and *Nim* leaves boiled water is given. When fever continues several days, the help of *Jhar-phuk* method and worship method is also taken. Syrup of *Bel* fruit is also served. Now-a-days, help of veterinary doctor is also sought.

Winter Fever

The change of winter season also brings diseases in cattle. The most common is winter fever. Boiled *Chiraita* leaves water and *Nim* leaves water is served to the patient animal. Mustard oil is applied over body, head and thorns. Mustard oil, onion juice, garlic juice, ginger juice and *gur* are served to the patient animal. Fire is kept burning in the shed nearby animal. Gentle hot water is served to the patient animal. If fever continues for several days, *Jhar-phuk* and worship methods are also used. If these methods fait, veterinary doctor is called for the treatment.

Mouth infection (Khoraha)

The disease of mouth infection is called locally as *Khoraha.* In this disease, the mouth tongue and throat of animal get infected. As a result, animal is not in a position to eat anything and drink water. In order to cure this disease, the mouth of patient animal is washed twice with *Nim* leaves boiled water and this water is also served the animal to drink. Loaf sugar is served to eat. This treatment continues for two to three weeks. This disease occurs in Ashwin-Kartik months or Chait-Baisakh month. *Jhar-phuk* and worship methods are also used to cure this disease. This is infectious disease. The animal suffering from this disease is isolated from other animals. Because it is a contagious disease. It spreads from cattle to cattle.

Hoof Infection (Khoraha)

This disease is also known as *Khoraha.* It is very dangerous disease which makes an animal disable to walk. Germs and wounds appear in hoof. As a result, the animal does not walk. The animal tries to clean hoof with mouth and tongue. Now, this disease spreads from hoof to mouth, tongue and throat. The hooves of animals is washed with hot *Nim* leaves boiled water twice in a day. Phenyle is dropped on hooves. *Nim* leaves paste is applied on hooves. *Jhar-phuk* and worship methods are also used to cure this disease.

Cut and Wound

In fields, the legs of oxen are cut. The cutting causes wounds. The wound occurs without cut too. The members of folk communities, cure cut and wound of animals by folk medicine. The cut or wound is washed with Nim leaves boiled water and *Nim* leaves paste is applied over it. Hot mustard oil and onion, garlic and ginger juice are dropped over wound at night. Now-a-days, dettol is also applied over it. A bandage with cloth is made. The paste of *Genda* flower leaves is also used as folk medicine to cure the cut and wound.

Swelling and Hurt

In quarelling with another animals, an animal receives hurt and swelling. To cure hurt and swelling folk communities use folk medicine. They soak the swelling with cloth wet in hot water. A hot paste of turmeric and lime is applied over the swollen part. This is repeated twice or thrice time in a day.

Severe pain

An animal suffering from severe pain is treated with folk medicine. For this purpose a special hot paste is prepared. This paste contains cowdung, leaves and seeds of *imali, babul* leaves and seeds, *mahua* flowers and seeds. All items are heated in a pot containing water. Mixture is heated for an hour. When a paste is ready, it is applied over the affected part twice in a day. *Mahua* liquor is also applied and served to the patient animal.

Fracture

Animals also get fracture. The fracture is cured by tieing the fractured leg with bamboo sticks and applying paste of *Harjorawa* plant, turmeric and lime thrice a day. The movement of animal is controlled.

Constipation

The animals also suffer from constipation. To cure the disease of constipation, *trifala churna,* vinegar of *Jamun,* loaf sugar and *ajawain,* and sisam leaves are used. Himalayan *Batisa* is a very commonly known Ayurvedic medicine to cure the disease of constipation in animal. It is known to every members of folk and peasant communities.

Loose Motion

To cure the disease of loose motion, folk people serve *bel* fruit, bamboo leaves, *sisam* leaves, churned curd, *trifala churna,* Himalayan *Batisa, Kala Namak* and Loaf sugar to control loose motion of an animal.

Cough and Cold

To cure an animal from cough and cold, the folk people serve dry *mahua* flower, *mahua* liquor, onion cooked in mustard oil, juice of garlic and ginger to patient animal.

Barrenness

As barrenness is considered curse for a woman, similarly barrenness is taken as curse for cow, she-buffalo, she-goat and she-camel or any other female animal domesticated. In order to cure the disease of barrenness, folk people use folk medicine. The concerned female animal is left in open field during night to have a dew bath. This is repeated for a months. New emerging bamboo is cut into pieces and served to the patient animal thrice a day for a month. Dry *mahua* flower, *gur* (jaggery) and mustard oil are served daily for a month. If these treatments fail, it is believed that God has cursed her or a black magician has done black magic. Hence *Jhar-phuk* treatment and *Puja-path* method of curing disease of barrenness are done. If these magical and religious methods are not successful, veterinary doctor is consulted and modern treatment is given.

Abortion

Abortion also takes place in some cases. To avoid abortion special care is taken. Nutritious feed is given and the concerned animal is not allowed to go in field for grazing grasses.

Delivery Related Behaviour

The expectant female animal is kept under supervision for successful delivery. Whenever there is complication, help of expert is taken. After delivery the calf and mother both require treatment. Mother is served light hot water, and turmeric cooked in loaf sugar for 21 days both ends. This medical behaviour helps mother to recover health very fast. It clears stomach and reproductive organ and increases the appetite. In the beginning light food is given. Cold water is not given to drink. But after 21 days, mother recovers her health. Now she becomes quite fit for giving good quantity of milk.

Not Flow of Milk

After delivery, the mother animals face the problem of not proper flow of milk. The flow of milk is so less that calf does not show interest in suckling. In order to increase the flow of milk, folk people serve turmeric cooked in loaf sugar and mustard oil regularly for a week. This increases the flow of milk. The calf start suckling more and more. Now, the cow or buffalo or other milch animals give sufficient quality of milk both ends. Now-a-days, help of Veterinary doctor is also taken to increase milk. Modern feeds are also served to the mother animal.

Thanail (Inflamated Nipple)

The milk giving animals sometimes face the problem of inflamated nipple. In this case, the mother does not allow the calf to suckle the nipples. She does not allow the milk man to milk because she suffers from pain. Oil and *ghee* is applied over nipples. Nipples are washed with hot water. *Totaka* is done with a wooden comb. Fire is burnt nearby the mother's nipples.

Sale and Purchase of Cattle

Sale and purchase of cattle take place in cattle fair. Cattle fairs take place in different places about which people know very well with the time, date and days of fair. The folk people visit the cattle fair to sell as well as purchase of cattle. Bargaining takes place in deciding the price of cattle. The buyer offers *pranam* to the cattle for selling to get money. The purchaser offers worship to cattle at his own house with *ghee*, vermillion, loaf sugar, rice grains and water.

Preparation of Manure from the Dung

The folk people know very well to prepare the manure from the dung. They put urine, ash and dung of cattle in a pit during rainy season. During rainy season dung fuel is not made because they do not get dried in rainy season. That is why all dung, urine ash and feed waste are collected and put in a pit. The dung gradually turned into a manure to be used in agricultural field.

Preparation of Fuel from Dung

During summer season, fuel is prepared from the dung which is locally known as *Goitha. Goitha* is used for cooking food. For making *Goitha,* dung is mixed in paddy-hey and made small round balls from this. The round ball is put on walls or on the ground and left to get dry in sun. In a week, *Goitha* is ready to use as fuel for cooking.

Worship of Cattle

Cattle worship occupies significant place in folk and peasant society. It is because their economy is based on cattle domestication. Cattle plough land, draw carts, pull *Rehat* (water lifting machine in wells), pull wheels of oil crusher, do thrashing, give milk, skin and calf. Thus, for agriculture, people are dependant on cattle to a great extent. It is quite natural that cattle worship has attracted attention to agriculturists and folk communities. The folk people observe *sohrai* festival for cattle. It is also known as *Gaydarh* festival. In this festival, cattle shed is cleaned and repaired properly. Cattle are washed in river or canal or stream. *Ghee* or oil is put on their head and horns. Vermillion is also put on head. Worship in the name of cattle God is done in cattle shed. *Khir-puri* is served to the cattle as *Prasad.* On each festive occasion, the worship of cattle is done and *Prasad* is offered to them.

Preparation of Cattleshed

In order to provide protection to cattle from heat, cold and rain, people erect shed. The structure of shed is like hut or house. The cattle shed has a number of wooden poles in which cattle are tied with the help of rope. In shed, the place of each cattle is decided. Each family has a shed. The shed has semi-circular earthen containers in which cattle are served food. The cattleshed is repaired each year after rainy season. It is offered worship in Sohrai after Dashera festival.

The cattle shed is cleaned properly each year. Dung and urine are cleaned. The entire shed is broomed.

Sterilization of Male Calves

Calves of cow and buffalo are used for ploughing the land, drawing carts, carrying back load and drawing oil crushing machine and water fetching machine. That is why the calves are sterilised. There are some experts in the village who do the work of sterilization. Now-a-days, the help of veterinary doctor is taken for this purpose.

Death Ritual of Cattle

Some rituals are observed on the death of a cattle. When a cattle, a domesticated animal dies with rope in neck or leg, death ritual of animal is performed like human. *Pinda* is offered in his/her name and a *shradh* ritual is done on 12th day after death. The dead body is buried with cloth on the body. This ritual is also observed for milch cattle. For other cattle this ritual is not observed.

Thus, from above account, it is quite clear that folk zoology is a mixture of science, humanism and religion.

Folk Botany

The science which deals with botanical knowledge of folk communities is known as folk botany. It deals with knowledge of domestication of plants and doing agriculture. The knowledge of domesticating plants and doing agriculture includes preserving or selecting seeds, preparing seedlings, transplanting seedlings, weeding, manuring, irrigating, harvesting, thrashing, winnowing, bringing produce in house and selling produce in market. It also deals with genetic counselling of plants and preparing hybrid variety of plants and seeds to get more and more fruits, flowers, vegetables and yields. Thus, folk botany (ethnobotany) is practice of botanical knowledge by folk communities. Folk biology is also known as ethnobotany.

Subject Matter of Folk Botany

Subject matters of folk botany are as follows:

- Folk classification of plants.
- Folk method of cultivation of plants.
- Rearing and caring of plants.
- Developing of high yield variety.
- Disease of plants.
- Treatment of Disease of plants.
- Preservation of produce.
- Sale of produce.

Classification of Plants

Folk people classify plants on following basis:

On the Basis of Species

Each plant represents a species. Each plant is known by a particular species name such as mango, guava, orange, papaya, *jamun, imali, ber, peepal, bargad,* potato, brinjal, pumpkin and so on.

On the Basis of Sub-Species

Each plant is further classified on the basis of subspecies. For example mango is classified as Biju and Langara. Paddy is divided into mansuri, dehradun, sonachur, katarani, sonam and others. Wheat is classified as Golden, Punjabi, Larma. Gram is classified as Dehati and Kabuli. Banana is divided into Chinia and Singapuri. *Mircha* (chilly) is classified as red chilly, green chilly, black chilly, Shimla chilly. Each plant species is divided into a number of sub-species on the basis of nature of fruits.

On the Basis of Taste of Fruits

Plants are classified on the basis of taste of fruits of plant. For example mango fruit is classified as sour and sweet. The tree is also identified as sour taste mango and sweet taste mango. Similarly, *Imali, ber,* apple, guava are classified on the basis of taste of fruit.

On the Basis of Size of Fruit

Folk people identify plant on the basis of size of fruit. For example Barka Aam, Chootaka Aam, Manjhila Aam, Golaka Aaam, Lawmaka Aam and Natawa Aam.

On the Basis of Colour

Plants are also classified on the basis of colour of fruits. For example yellow, red, green fruit mango tree. Red, green, yellow fruit guava tree.

On the Basis of Size

Folk people classify plants on the basis of their size. They are as follows:

Per **(Tree):** Trees are big in size. They give flower, fruits, seeds and for years on cultivation only once time. For example mango, guava, papaya, jamun, ber, bel, coconut, Nim and others.

Paudha **(Crops):** The small plants which are cultivated once or twice in a year and give flower, fruits and seeds are called crops. For example, paddy, maize, oilseeds and others.

Sag-Pat **(Leafy vegetable):** Very small crops whose leaves are used as vegetable are called sag-pat. For example karmi sag, Beng sag, gendhari sag and others.

Latar **(Stem or creeper or climbers):** The plants which creep and climb on roof to yield flower, fruits and seed are called latar. For example, kaddu, kohra, nenua, bhatua and others.

On the Basis of Time taken to ripe

Folk people classify plants on the basis of time taken to ripe. They are as follows:

Half yearly. There are some crops which are cultivated twice in a year. They are called half yearly crops. For example maize, paddy. Leafy vegetables and vegetables.

Annual crops

Some crops are cultivated annually to get yield. For example wheat, oat, millet, *arahar,* gram, *masoori,* and others.

Perennial

There are trees which give flower, fruit, seed, wood for lifelong, when cultivated once. They are termed as perennial tree. For example mango, *sal, katahal, imali, aam, jaumn, ber* and others.

On the Basis of Domestication

Folk people classify plants on the basis of domestication. They called cultivated plants as domesticated plants and self-germinated plants as wild plants.

On the Basis of Value

Folk people classify plants on the basis of values. They are as follows:

Wood Value Tree

There are some trees which has wood value. For example, *sisam, gamhar, sakhua, sagwan.*

Fruit Value Tree

There are some trees which have fruit value. For example, guava, *sharifa,* apple, papaya.

Flower Value Tree

Some plants have flower value. For example *Genda*, *beli*, *chameli*, *ratrani*, *champa, harsringar* and others.

Decorative Value

Some trees and plants have decorative value. For example, *Ashoka,* show plant, money plant.

Milk Value Tree

Some trees yield milk like substance. They are *peepal, ber, pankar, gular, katahal* and ruber plant.

Grain Value Crops

There are some crops which have grain value. For example paddy, wheat, pulses.

Oil Value Crops

Some crops yield oilseeds. They are *saraso, til, tisi, jaitun, suryamukhi, champa, chameli.*

Toddy Value Tree

Some tree yield toddy. They are *Tar, Khajur, Nim.*

Wine Value Tree

Some trees yield wine. For example Mahua and Grapes.

Medicine Value Tree

Some plants have medicinal value, for example *Ashwa Gandha, Nim, Harjorawa, Gurmar, Chiraita, Sahejan, Sarpagandha, Aam, Bel, Jamun* and others.

Vegetable Values

Some crops yield vegetable. They are *Kaddu, Kohra, Bhatua, Nenua,* Potato, Radish, *Gajar.*

Leafy Vegetable Value

Some crops have leafy vegetable value. For example *Chana, Khesari, Palak, Gendhari, Saraso* and others.

Religious Value

Some crops and trees have religious value. They are *Tulsi, Pipal, Ber, Aam, Amla, Pankar, Gular, Nim* and others.

Fence Value Crops

Some crops have fence value. They are *putus* and *thethar.*

Cultivation of Crops and Plants

For cultivating plants and trees, folk people prepare land first of all. The preparation of lands includes digging or ploughing. Different methods are employed to prepare land for plantation of trees and crops. People plant trees on barren lands where there is no scope of agricultural crops. They cultivate plants of wood and fruit value on barren lands or on the bank of agricultural field. Folk people cultivate vegetables in the kitchen garden. They cultivate mango, guava, papaya, jack fruits in land situated in front of house. They cultivate flower in courtyard or outside. They do agriculture in agricultural field.

Plants Cultivated on Barren Land

In folk communities, each family has some barren land over which plants of wood and fruit value are cultivated. The cultivation of tree plants is done in the month of Ashad, i.e. beginning of rainy season. As soon as first rainfall occurs, pits are dug for the cultivation of tree plants. The pit is left for some days. When rains, the cultivation of seedling of tree is done. During rainy season there is no need of irrigation and the roots of tree seedling spread in soil. In this way plants are cultivated on barren land. Now, root is dug each year to absorb more and more water during rainy season. After rainy season the root is filled with soil. This process is repeated each year till the plant does not grow into a tree.

Cultivation in Kitchen Garden

The folk people cultivate vegetable in kitchen garden. They cultivate *kaddu, kohara, bhatua, nenua, vindi,* tomato, brinjal, chilly, potato etc. For this purpose, they prepare land with spade, *khanti* and *khurapi.* They cultivate these vegetables plants during rainy season. They start getting vegetables in one and half months.

Cultivation of Flower

The folk people cultivate flowers like *Genda, Bajentri, Kanaili, Urahul, Beli, Sadasuhagin* and others in their courtyard and by the side of entrance gate.

Cultivation of Paddy

The folk people cultivate paddy in their agriculture fields. The agriculture is carried out by following process:

- Ploughing fields of paddy in first rain fall.
- Manuring Agricultural Fields.
- Sowing Paddy Seeds.
- Preparing wet field for transplanting seedlings.
- Transplantation of seedlings.
- Weeding.
- Watching.
- Irrigating.
- Harvesting.
- Making bundles of paddy crops.
- Bringing paddy crops in thrashing field.
- Thrashing paddy crops.
- Winnowing.
- Storing grains in house.
- Merry making.

Method of Cultivation of Paddy

Paddy is cultivated by two methods: (i) Dry method and (ii) Wet method.

(i) In dry method, coarse variety of paddy seeds are sown in the field after first shower of rains. They are left to germinate and grow. Other agricultural processes are same as in case of wet method.

(ii) In wet method, agricultural fields is filled and prepared in water to transplant paddy seedings. As paddy seedlings are transplanted in water, it is known as wet method. By this method, Jarhan or Agahani Paddy crops are cultivated.

Besides manuring and weeding, chemical fertilizers are also used to get more yield now-a-days. Pesticides, insecticides and weedicide are also used to remove crop disease.

Cultivation of Rabi Crops

Wheat, gram, khesari, *chana, masur, tisi,* mustard are known as Rabi crops. These crops are cultivated by dry method. Wheat and mustard are irrigated thrice times. Other crops are not irrigated.

Cultivation of Garma Crops

Now-a-days, folk and peasant people have assured means of irrigation like canal, well, tubewells, boring, diesel machine. With the help of these means, they are able to provide irrigation to crops cultivated in summer season. They cultivate, maize, paddy vegetable, cereals and *til* in summer season as Garma crops.

Weeding

Weeding is an important agricultural process. In weeding grasses are removed from the field of standing crops. The folk and peasant people do weeding with the help of their hands. They pull out each grass from the field one by one. Now the field has only crops. If weeding is not done, it affects the health of crops and finally yield. Weedicides are also used to weed out grasses.

Spraying Urea Fertilizer

After weeding the folk and peasant people spray urea in the field of crops to provide nutrition. Sometimes, solution of urea fertilizer is also sprayed on crops.

Watching the Field of Crops

The folk and peasant people watch the crops regularly to avoid destruction from wild animals, birds and theft. They erect a hut on a corner of the field. Also make a human effigy in the field to frighten the animals and birds. They play tin to create noise to drive away wild animals and birds. They sleep in hut and watch crops during night. The crops are watched till harvesting is not done.

Harvesting

When crops are ripe, they are harvested. The folk and peasant people do manual harvesting. They harvest crops with the help of sickle. They make bundles of the crops and bring each bundle in thrashing field by head load. Now-a-days, harvesting is also done by harvester.

Thrashing

The folk and peasant people do harvesting generally manually. They also use animal for the purpose by thrashing crops to get grains out from the straw or stalk. These days harvester does harvesting, thrashing and winnowing. But folk people are still dependant on manual thrashing.

Winnowing

In order to get grains separated from hey, winnowing is done. The folk people do winnowing manually with the help of winnowing tray.

Storing Grains in House

After winnowing grains are carried in house for storing. But before bringing grains in house, the heap of grains is offered worship by the owner by burning *dhup* and *agarbati.*

Merry-making

When grains come in the house, it is a joyous occasion for the family. New grains are prepared and cooked. It is served to ancestors, Gods and Goddesses of the house and village. Then all family members share it. They enjoy by singing and dancing.

Preservation of Grains

Grains are preserved in big earthen pots for daily and future use in folk communities.

Sale of Produce

The folk people sell their agricultural produce in the hands of middleman of the *haat* bazaar to get cash. From cash they purchase food and other items of daily consumption.

Crop Diseases and their Treatment

The fungus and insects attack on crops in the field. They destroy the leaves and sometimes entire crops. The folk people spray *karanj* oil and ash to drive away insects. But, now-a-days, insecticides are also used and urea solution is also sprayed.

Creation of Improved Variety of Plants

The folk people create improved variety of plants and crops by grafting method and crossing method together. In grafting method, they flake the newer branch of the same plant and tie a cloth having ash on scaled part. Water is spread daily. As a result root comes out. Then the branch is cut and transplanted. The fruits of grafted plants are bigger than plants emerging from seeds.

In crossing method, two different plants are selected and crossed with each other. For this purpose both selected plants are tied together by removing flakes. The crossed spot is tied with a cloth having ash. Water is spread. The roots gradually appear. Now, the gene of one plant is mixed with gene of other plant. Thus, improved variety is created. Brinjal can be crossed with pumpkin, tomato can be crossed with potato, papaya can be crossed with *Kohara* or *Bhatua.* These are folk method of creating improved variety of plants.

Preservation of Seeds

The folk and peasant people preserve seeds of paddy, wheat, maize, oil seeds, gram, vegetables and leafy vegetables with great care. They do not select seeds of diseased crops. Rather they select seeds of healthy crops. They preserve seeds in earthen pots with tight lid. The lid is sealed with wet soil. It is opened before sowing in fields. Now-a-days, folk and peasant people have started purchasing HYV seeds from the market. But the seeds of HYV crops are not preservable. So, they have to purchase seeds each year from the market.

Bibliography

Atal, Yogesh 1965: *Adivasi Bharat*, Delhi: Rajkamal Prakashan.

Basavaraddi, Ishwar V. 2015: Yoga: Right Path to Health and Wellness, *Yojana,* Vol. 59, pp. 7-12, June.

Bhowmick, P.K. 1963: *The Lodhas of West Bengal*, Calcutta: Punthi Pustak.

Bose, N.K. 1970: *Tribal Life in India*, Bombay: Asia Publishing House.

Carstairs, G.M. 1963: *Medicines and Faith in Rural Rajasthan*, New York. Academy of Social Science Series, Vol. 30, No. 41.

Das, A.K. and S.K. Banerjee. 1962: *The Lepchas of Darjeeling*, Kolkata: Cultural Research Institute.

Das, A.K. and A.N. Banerjee 1964: *Impact of Industrialization on Tribes of West Bengal.* Kolkata: Cultural Research Institute.

Das, A.K. and M.K. Raha. 1963: *The Oraon of Sundarvan*, Kolkata: Cultural Research Institute.

Das, A.K., M.K. Raha and B.K. Choudhary 1966: *The Malpaharia of West Bengal*. Kolkata: Cultural Research Institute.

Dube, S.C. 1954: *The Kamar*, Lucknow: University Publisher.

Dube, S.C. 1955: *Indian Village*, London: Cornell University.

Dube, S.C. (ed.) 1977: *Tribal Heritage of India*, Delhi: Vikas Publishing House.

Elwin, Verrier, 1939: *The Baiga*, London: Johnmurray.

Elwin Verrier, 1942: *The Agaria*, London: Oxford University Press.

Elwin, Verrier, 1943: *Maria Murder and Suicide*, Groeffery Cambridge. Oxford University Press.

Elwin, Verrier, 1947: *The Maria and Their Gothul*, Groeffery Cambridge. Oxford University Press.

Elwin, Verrier, 1950: *Bodo Highlanders*, Bombay: Oxford University Press.

Elwin, Verrier, 1954: *Tribal Myths of Orissa*, Bombay: Oxford University Press.

Ghyre, G.S. 1979: *Vedic India*, Bombay: Popular Prakashan.

Giriffith, W.G. 1946: *The Kol Tribes of Central India*, Calcutta: Royal Asiatic Society of Bengal.

Grierson, W.G. 1938: *The Maria Gonds of Bastar*, London: Oxford University Press.

Gurdon, P.R.T. 1906: *The Khasi*, London: McMillan.

Haldar, A.K. and Gaya Pandey. 2001: *Artisan Tribes of Bihar and Bengal*, Kolkata: R.N. Bhattacharya.

Hasan, K.A. 1960: 'Role of Anthropology in Social and Preventive Medicine', *Journal of Medical Association*, Vol. 35, No. 1.

Hassan, K.A., 1964: *Folk Concept of Etiology and Illness in North Indian Village*, Spring Krober's Anthropological Society, Paper No. 30.

Krishnamachary, 2015: 'The Siddha System of Medicine', *Yojana*, Vol. 59. pp 55-59, June.

Katoch, D.C. 2015: 'Emergence and Growth of Ayurveda', *Yojana,* Vol. 59, pp. 13-18, June.

Malinowski, B.K., 1944: *Scientific Theory of Culture and Other Essays,* Chapel Hill: University of Carolina.

Manchanda, Jajk. and Harleen Kaur, 2015: 'Homoeopathy: The Gentle Medicine', *Yojana,* Vol. 59, pp. 19-23, June.

Nair, R.M. 2015. 'Naturopathy and India's Health Care Challenges', *Yojana*, Vol. 59, pp. 51-54, June.

Pandey, Gaya, 2006: *Bhartiya Janajatiya Sanskriti*, New Delhi: Concept Publishing Company.

Pandey, Gaya, 2008: *Development Anthropology*, New Delhi: Concept Publishing Company.

Pandey, Gaya, 2017. *Chikitsatmak Manavshastra*, New Delhi: Concept Publishing Company.

Prasad, N., 1964: *Land and People of Tribal Bihar*, Ranchi: Bihar Tribal Welfare Institute.

Rahman, Raisur, 2015: 'Unani Medicine: The Art of Health and Healing,' *Yojana,* Vol. 59, pp. 43-50, June.

Roy, S.C. 1912: *Munda and Their Country*, Kolkata: City Bar Library.

Roy, S.C. 1915: *Oraon of Chotanagpur*, Ranchi: Bar Library.

Roy, S.C. 1925: *The Birhor*, Ranchi: Man in India Office.

Roy, S.C. 1928: *Oraon Religions and Custom*, Ranchi: Man in India Office.

Roy, S.C. 1935: *The Hill Bhuiya of Orissa*, Ranchi: Man in India Office.

Roy, S.C. 1937: *The Kharia*, Two Volumes, Ranchi: Man in India Office.

Report, 2001: *Census of India*, New Delhi: Publication Division.

Report, 2005: *Task Group on Development of Scheduled Castes and Scheduled Tribes*, Planning Commission, Government of India.

Shukla, R.K. 1998: *Forestry For Tribal Development*, New Delhi, Department of Forest.

Singh, A.K., Gaya Pandey and P.K. Singh. 1997: *Forest and Tribals*, New Delhi: Classical Publication.

Tylor, E.B. 1871: *Primitive Culture*, London: Jay Murray.

Vidyarthi, L.P. 1963: *Maler: Nature-Man-Spirit Complex in a Hill Tribe in Bihar*, Calcutta: Bookland.

Vidyarthi, L.P. (ed.) 1968: *Applied Anthropology in India*, Allahabad: Kitab Mahal.

Vidyarthi, L.P. (ed) 1973: *Applied and Action Anthropology in India*, New Delhi: Concept Publishing Company.

Vidyarthi, L.P. and B.K. Rai, 1976: *Tribal Culture of India*, New Delhi: Concept Publishing Company.

Vidyarthi, L.P. and R.K. Prasad, 1980: *Dietary Patterns and Habits*, New Delhi: Concept Publishing Company.

Index